"Just Like Other S

The preparation of the text for the English edition was supported by the Hungarian Cultural Centre, London and the Hungarian Ministry of Education and Culture.

"Just Like Other Students":
Reception of the 1956 Hungarian Refugee
Students in Britain

By

Magda Czigány

CAMBRIDGE
SCHOLARS

PUBLISHING

"Just Like Other Students": Reception of the 1956 Hungarian Refugee Students in Britain, by Magda Czigány

This book first published 2009. The present binding first published 2009.

Cambridge Scholars Publishing

12 Back Chapman Street, Newcastle upon Tyne, NE6 2XX, UK

British Library Cataloguing in Publication Data
A catalogue record for this book is available from the British Library

ISBN (10): 1-4438-0550-5, ISBN (13): 978-1-4438-0550-6

To my grandson, Daniel

TABLE OF CONTENTS

FOREWORD

When nearing the end of the compulsory seminar which prepared us for the leisurely years of our retirement, we were asked to outline what activities we were planning to fill all those empty hours with. I had an easy time. There was no need for me to repeat the obvious; what dozens of other future senior citizens had said—to travel widely and to see the world—nor to concoct implausible projects to be accomplished in the years to come. I was able to give a ready-made answer, since I had already decided to devote my time and energy to researching the reception of the Hungarian refugee students who came to Great Britain after the Soviet Army had crushed the 1956 revolution.

Being myself one of the refugee students, the memories of those "heroic" first years in Britain have always stayed with me, maybe somewhat faded, but never forgotten. Then, with the passage of time, I began to turn from the future to the past and my curiosity about the background of the so-called Hungarian students scheme was awakened. On our arrival in Britain we were received with much good will and generosity, and we were well looked after both during the months spent preparing to enter university life and during our years of study. However, we knew little or nothing about the people who organized our reception or how it was done. I wished to learn therefore what had induced the universities to offer their help and about the presumably very large organizational effort which had made it possible for hundreds of Hungarian students to come to this country and continue their studies here. I wished to find out how we were selected and allocated to universities, taught English in special language courses set up for us, and by what means the universities had secured the necessary financial resources to fund all this activity. I also hoped to discover how the students fared; the problems they had faced and the successes they had achieved. Briefly, I wished to research and write up the story of my generation during what was perhaps the most exciting period of their lives.

It came to my knowledge that the papers and documents of the Hungarian Office which had been entrusted with the administration of the Hungarian students scheme, and which operated between 1957 and 1962 within the University of London, had been deposited in the University's Central Archives. I assumed that these, supplemented by the records kept by each university participating in the scheme would provide the necessary information. I hoped to rely on the help of my former colleagues—the chief librarians of British universities—to map the location and extent of these collections and to gain access to them, or to advise me whom I should approach in order to be able to carry out my research. I am happy to say that the help was more than forthcoming; I am truly grateful for all the assistance I have received from university librarians, archivists, keepers of student records and other officials who often painstakingly carried out the time-consuming groundwork for me.

The universities, former polytechnics and technical colleges I approached for information and which kindly responded to my request are listed under the sources at the end of the book. I would, however, like to single out the universities which, acting as regional centres, took the lion's share in looking after the refugee students by offering temporary accommodation on their arrival and by organizing the intensive language courses for them, and which have so readily opened their files for me: Birmingham, Cambridge, Edinburgh, Leeds, London and Oxford as well as the Modern Records Centre at the University of Warwick, which houses the archives of the Committee of Vice-Chancellors and Principals, under whose aegis the Hungarian students scheme had been set up. The Corporation of London Records Office allowed me access to the documents relating to the establishment and management of the Lord Mayor's Fund, and the London Metropolitan Archives provided valuable information in the compilation of the list of students who had received Major County Awards which enabled them to continue their studies in the polytechnics and technical colleges of the capital.

It is regrettable that over the years some archival material had been lost, mainly in the archives and student records of the former London polytechnics, due to the major reorganization of British higher education during the past fifty years. Even more unfortunate is the loss of the archives of the former World University Service (WUS) during a transfer, since it had contained the details of over three hundred Hungarian students registered by WUS, of whom nearly one hundred had been awarded WUS scholarships for their university studies.

A substantial and probably the most interesting part of the main collection in the University of London Archives is still closed; it contains the personal records and documents of the students: notes on the interviews conducted with them and on their allocation to various universities, detailed reports issued yearly on their progress and the students' personal correspondence with the Hungarian Office. The exceptionally long closure of the archives was set up to protect the students, and because the files will become open near the middle of this century, the students themselves will not be able to look at them or comment on them. Similarly restrictive is the strictly interpreted Data Protection Act, which prohibits referring to the names of living people unless they specifically give their consent.

Because of these restrictions, I decided to contact a number of former refugee students either through personal acquaintances or with the help of alumni offices. Many of them were willing to share their recollections with me and kindly gave their permission to quote them—often extensively—and to refer to them by name. I would like therefore to record here my thanks to the following former fellow-students: Félix Allender, László Antal, István Bátori, Tamás Csáthy, Géza Fehérvári, Péter Halmos, László Huszár, Katalin Jámbor, Ambrus Jankó, the brothers Mihály and Miklós Kruppa, Ferenc Lengyel, István Opalka, Antal Ormay, Péter Pallai, András Sándor, István Selmeczi, András and Kornélia Szabó, Kálmán Száz, András Szűcs, Béla Ulicsák, Sándor Váci, Pál and Péter Wonke, Marietta Záhonyi, Albin Závody, Iván Zmertych, Péter Zollman and András Zsigmond. After the publication of the Hungarian version of the book, further material was kindly put at my disposal by András Barabás and István Pálffy to be included in the English version.

I would also like to express my thanks to other people who were willing to be interviewed by me, among them Mrs Judith Juhász, widow of Csaba Juhász, one of the students at Imperial College and D. Mervyn Jones who, during the late 1950s was a college tutor at Exeter College in Oxford and had four Hungarian students in his charge, providing additional English tuition for them. Being a contemporary of many of the prominent people involved with the refugee students, Mervyn Jones kindly supplied me with valuable insight into their motivations and actions.

Initially, my intention was to include only the facts and figures of the Hungarian refugee students scheme in the narrative, illustrating perhaps certain aspects with the selected recollections of the former students. When writing this book however, I felt that to help the reader to understand the students' attitude and the way they responded to their new circumstances, the inclusion of more personal details might be desirable. Drawing on my own reminiscences, told and retold in the family circle over long winter evenings, I decided to regale the readers with my own motivations and experiences: what had forced me to leave Hungary and escape to the West; how I got to England by chance and after some escapades; how I was enrolled as a student at Westfield College where I was kindly received into a small student community and what hurdles I had to overcome to obtain the much coveted degree at London University.

Recalling and sharpening the memories of the student years, I was greatly helped by my husband, Lóránt Czigány, a fellow student since we began our studies at the University of Szeged in Hungary, with whom I shared all the trials and tribulations of settling down in a new and alien environment and with whom I was able to discuss all the aspects of my research and shaping the findings into a narrative. I am grateful for his advice, for his reading both the Hungarian and the English versions of the text, and providing comments, corrections and guidance. Without his encouragement, neither the research would have been carried out fully, nor the laborious task of writing the book accomplished. I am equally grateful to my daughter Judith and son-in-law John Pinfold for meticulously going through the text of the English version of the book and suggesting many necessary changes and corrections.

In depicting the slow and often tiresome process of assimilation of the students to their new circumstances I was able to draw on the findings of the survey of the Hungarian refugee students carried out by two students of sociology at the LSE, Alan Dare and Paul Hollander, in the autumn of 1958 as a project for their diplomas. They questioned a large number of the Hungarian students about their views and attitudes in great detail; the tables compiled from the answers and the comments by the students quoted extensively in the text of the report, provided an insight into their feeling at that time, undimmed by later experiences. Quotations from Hungarian sources were translated into English by myself; I alone am responsible for any misquotations, misinterpretations and mistakes.

In the 1950s, with the memory of our experiences still fresh in our minds, we often said that we had a more than ample collection of stories to tell our children and grandchildren. It is therefore a source of great happiness for me that, inspired by the celebration of the fiftieth anniversary of the 1956 Hungarian revolution, my own grandson shows an increasing interest in the past of his grandparents, especially in their participation in the revolution and their student years in this country. I hope that this book will help to preserve the memories of the past and pass them on to the next generation. Therefore, I dedicate it to my grandson, Daniel.

London, 15 March 2008

CHAPTER I

THE EXODUS

The room was sparsely furnished, with a large, well-scrubbed wooden table in the middle. The faint light shed by the naked light bulb hanging from the centre of the ceiling barely enabled the three students, all from the University of Szeged, to read the names of the villages on either side of the Austro-Hungarian border, since the letters on the old, well-worn map, spread out on top of the table, had become blurred. Not as if they had any chance to choose in advance the spot where they would try to leave the country in a few days time. They only knew that they had to escape, because they had no other choice. It was mid-November and they were ready to depart. During the revolution one of them, Lóránt Czigány, had taken up arms and joined the university battalion, which was put in charge of the barracks on the outskirts of the town, after they had been vacated in a hurry by the ÁVH, the hated secret police. Although he had never fired a single shot, he was convinced that severe punishment would be meted out to him. István Bátori, the other student, had gone home at the end of October to the nearby town of Szarvas, where he had volunteered for the newly set up local revolutionary home guard. Now, having returned to Szeged, he also had reason enough to fear what might happen to him if he decided to stay.

I was the third student, an elected member of the University Revolutionary Committee, who, in the belief that we would win the revolution, also had gone home to Kalocsa, a small town on the Danube in Southern Hungary, to check that my family was all right. After November 4th, when the Russian tanks had crushed the revolution, I returned against all advice to Szeged, because I was unwilling to accept that the promise of the glorious, intoxicating days of late October would never be fulfilled, or that the freedom we had only just won would be engulfed again by the all-pervasive slavery of communist ideology and practice. The student hostels were closed and we congregated in the flat of our fellow student, Marica Csetri, whose parents most generously—and not without risk—opened their doors to us, and offered a bed to those who had no other accommodation in town. We fervently debated what might happen to the country, to the university, to us. Our hope diminished day by day, as we were forced to realize that only the worst possible scenario could follow. I would be dismissed from the university – and this would be only a "mild" retaliation. My background and pervious history offered enough ammunition to the university authorities to judge my participation in the revolution with the utmost severity.

I had already been told firmly and unequivocally, at the age of fourteen, that because of my "clericalist and bourgeois" family background, I would not be educated "at the expense of the working class", would not be allowed to pursue any intellectual career or to be offered a white collar job in my life, but was destined to do physical labour, to which, rather to my surprise and regret, I was little suited. It was the summer of 1950 and I had just finished class VIII in the newly restructured school system. I loved studying and regularly achieved top marks and had no doubt that I would proceed to the local grammar school in September. So, when we heard that the pass list had been posted on the door of the class room, I rushed to inspect it. To my astonishment, the space where the name of the school, in which I was supposed to continue my studies should have been inserted, was left empty. It must be a mistake, an unfortunate omission, I thought. However, after sustained enquiries I was told, that as a child of a family, which could only be regarded as the "enemy of the people", I would receive no further state education.

Private education in my home town, of course, did not exist.

True, the family might have been accused to be under the influence of the Church, as one of my uncles was a priest, a Franciscan friar, in charge of the instruction of novices to the order in Hungary. Or, rather, he had been, since after the dissolution of the order in the previous year, he had been working as an unskilled labourer in one of the depots of the Hungarian railways. That we also had a nun in the family, we never even whispered about. She entered a convent as a young girl in Pozsony, and when my grandparents and their other children were expelled to Hungary after the First World War and the town became Bratislava in the newly created Czechoslovakia, she stayed there, so it was easy for us to keep silent about her existence. My father represented the "bourgeois" element. With great determination he had left the peasant existence of his family behind, learned a trade and opened a watchmaker and jeweller's shop in Kalocsa. He was respected in the town, widely liked and supported and due to his hard work, he was able to save enough to have a new house built in the desirable suburb called Burghers' Garden, after his first, more modest house had been swept away by the disastrous flood of the Danube in the spring of 1941. Before the Second World War he may have employed an assistant, but I was never aware of it; to my knowledge, he certainly never was or exploited anyone as a "capitalist ogre". One might say that the "bourgeois" and "clericalist" strands were combined in the commission he received from the local archbishopric: he was put in charge of all the clocks in the diocese. It was obvious that his enemies wished to punish him by barring me from further education.

The family refused to acquiesce in the decision: petition after petition was sent to anyone who might be able to advance our cause. Private teachers were sought out— retired, elderly men, who were brave enough to teach the children barred from the grammar school—and employed to give lessons in mathematics, chemistry and physics in order to prepare them for joining their classes if the decision were to be suddenly reversed. Slowly, a year went by and we had to accept defeat; all hope for a change seemed to be in vain, the regime stood firm, the unrelenting oppression reached and controlled all walks of life. Some of the replies to the petitions, however, outlined a possible, although rather long-term solution; after years of physical labour, which—one could only assume—"purified" the worker from all "bourgeois" tendencies, he would be allowed to follow part-time studies for the Hungarian equivalent of the GCE certificate. Accordingly, I was sent to work. First in a remote state-owned agricultural establishment, where concrete bunkers without any facilities served as accommodation for the labour force—food was brought to us in the fields. We hoed and weeded the unending rows of potatoes, marrows and cucumbers, or picked fruit and vegetables from sunrise to sunset. I desperately tried to do my best, but to no avail; I was the last among the hoers and never reached the target set for the pickers. At the end of season I was transferred to the paprika mill in my hometown, which is famous for producing the best "noble sweet" paprika powder in the country. My task was to thread the newly harvested red spice peppers onto a long string for hanging them up to dry in preparation for the milling. Again, I was rather useless: the needle pricked my fingers more often than passed through the stems of the paprika and no group of workers accepted me willingly as a member, because my contribution seriously lowered their required output.

By late autumn a new job was on offer, perhaps I would be more suited to help out in a kitchen. A simple, basic lunch was provided for about fifty to sixty people by two of us: a middle-aged cook and myself. I had to do all the preparation, such as peeling potatoes, cleaning the vegetables, washing up the dirty dishes and helping with the serving of the food. As the kitchen had no running water, it was also my task to fetch buckets of water from the well in the yard. So, I was rushing out umpteen times a day from the hot, steaming kitchen into the freezing air outside and it was no wonder that before the end of the year I contracted rheumatic fever, which then, in the absence of antibiotics, often proved fatal. My illness however, seemed to give me my lucky break. I was assigned to the care of Dr. Szántó, a GP and prominent party member, who might have felt some pity for my plight and interceded with the authorities on by behalf. Or, as the timing of my convalescence coincided with one of the temporary relaxations of the unremitting persecution of the "enemies of the people", the authorities might have relented and, to my delight, in the middle of January 1952, I received the long awaited permission to enter class I of the grammar school. Due to the instruction I had received, and to the extensive reading of literature and history books, which my mother had encouraged me to do, I sailed through the end of year exams in June and was allowed to take the second year exams during the summer. My teachers bent over backwards to extract from me the right answers—most of the exams were oral—and readily gave me the marks necessary to pass in all subjects. In September I was therefore able to rejoin my former class-mates and to obtain the GCE with distinction in 1954.

My experiences made me cautious in applying for a university place. Although I would have liked to pursue medical studies to become a doctor, I did not dare to put my name forward for this much coveted subject. I decided to study Hungarian language, literature and history instead. Nor did I dare to submit an application to any of the universities in Budapest, but chose a provincial university, the University of Szeged, in the hope that no particular attention would be paid to me and my background among the other applicants, probably relatively few in number and just about enough to fill the university's prescribed quota. Again, my luck held: during the interview I was quizzed about my favourite author and I took the chance to talk about Dickens, many of whose novels I had avidly read in Hungarian translation among the remnants of my uncle's discarded library which had come into my possession. One of the professors conducting the interview happened to be also a fan of Dickens and after a brief discussion of *A tale of two cities*, he more or less indicated that I would be accepted as a student. Moreover, I was awarded a so-called "Rákosi scholarship", a much larger monthly sum than the "ordinary" grant, named after the Communist dictator, Mátyás Rákosi. My friend, who was also interviewed for a university place, and I had discovered the notice about the grant posted on a board in the corridor of the Faculty of Arts, obtained the relevant forms and against the stern advice of our headmaster, submitted the application and during the rest of the summer holiday, we happily forgot all about it. Most probably no one else applied from Szeged and to our surprise—and consternation—we were singled out as the two freshers who had been awarded this "prestigious" grant. I was convinced that I would be regarded with suspicion by the other students as a stool pigeon of the party amongst them. Comrade Karácsonyi, the university's party secretary however, soon discovered the truth: instead of being a promising young Communist cadre, I was an unreliable "class alien". He warned me not to apply for the continuation of the grant the following year, as he would make sure that I would not get it. During the first two academic sessions therefore, I endeavoured to be as inconspicuous as possible: willingly participating in all compulsory activities but never assuming any leading role, happy being counted amongst the hard working elite but never excelling in any particular subject.

It was therefore utterly unexpected when Comrade Karácsonyi issued to me an unequivocal order just before the summer break, that I should take on the role of DISZ secretary in my class during the coming 1956/57 session. DISZ (Union of Working Youth) was the Communist party's youth organization, and the appointed secretaries were either trusted current or potential party members. Comrade Karácsonyi knew very well that I was neither. That spring, there was general dissatisfaction with, or even agitation against Rákosi and his regime. We, the students at Szeged we were aware of it, but at that time, having lost my father in February, I cared little about politics. Instead, I practised every evening with the university choir; we were to participate in the international festival at Llangollen. Of course, nothing came of it and, at my instigation, some of us began corresponding with the third year students in the University of Kolozsvár (Cluj in Romania), who were also studying Hungarian, with the aim of visiting each other and even spending a semester at each others' institutions. This idea must have sprung from the liberating unrest felt in the whole country and we were convinced that it was bold but achievable, when in truth, it was no more than a naive and rather dangerous dream. (Imagine the Romanian government's reaction to it: an attempt to export the unrest to another socialist country—the reason why the satellite countries in East Europe were hermetically sealed not only from the West, but also from one another—and to awaken the slumbering nationalistic feelings in the Hungarian minority in Transylvania!)

I dared not argue with Comrade Karácsonyi and was looking forward to my DISZ role with dismay. We—the newly appointed DISZ secretaries, some party members and students who were deemed reliable comrades—were called in by telegram a week before the semester started to attend a special seminar discussing university reforms. Leaders of the university's

Communist party informed us of the introduction of free choice: not all subjects would be compulsory, not even Russian, not all lectures need be attended, not even the Marxist-Leninist courses and we ourselves could draw up within limits our own course plans and timetable. There would be no more organized excursions into neighbouring villages to "admonish" the peasants about their "socialist duties" and no more forced participation in seasonal agricultural work, where the students in any case did more harm than good. Responsibilities for us, for our studies and education, up to then the privilege of the university authorities, would be devolved to us and we must be prepared to take them on. Heady stuff, but as the seminar progressed, we began to realize that what the party really wanted was to retain control, at least indirectly. Through us, the leaders of the students, the party could ensure that the new rules would be still shaped according to their rules and instructions. The students would trust us, because we would be communicating these exciting changes to them. And, of course, we would report back to the party. What the party members did not realize was that they had let the genie out of the bottle. We rightly interpreted their fake enthusiasm for the changes as disguised fear and it fuelled our demands for more substantial reforms, their cautiousness spurring us into action. With responsibility bestowed on us, we also embraced power; we felt liberated to voice our wishes and act upon them. And this was only the beginning.

October 1956 was immensely busy and exciting. We attended only those lectures we deemed relevant and interesting, developed our own study projects and, for the very first time, carried out our own research. The political changes taking place were fervently debated, the demands of the students formulated and re-formulated day by day. In addition, during the night we shovelled paprika into wagons at the local railway station in order to earn money for our planned excursion to Kolozsvár University. We were aware that at the general meeting of all students on 16 October, when we decided to set up our own union, called MEFESZ (Union of Hungarian University and College Students) in defiance of DISZ, we had boldly taken an irrevocable political stance against the whole Communist regime. Fear and timidity deserted us; the daring we exhibited was based on the firm conviction that we did not act alone, but that the whole country was behind us. So, on the evening of October 23rd, when in support of the students' marches in Budapest, we and with us the whole population of the town occupied the streets and squares, shouting, singing, reciting poetry, each one of us alone and all together with one single voice, we swept away the lies of the past eight years and dared to break the silence of fear imposed on us against our will.

Over the next few days the authorities tried to regain their lost ground. They mobilized the police force, posted the secret police and the army at strategic points, prohibited any assembly in public places and threatened those who dared to demonstrate with armed response; they were ready to shoot into the crowd. A curfew was declared after dark. Small groups of students played cat and mouse with the police to try and break it. The leaders of the university—among them the rector, Professor Dezső Baróti himself—were aware of the seriousness of the situation. They tried to collect the students and take them off the streets and move them to the nearest student hostel for safety. It was thus that we female students ended up in the hostel for male students for the night. In the morning we were allowed to return to our own hostel. In the porter's lodge Comrade Karácsonyi awaited us, with a notebook in his hand to enter in it the names of the disobedient students. "You too, Comrade Salacz?" he asked me. "Yes, me too, Comrade Karácsonyi", I replied defiantly. By the end of October the revolution seemed to be victorious and at the next general meeting of the students we set up the Revolutionary Committee of the University. My name was put forward to represent the students of the Arts Faculty on the Committee and I was duly elected. Although I was somewhat dubious about the person who proposed me—a devout party member in year four—and suspected his intentions as nothing but provocation, I was happy to serve even if our miraculous experiment were to fail and I were to reap all the consequences of my actions.

These were my thoughts in the flat of Marica's parents in mid-November. Surely, there was no future for me at Szeged and I would be lucky if my punishment was merely expulsion from the university. People were imprisoned for lesser "misdeeds". Were they to allow me to complete my studies, I would be in no better position. A teacher of Hungarian history, most probably in a provincial grammar school, I would have to stand in front of the class and talk about the "counter revolution" of 1956, staged by a bloodthirsty reactionary mob. I would have to repeatedly tell lies to my pupils, therefore knowingly defaming that glorious unique moment that we all felt had been worth living for. I had no other choice but to leave my home and escape to the West.

It is far from my intention here to write a personal history. However, during the last fifty years accusations have occasionally been levelled against the Hungarian refugees, in particular against the younger men and women among them—in some cases even in the guise of genuine research, seemingly supported by independent sociological surveys—that the great majority of those who escaped did so purely to seek adventure and an easy route to riches. It was alleged that they did not take part in the revolution, did not fight the invading Soviet Army—even if they claimed so subsequently—and probably held no political views at all, but seized the opportunity offered by the brief opening of the border with Austria and crossed the Iron Curtain in the hope of a better, more prosperous life in the West. They were no more than adventurers, in search of quick gains. As long as these accusations were made by historians, first and foremost by Julianna Puskás[1], commissioned by the Kádár regime to carry out research on Hungarian émigrés in the United States, there seemed to be no need to refute them, since their motives were more than transparent. It was well known that to obtain permission for undertaking such a project, the researcher must have been vetted and found to be a reliable cadre who was willing to accept the strings attached to the commission, including a pre-determined slant on what the findings should be. It is therefore regrettable that their distortions have found their way into scholarly works such as Béla Várdy's justifiably acclaimed magnum opus on Hungarians in America, in which he describes the 1956 refugees thus: "The vast majority of them were totally apolitical who left their home simply because the borders, closed till then, suddenly and unexpectedly were opened. They left partly in the hope of greater opportunities, partly driven by the sense of adventure dormant in all youth, to find out what the West could offer to them."[2] Or, a few paragraphs later, quoting Puskás's "well phrased" assessment of the young 1956 refugees verbatim: "Their pampering only stopped… when after the initial enthusiastic propaganda it began to come to light that very few of them actually fought in the revolution and the motivation of their flight was not political at all."[3] While Puskás acknowledges that their escape might also have been induced by fear, she limits that to the experiences they might have gained in the first half of the fifties, as if there had been no persecutions, trials and severe, often inhuman, punishment after the revolution was crushed. The premonition of these horrors to come by those who decided to leave was, indeed, truly justified. Assuming that Puskás was also well aware of this possible

[1] See Puskás, Julianna: Elvándorlások Magyarországról 1945 óta és a magyar diaszpóra néhány jellegzetessége az 1970-es években. (Migrations from Hungary since 1945 and some characteristics of the Hungarian diaspora in the 1970-ies.) In: Molnár, J., Orbán, S. and Urbán, K. eds.: *Tanulmányok a magyar népi demokrácia negyven évéről.* (Studies about the forty years of the peoples' democracy). Budapest, 1985. p.251.
[2] Várdy, Béla: *Magyarok az Újvilágban: az észak-amerikai magyarság rendhagyó története.* (Hungarians in the New World: an irregular history of the North-American Hungarians.) Budapest, 2000. p.450.
[3] Ibid. p.451.

motivation, she could not express it in the Kádár years without forfeiting the publication of the results of her research or even without endangering herself. Várdy has, however, little excuse for accepting Puskás's statements without critical evaluation. His references are still overshadowed by the bitter prejudice and ill-concealed displeasure with which the former "displaced persons" or "DPs" regarded the hordes of refugees. The "DPs" like himself, had endured hardship when after the Second World War they settled in the USA, while desperately trying to maintain standards. To them the newcomers were loud, uncouth and likely to be imbued with Communism, yet they were welcomed by the West with open arms and open purses.

My own experiences and ponderings were only one of many: the recollections of the former refugee students then and now speak unanimously of grief and the feeling of hopelessness and fear. They anticipated the worst. One of them, a well-regarded businessman with a successful career in electronics in Canada, for example, writing to the alumni association in his old university at Glasgow, begins his brief biography with the sentence: "Had they [the Russians or the Hungarian authorities] caught me, I would have certainly been hanged within weeks." He does not exaggerate; elected to the Revolutionary Committee of the Technical University of Budapest, he was soon delegated as the student representative to the Revolutionary Committee of the Armed Forces in charge of the capital—to which he modestly does not even refer in his letter. Hiding after the Russian invasion in a nearby village, he heard that the newly formed workers' militia was looking for him and there and then decided to leave the country.[4]

But the prerequisite for punishment did not need to be a heroic action; a small gesture was deemed to be enough: smiling encouragement for the demonstrators from an upstairs window, being one of the crowd surging ahead on the street, shouting with the others "Russians go home", helping to cut out the Soviet-style coat of arms from the Hungarian tricolour, pulling down the red star from the top of a building, printing or distributing leaflets listing the demands of the people, editing a "free" newspaper, publicly voicing an opinion of dissent, tending the wounded, burying the dead, or serving in the new institutions of the revolution. The simple knowledge that the ever-present and vigilant comrade karácsonyis had scribbled a student's name and his "misdeeds" into their notebooks, gave him enough reason to contemplate escape. It was the fear of reprisal that pushed the thousands of students across the Hungarian border.

---

[4] Interview with Tamás Csáthy. 16 Feb. 2006.

Paul Hollander, a refugee Hungarian student reading sociology at the London School of Economics and his friend and fellow student, Alan Dare, carried out in 1958 a survey among the Hungarian students studying in Great Britain. Their aim was to discover how the students had managed to settle down and with what degree of success they had begun the lengthy and often painful process of assimilation.[5] They distributed 350 questionnaires of which 279 were returned, a very high proportion, especially if we consider the suspicion with which such requests were received and the reluctance of the students—who still vividly remembered the bitter experiences of the Rákosi years—to reveal anything about themselves, even anonymously. Among other details, the students were quizzed about their background, when and why they decided to emigrate. They could choose from seven possible answers, but the choice was not limited to giving only a single one. In some cases, especially those picked by most students, the wording and therefore the content of both the questions and answers somewhat overlapped, and would have influenced the interpretation of the responses, had they not registered overwhelmingly the chief reasons for leaving Hungary as: "lack of individual rights", quoted 182 times, "danger to life and personal freedom" chosen by 167 students and "collapse of the revolution" – which, of course, echoed the sentiment of the previous two replies - nominated by 126 persons. 113 students indicated that they had also considered the opportunity to study in the West when they made their decision, but a large majority of them still believed that after they had acquired foreign languages and obtained their qualifications abroad, they would return to Hungary. The range of possible answers included the ominous "curiosity, desire for adventure" and it duly featured as the reason for leaving Hungary in 51 of the returned forms. However, two years after the revolution, a large majority of the students studying in Britain still clearly stated that they were forced to become refugees through sheer desperation and by the fear of reprisals.[6] The replies to the previous question ("When did you first think of leaving Hungary?") reinforces this perception; during the revolution only five persons contemplated leaving, while after the Soviets crushed it, 149 of them considered emigrating.[7]

Dare and Hollander encouraged the students to send in their comments; some of these read as moving personal confessions about the years of oppression: they talk of the lies everyone had to adopt simply to survive,

---

[5] Dare, Alan and Hollander, Paul: *Hungarian students in Great Britain. Past experiences – present attitudes.* London, 1959. Typescript.
[6] Ibid. Table 30, p.XXXV.
[7] Ibid. Table 29, p.XXXV.

of the enforced hypocrisy of the whole Communist system and of the desperation that all of this would now surely return. "I was always afraid"—writes one of them. "Even in comparison with my countrymen, I was more frightened and had fewer rights. The Communists lied constantly and they wanted to make me lie as well. One was always forced to be deceitful." Or, another statement: "The regime's propaganda that progress towards Communism was the supreme object was only a lie; this fundamental lie and the contradictions following from it made life unbearable." And listing what was unbearable: "The basic contradiction in the system, between theory and practice; the constant obligation to lie; the unbearable lack of confidence..."[8] This is what induced most of the students to leave their homeland. Having sampled freedom for a few intoxicating days, they refused to accept that the restrictions on every aspect of life would return. They wanted to start a new life without lies and fear in a country where one had personal freedom and rights and need not expect reprisals.

The scale of the reprisals only came to light after the change of regime in 1989, when at least some of the classified documents relating to 1956 were released. Even for a seemingly insignificant action during the so-called "counter-revolution" the perpetrator might have had to stand trial, be found guilty and sent to prison. A relatively mild punishment for a student included suspension for one or two semesters, however, a large number of them were expelled. The Council of the University of Szeged, at its meeting on 21st December 1989, named all those who had participated in some way or other in the revolution and suffered recrimination in 1957: the list contains the names of 38 university teachers and 82 students. As in the academic year 1956/57 the number of day students at Szeged University reached only 890, almost 10% of the student population was singled out for punishment. According to the Council minutes, 48 students from the three faculties of the University (Arts, Law and Sciences) were expelled during the spring and summer of 1957 and were barred from studying at any higher education institution in the country. The expelled students included those 31 who were known to have left the country. Six students were suspended for an academic year and another six indefinitely, fifteen received a severe reprimand, four a reprimand and two were cautioned. Four students were acquitted and the disciplinary procedures were still ongoing in the case of two.[9]

---

[8] Ibid. p.60.
[9] Bólya, Lajos, rector: *Jelentés a Szegedi tudományegyetem 1956-57. tanévi munkájáról. Hallgatói fegyelmi ügyek.* (Report on the work of the University of

The minutes of the Council of the Arts Faculty in September 1957 provide details of the punishment meted out to twelve named arts students. The student receiving the heaviest punishment, suspension for two semesters, was my fellow third year student, Etelka Fekete. Her "crime" is explained in the table, compiled for the book on the history of setting up MEFESZ, which also includes material on the reprisals: Etelka was among the students who collected donations to help cover the burial costs of the single victim of the revolution at Szeged, an eighteen year old worker, named Lajos Schwarz, who was shot by an army squad in the early days of the revolution.[10] This small, humane gesture proved to be enough for the then university authorities to set an intimidating example in her case. Yet, her background met all the requirements of the regime: her mother worked in a kolkhoz, lived in poor circumstances, and, according to the notes taken, she would not have been able to support her daughter during the suspension year. The Council therefore decided to recommend that Etelka should work as a semi-skilled labourer during her punishment.

The students who instigated the break with the Communist youth organization (DISZ) and were instrumental in setting up MEFESZ, received, after lengthy detention and trial, several years of imprisonment. And for those released from prison during the Kádár years punishment continued uninterrupted until 1989: they and even their families were stigmatized and discriminated against. They had no rights, received no recognition and in a sense existed outside society. It was therefore right and proper of the Council of the University of Szeged in 1989 to pass the following resolution: "Many of the University's respected members and students became the victims of politically motivated and denigrating procedures and of their serious consequences... The Council declares those procedures and the decisions then reached at the time to be contrary to the spirit of *universitas* and distances itself from them; it expresses its regret to those persecuted and to their relatives and regards them as belonging in perpetuity to the community of the *alma mater*." [11]

Although most students shared the main reasons for choosing to emigrate, the road leading to the final decision varied greatly. Some of

---

Szeged during the session 1956-57. Disciplinary action against students.) MOL, Box XIX-I-2-f/241.
[10] Kiss, Tamás: *Magyar Egyetemisták és Főiskolások Szövetsége 1956 – Szeged.* (The Union of Hungarian University and College Students 1956 – Szeged.) 2nd ed., Budapest, 2002, pp.169-173.
[11] A Szegedi Tudományegyetem Egyetemi Tanácsa: *Jegyzőkönyv az 1989. december hó 21-én megtartott ülésről.* (Council of the University of Szeged. *Minutes of the meeting of 21 December 1989.*) Resolutions no. 114-115/1989.

them left the country during the revolution on a specific mission, representing, for example, the revolutionary committees of the universities and seeking the support of the West, first and foremost of the national and international student organizations. When they heard the news of the invading Soviet army, they realized there was little merit in their returning as they would be soon caught by the military, Russian or Hungarian. They would be able to do more, and more effectively for Hungary, if they stayed abroad.[12] Some of them were warned by their parents not to go back and indeed, some of the parents themselves decided to leave the country. It is ironic, that the mother of András Sándor, one of the delegates of the Revolutionary Committee of the Budapest ELTE University, arrived in Vienna on 26th November to dissuade him from returning to Hungary, on the very same day as András, on board of one of the specially chartered aircraft to bring Hungarian students to Britain, landed at Blackbushe airfield. His mother also decided to stay in the West and they met only years later, in 1963, in New York.[13] Other students were in the delegation of Hungarian politicians, who in the name of the Prime Minister, Imre Nagy and the revolutionary government of Hungary, sought intervention by the United Nations.[14] Initially, a large number of students decided to await the outcome, many of them in hiding, hoping that all was not yet lost and that at least some of the demands expressed during the revolution might still be met, or that help would be coming from Western countries, first and foremost from the United Nations. When the West did not stir and persecution began to grow, they also left for the Austrian frontier. One of the most heartrending stories was that of a boy, only eighteen years old, who, when going home in a dark November evening, was met a few streets away from their house by his father, who was waiting for him. He was told that he could not go home as someone had denounced him as having taken up arms during the revolution and the police had already searched the house with a warrant for his arrest. He gave his son a small bundle with a few items deemed necessary for the journey into the unknown, advised him whom to seek out should he arrive safely in the West and bade him farewell then and there, seeing him perhaps for the last time.[15]

---

[12] See: Gömöri, György: Oxfordi egyetemisták a magyar szabadságért. (Students of Oxford for Hungarian liberty.) In: *Az 1956-os Magyar Forradalom Történetének Dokumentációs és Kutatóintézete. Évkönyv III.* 1994, p.27-34.

[13] Interview with András Sándor. 31 Oct. 2004.

[14] See, for example: Bujdosó, Alpár: *299 nap.* (299 days.) Budapest, 2003.

[15] Interview with Péter Pallai. 25 Sept. 2004. See also: Bogyay, Katalin: *The voice of freedom. Remembering the 1956 revolution.* London, 2006, p.96.

Many of those whose application for a university place had been rejected on political grounds or those who were expelled from the universities for reasons often not even explained to them, also decided to emigrate. Their aim was to study abroad and to build their careers without obstruction, something which was denied to them in their own country. Perhaps they could be labelled "economic migrants", but hardly adventurers. Although not as students, they might have participated in the events of late October, might even have fought the Russians and they had reason enough to fear the reprisals. But even for those not involved in the uprising, what could the future offer? They had already been cast away by the previous regime, and the new one, taking an equally hard line, would not be more lenient. For the men and women, imprisoned during Rákosi's regime and freed by the revolution, there was only one option: they also had to leave Hungary. They knew that they would be rounded up, thrown back into the jails, accused with "new crimes" they had probably not committed, and their sentences would be increased manifold.

Such prisoners were László Jámbor and his wife, Kati. László Jámbor initially entered the medical university in Budapest to become a doctor, but after two years wanted to transfer to the University of Economics. His request was refused on the grounds that "he had already wasted enough money of the Peoples' Republic", but he was allocated a place in the Russian Institute, where, understandably, there were plenty of vacancies. By the early 1950s he had become involved with a group of malcontents who were, rather naively, plotting resistance, stockpiling Second World War ammunition found in the Buda hills, so that they would be ready for fighting as partisans if and when Hungary would be freed by the West. The group and its activities were revealed to the ÁVH, the secret police, and all its members were arrested, except László, who managed to escape and hide in a picturesque village, called Kesztölc, in the Pilis mountains, where local resistance was also fermenting. He helped with the production and distribution of leaflets—they had so little funds at their disposal that they stole a radio from the workers' club and sold it in order to cover at least some of the printing costs. Kati, László's fiancée, an arts student in Budapest, acted as a liaison person between members of the resistance group and participated in the leafleting action. When the undercover agent of the ÁVH, who had infiltrated the group, demanded the delivery of the text for a new batch of leaflets, Kati gave it to him and he promptly passed it to the police. Both László and Kati, together with the other members of the group were taken into custody. A show-trial was mounted and exemplary sentences were passed on 7 October 1952: two of the Kesztölc leafleteers were executed, László got life-imprisonment, Kati first fifteen, then after appeal, ten years in prison.[16]

They met again only four years later, in early November 1956, after the political prisoners had been set free by the revolutionary forces. A friend offered temporary accommodation to them in her parents' house in Budapest, until they could decide what they wanted to do. Kati's mother, a devout and conservative woman, would only acquiesce to this arrangement if they promptly got married in a church—not an easy task to arrange a wedding ceremony in the general upheaval. Fortunately, the local vicar lived only a few houses away and was willing to do the honours. Within days, László and Kati knew they had no other choice, but to leave the country. The first step was to obtain an official marriage certificate from the registry office in the local town hall. One could assume that this type of request was not unique when thousands contemplated emigration; the registrar pulled in witnesses from among the passers-by in the street and issued the documents without any delay. The small group of political prisoners embarked on their journey to the Austrian frontier mid-November. They had no money, with the exception of a few hundred forints, a tiny sum given to one of them, a girl called Juli, by the Israeli consulate, because when seeking support, she said that she intended to emigrate to Israel. Yet, she nearly gave it up and only at the strenuous encouragement of the others climbed onto the back of the lorry. What they could rely on however, was the network of former fellow prisoners who provided them with accommodation, food and advice on their way across Transdanubia. A few days later László and Kati Jámbor crossed the border at the small village of Sopronhorpács and headed first to Vienna, and then to England.[17]

Finally there should also be mention of those who left, or tried to leave Hungary before 1956. Many of them were Jewish children, who were herded up during the last months of the Second World War, to be taken to the concentration camps abroad and of whom only a few survived. Some others left the country with the retreating Hungarian Army, but returned home in 1945 with their families. There were also those, who wanted to emigrate after the Communist takeover but were caught and duly punished for their failed attempt. The story of Sándor Váci, now an independent architect, working mainly in the City of London, might be singled out as

---

[16] For the details of this small resistance movement see: Fáy, Zoltán: Röplapszórók. Egy ellenállási mozgalom 1952-ben: a kesztölci összesküvés. (The leafleteers. A resistance movement in 1952: the Kesztölc conspirary.) *Magyar Nemzet*, 16 Oct. 2004.
[17] Interview with Katalin Jámbor. 6 Jan. 2005.

an example. Still a baby, he was taken by his family to France a few months before the outbreak of the war. They hoped to settle near Lille and to set up a factory manufacturing putty, for which there was enough demand by the local vegetable growers for the insulation of their greenhouses. They had barely settled down in their new environment, when war was declared. They were expelled as aliens and after many vicissitudes ended up at Trieste in Italy, and finally, now penniless, returned to the Hungarian town of Vác, from where they had started their epic journey. Sándor Váci's father died on the Eastern front where he was serving in a forced labour unit of the Hungarian army. His mother's attempt to cross the border to the West in the 1950s was unsuccessful. Lumbered with all this emotional package, Váci grew up and obtained his GCE in June 1956, but being of bourgeois origin, he was not admitted to the College of Design, where he wanted to study. However, he is now convinced that the deprivation he received as a boy bolstered both his compassion and self-esteem: people never felt greater solidarity with each other than during the tyrannical Rákosi years, when everyone received an equal share of misery, persecution and poverty. During the revolution he was more of a bystander; he witnessed the important events, but did not take up arms. He does not regard himself a hero, but still despairs about losing a little piece of Stalin's monumental bronze statue which was pulled down and broken up by the joyous crowd. He left Hungary again with his family in1956, more curious than expectant about finding opportunities only freedom could offer.[18]

During November and December Radio Free Europe incessantly broadcast coded messages under assumed names of those who had managed to escape. These were to allay the anxiety of members of their family and friends still in Hungary. However, they also encouraged those who prepared themselves to head for the border. "If they were able to escape, why not us?"—many posed the question, hoping for the best. Crossing the border was not without danger. The first refugees, who crossed soon after 4th November, were mostly from nearby towns and villages. They were able to walk across the open border and needed not to fear the mines, barbed wire or soldiers firing at anyone crossing no man's land. The Western media, in full gear, waited for them on the Austrian side, taking pictures of their smiling faces or of them tearfully gathering a last handful of earth from their homeland.

By mid-November however, the Russians and some of the Hungarian border guards had closed in and on 22nd November the first snow of the

---

[18] Interview with Sándor Váci. 23 Feb. 2006.

winter fell, making the escape more difficult: it was easy to pinpoint and apprehend the escapees haltingly negotiating the frozen furrows in the snow covered fields. Every refugee has his or her own story. The experiences they gained would furnish them with ample material to tell their children and grandchildren in years to come: how they managed to secure the last place in an already overloaded lorry, how they alighted from the train stopping on the open track, miles away from the nearest city, where the police were waiting for them at the railway station. How kindly the villagers helped them, put them up for the night, fed them and offered advice on the best way to avoid the quickly moving Russian troops. How much they had to pay to the guide who would take them right up to frontier and how anxiously they hoped that it really was only a few steps away when he left them alone. How they caught their breath when a fallen twig broke under their foot, making a terrifyingly sharp burst of noise in the silence of the woods. How they listened petrified to the barking of the police dogs and waited by lying down in the furrows for the darkness to envelop them again when the flares, fired by the army, brightly illuminated the whole landscape. How would they know that they arrived on Austrian soil? Was this the last icy stream they had to cross, the bridge leading to the other side? Or, had they gone back into Hungary because of the irregularities of the border? Were they walking towards a single source of light—presumably a village in Austria—or going around it in circles? Of the common experience of all refugees, let us quote one story, which demonstrates not only the vicissitudes they had to overcome, but also their determination, courage and perseverance which drove them towards freedom.

Antal Ormay, an arts student studying journalism, was a member of the delegation from Budapest visiting Győr, a major town in Transdanubia, where the Revolutionary Council was still resisting the invading army, and operating the last remaining "free radio" in the country. Ormay, who was relaying and collecting messages, offered his help to the Council, trying to bury his desperation in feverish activities. However, he soon realized that all was in vain, and that the revolution was irrevocably crushed. He was warned that the police were looking for him; they had already searched his lodgings. It would have been futile to go back to Budapest, as he would be caught there too. Ormay decided to emigrate. He recalled what he had learned in his geography lessons: Győr is a town where three rivers meet to join the Danube, one of them, the Rábca, has its source somewhere in the swamps of Lake Fertő, which straddles the Austro-Hungarian border. The Rábca could serve as guide for him; he only has to follow it upstream. This was a route no one took. Alone, he had not only to conquer the considerable distance, but also the creeping November frost, his numbing loneliness and awakening doubts. Some workmen repairing the river bank said that if he kept going, he would reach a hut before dusk fell, where he would be welcomed to stay overnight. But the hut was dark, its door locked, seemingly abandoned. Ormay, utterly exhausted, prised open one of the windows, climbed in and slumped on the bed and fell asleep as he was, with his overcoat and shoes still on.

At dawn he was woken up by someone banging on the door. There was no choice: he could not hide or flee unseen, he had to open it. The visitors were friends of the people normally inhabiting the hut. Listening to Ormay's tale, they gave him food and a detailed explanation of how to get to the border safely through the labyrinthine marshland of rivulets, canals, stagnant water and the reed beds of Lake Fertő, where only those in the know could find their way. Even the border was peculiarly drawn; one segment of it protruded deep into Austria, and Ormay had to take care not to cross it twice, coming back into Hungary. After two days strenuous walking he successfully reached Austria. To complete the story, and to record that his inventiveness had indeed not deserted him in London, it is worth recounting his escapade in the Lancaster Gate Hotel. Ormay flew in with the first of the chartered aircraft bringing Hungarian refugee students to Britain and the British Council for Aid to Refugees put them up in the Lancaster Gate Hotel before transferring them to Oxford. Ormay woke up in the morning feeling very hungry but he had no notion what one was supposed to do in such an elegant place. His knowledge of English was practically non-existent, but thinking hard, the word "breakfast" came into his mind. Picking up the telephone, he half-heartedly placed an order by shouting the magic word into it. He was amazed when few minutes later the door opened and a trolley loaded with a full English breakfast, was wheeled in.[19]

It is estimated that over 200,000 refugees left Hungary, among them between 7000 and 8000 university students. Today, listening to their stories, their first acts in the West seem almost comical, though, knowing the background, completely understandable. With their few Austrian Schillings they went out to buy an illustrated magazine, a bunch of bananas and a bottle of coca-cola. Western magazines were not allowed across the Iron Curtain, where the papers were drab and contained only propaganda. Everyone imagined that magazines published abroad were immensely exciting and the true purveyors of Western style living and culture. Bananas were also not available in Hungary—heaven knows why.

[19] Interview with Antal Ormay. 25 Nov. 2004.

When in a recently released Hungarian film, one of the cast peeled a banana and ate it, audiences in every cinema heaved a huge sigh of desire. Coca-cola was not only banned, but labelled as a dangerous mind-blowing drug, the symbol of the depravity of the West. Not surprisingly, refugees in the camps surrounded those who had been singled out to drink a bottle of the demon drink, with a great expectation of what would happen. They were more than disappointed when it produced no discernible after-effect.

The whole world, from which the population of the satellite countries had been almost hermetically sealed off, suddenly opened up and that was truly mind-blowing for the refugees. They could go anywhere, chose any country to live in—but why, on what grounds? What might seem incredible today is that most of the students firmly believed —in spite of their experiences under the Communist regime, of their bitterness at losing the last chance of a better life the revolution had promised and of their fear of the reprisals which could last for years—that they were destined only for a short stay in the West. After completing their studies, learning languages and gaining new experiences, they would return home. The years spent as wandering scholars would be of benefit to their home country. (Gyula Várallyay's book on setting up the organization of Hungarian refugee students in the West, the Union of Free Hungarian Students, is "On a study-tour", clearly referring to this belief. The students were preparing to learn as much as they could in the shortest possible time, and then to go back home.)[20] This self-induced delusion, flying in the face of experience and commonsense, could only have sprung from the pain and desperation of leaving one's home with little hope of ever returning. The students knew that the belief in a study-tour was only an irrational make-believe to enable them to accept the seemingly unacceptable.

The choice for those with some knowledge of a foreign language was easier, as it was for the escapees who had relatives in a Western country. Most of the refugees, however, stood bewildered at the almost limitless opportunities opening up for them and felt under immense pressure to decide instantly their own fate and that of their families. One of the most poignant descriptions of this mind-numbing feeling can be found in Stephen Vizinczey's book, *In praise of older women.* Himself a refugee, he depicts a scene he experienced in a small Austrian village near the Hungarian border: "On the Austrian side of the border we found a road, a passing milk truck picked us up and drove to the nearest village. The

---

[20] Várallyay, Gyula: *Tanulmányúton: az emigráns magyar diákmozgalom 1956 után.* (On a study tour: the movements of émigré Hungarian students after 1956.) Budapest, 1992.

village square was already crowded with refugees, who were stamping their feet against the cold and staring at a line of brand new silver buses. These had yellow, hand-painted signs proclaiming the points of their destination: Switzerland, U.S.A., Belgium, Sweden, England, Australia, France, Italy, New Zealand, Brazil, Spain, Canada, West Germany and, simply, Wien. At the police station on the other side of the square, Red Cross officials were dispensing the first aid of hot coffee and sandwiches, while nurses in black coats and white caps scurried through the crowd in search of the wounded and babies in need. Other officials, appearing less sympathetic, were prodding the refugees to pick a bus and get on it.

'That revolution must have made bigger headlines than I thought' a young man commented. 'We're getting the red-carpet treatment reserved for victims of sensational disasters.' Still, most of us were bewildered by the sight of that muddy village square with its buses going to the four corners of the earth. Less than an hour before, we couldn't move without being shot at; now we were invited to choose our place under the sun. It did not make sense to the senses, things didn't connect... Where to spend the rest of one's life? A couple with a small baby, who had already boarded the bus for Belgium, got off and rushed to the vehicle marked New Zealand. There were others who walked up and down the lines of buses, reading and re-reading the names of countries with studious expressions, but without being able to make up their minds. And where was I finally going to get my Ph.D.? In what language? It was impossible to believe that by taking a few steps in this or that direction I would settle these questions for good. I happened to be standing beside the yellow letters 'Sweden'. If I stepped on that bus, I would meet a woman in Stockholm and we'd fall in love – but if I moved on to the next vehicle, we'd never even learn of each other's existence.'[21]

The three of us, students from Szeged, also lived through these incredible days in the state of an emotional see-saw: we were overjoyed that we had managed to escape, but anxious as to where would eventually end up, grateful for the care we received, but afraid that somewhere, someone whom we did not know, would decide our future. We were full of plans that changed daily, because no one could assure us that they were feasible. If we wanted to make our own decision, there was no time to waste, even if we chose to leave our fate to chance. We enrolled simultaneously for the quotas destined to go to England, France and Sweden and planned to leave with the first contingent to depart from the camp. At the beginning of December, the British representative distributed

---

[21] Vizinczey, Stephen: *In praise of older women*. London, 1966, pp.135-137.

to each member of the group leaving for England a nice, soft plaid and herded all of us onto the waiting bus. First we were taken to Graz, then to Linz and from there by aeroplane to Blackbushe airfield in Hampshire. We crossed the Hungarian border on 21st November and arrived in England on 7th December.

Hollander and Dare's survey reveals that our decision to leave the final outcome to chance was by no means unique: of the 279 replies they received, 45 stated that they acted similarly—15 of them wanted to leave the Austrian camp as soon as possible and 30 students, without really knowing why, joined the groups of refugees going to Britain. 59 respondents quoted the efficiency of the British in organizing the transport and the promise of grants to continue their studies. The rest made up their minds after careful consideration of the advantages of settling in the United Kingdom: it offered a reliable safe haven, personal and political freedom, democratic rights, peaceful existence, a feeling of well-being and wide ranging social welfare provisions and, last but by no means least, it was the furthest in Europe from the Iron Curtain. "I heard a great deal about Britain"—writes one of them. "It seemed to be a country where I could most quickly build up the moral basis necessary for starting a new life, and where I would most likely find peace and security." Or, quoting another reply: "I always wanted to go to a British university. I wanted to stay in Europe but to be as far away as possible from its trouble spots."[22] As László Cs. Szabó, a Hungarian writer, living in exile in London expressed perhaps most eloquently the common sentiment: "Give back my human dignity, my last refuge, my castle built on a rock, England!"[23]

Being able to speak some English certainly influenced the choice to come to England. Those, who had a smattering of English hoped to find their way and settle down quickly, whilst those who did not, knew that after learning it, they could settle down anywhere in the world. To the question "Why did you come to Britain?" two answers could be chosen from a list of eleven. 38 respondents gave as their first choice "Language—familiar, useful, important" while 68 picked it as the second choice.[24] The responses to the survey were made two years after coming to Britain and were likely to be influenced by other factors, namely, the experiences gained on and after arrival, first and foremost by the exceptionally warm welcome the refugee students received and the help they were given. As one of them summarizes it in his answer: "When I

---

[22] Dare, Alan and Hollander, Paul: Op. cit.. p.52.
[23] Cs. Szabó, László.: A bujdosó hegedős. (The fugitive fiddler.) *Irodalmi Ujság*, 15 March, 1958.
[24] Dare, Alan and Hollander, Paul: Op. cit., Table 33, p.XXXVI.

came, I did not care where I was going, but now I am glad that I came
here." Or, quoting from another answer: "I came to Britain by sheer
chance; but even if I had had a choice I would have come here. I think it is
the most democratic and the freest country in the world." And, striking a
less high note: "I like the British; one can live here in peace; but I had no
idea that the weather was so bad."[25]

---

[25] Ibid. p.53.

CHAPTER II

THE LORD MAYOR'S FUND

The authorities in England placed the three of us, like most of the Hungarian refugees, into barracks recently vacated by the army which had been dispatched to Suez. It was therefore at the Crookham military establishment where I received my first cup of English tea, the first bowl of cereal—both of them causing quite a shock—and, before being corralled into the sleeping quarters, issued with a pair of man's blue and white striped pyjamas, tied with a string, which I kept out of sentimentality, for years. Only a few days had passed when the interpreter, full of excitement, whispered: "A great honour is to be bestowed on us, the Lord Mayor of London himself is to pay a visit to the camp!" All Hungarian children know something about the Lord Mayor: they all learn by heart the poem by János Arany on the fate of the bards of Wales, who went to their death at the stakes rather than hail the conqueror of their country, King Edward I. Arany wrote the tersely composed allegorical ballad in response to the summons by the Austrian authorities to eulogize the Habsburg emperor, Francis Joseph, when visiting Hungary after crushing the 1848/49 freedom fight with the help of the Russians. Returning from Wales, King Edward suffers from nightmares: he seems to hear the song of the martyred bards in his dreams. He threatens the Lord Mayor of London with hanging should the slightest noise disturb the silence of the night.

In my recollection, the newly installed Lord Mayor of London, Sir Cullum Welch, was smallish, slight in stature but exuding authority. We appreciated however his somewhat medieval looking official black attire and the heavy, superbly wrought gold chain around his neck more than the man and his position. We did not comprehend why he was received with such circumspection in the camp by all the officials and why we were admonished by the interpreters to show the greatest respect to him. Fortunately, our non-existent English—we were unable to put our amazement into words or ask silly questions—hid our shameful ignorance. How were we to know that all the Hungarian refugees owed the excellent organization of their reception to him: the quick transfer from the camps in

Austria to England, the immediate registration without any fuss, the help offered for learning English and learning about England, for finding jobs, settling down and building a new home, a new existence for themselves in a foreign country? And how were we, Hungarian refugee students, to know in the Crookham barracks that the financial support we would receive for the continuation of our studies will be met to a large extent from the grant received by the universities from the Lord Mayor of London's special appeal fund? The fund, though set up by the Lord Mayor barely a month's ago, had by the time of his visit to Crookham collected over a million and half pounds. It was a nationwide response to the crushing of the Hungarian revolution by the Soviet Army, fuelled by the remorse people felt about the inadequacy of the "free world" to help Hungary when she most needed it and to come to the aid of the people desperately fighting for their rights and freedom. The remorse was doubly felt in Britain because of the Suez crisis; an ill-judged action, condemned by the majority of the population, which pushed the news about the Hungarian revolution to the background at a crucial time and rendered hypocritical the protests against the neo-colonial aggression of the Soviets.

Hungary, of course, had been in the news since the middle of October, the papers linking the growing unrest there with events in Poland, as being part of the general "ferment" in Eastern Europe. After 23rd October the revolution in Hungary became a main news item; all the newspapers followed it with keen interest, reporting on Downing Street's admiration for Hungary, the government's offer of £25,000 to the Red Cross for medical supplies and the departure of the 21st Royal Air Force planes to take supplies to Budapest. Oddly enough, on 23rd October, the day when the revolution broke out, the question of refugees and their reception in the United Kingdom was raised in Parliament: it was, however, on the potential influx of Poles to Britain. Would the government be ready to amend the existing quotas? On behalf of the Home Office, the Parliamentary Secretary, Mr. Deedes, reassured the House of Commons that there was no intention to change the policy on set limits: "If we abandoned the limits of our present policy, there would be not hundreds but thousands of potential immigrants to the UK from behind the Iron Curtain."[1] In respect of Hungary, readers felt that whatever the government did, it was by no means enough. In a letter John Appleby belittled the sum earmarked for instant relief and argued that someone should set up a national appeal to double, or even quadruple the £25,000

---

[1] Reported next day in *The Daily Telegraph*. Iron curtain immigrants: flood from Poland. 24 Oct. 1956, p.13.

set aside for this purpose.[2] The publication of the letter, however, coincided with the outbreak of the war in Suez and the exploding crisis pushed the news on Hungary to the background. While, over the next few days, the newspapers could not resist showing the severed head of Stalin's statue in the dust of a Budapest boulevard, or the picture of Cardinal Mindszenty being freed from prison, the column inches dealing with the Hungarian revolution shrank dramatically and were more or less banished from the pages devoted to main foreign news items. No wonder: the Suez crisis was of overriding interest and importance to the people of Britain and the Hungarian revolution had, in any case, been declared "victorious" by Imre Nagy, the new prime minister, as quoted, for example, in *The Times*.[3] It was time to concentrate all attention on the government's folly at Suez.

The invasion of Budapest by the Red Army on Sunday, 4th November, changed everything. The brutal crushing of the uprising was the main item in all the newspapers; the title of the leader in *The Daily Telegraph* providing the catchphrase: "Martyrdom of Hungary".[4] The following day the linking of events in Hungary and Suez already appeared in the papers, most forcefully in the readers' letters. To cite only two examples: a telegram by four Liberal candidates, among them Jeremy Thorpe (later leader of the Liberal Party), addressed to Anthony Eden: "Your example has deprived us of the right to protest at the murder of Hungary"[5] and a letter by Robert Speight and Malcolm Muggeridge in *The Times*: "The bitter division in public opinion provoked by the British intervention in the Middle East has already one disastrous consequence. It has deflected popular attention from the far more important struggle in Hungary. A week ago the feelings of the British people were fused in a single flame of admiration for the courage and apparent success of the Hungarian revolt. Now, that success seems threatened by Russian treachery and brute force and Hungary has appealed to the West... The Prime Minister has told us that 50 million tons of British shipping are at stake in his dispute with President Nasser. What is at stake in Central Europe are more than 50 million souls."[6]

The newspapers also reported on the widespread protests, often violent, in Europe's major cities and on the first refugees crossing the border from Hungary to Austria. By Wednesday protest marches in the

---

[2] *The Daily Telegraph*, 31 Oct. 1956.
[3] *The Times*. Revolution victorious. 1 Nov. 1956, p.10.
[4] *The Daily Telegraph*. 5 Nov. 1956, p.6.
[5] Ibid. 6 Nov. 1956, p.12.
[6] *The Times*. 6 Nov. 1956, p.11.

United Kingdom also began; more than a thousand Glaswegian students poured onto the streets to express in a dignified, silent march their solidarity with Hungary. Their action was repeated on Thursday by students in Dublin and Cardiff and on Friday in London, where students marched from the Royal Albert Hall to the Soviet Embassy in Kensington Gardens, four abreast, with black armbands, waving Hungarian and Polish flags. Students were also ready to embrace direct action: four Oxford undergraduates[7] left immediately for Hungary without even seeking permission from their colleges and the students of Nottingham University put forward the idea of forming a volunteer student force to fight in Budapest. They received strong support from the students of London University; *The Times* quoted the call to arms by J. Ashbourne: "We want everyone who can carry a gun and use a gun and willing to go."[8]

The tumultuous events of the week, presented most forcefully by the media, resulted in an unprecedented outpouring of sympathy, the voicing of remorse and frustration of not being able to offer direct help to Hungary, and in the urge to do something concrete and practical at once. The first pictures and reports on the growing number of refugees also appeared in the papers inflaming the smouldering dissatisfaction with the government's belated action or lack of action—although notwithstanding the statement about strictly keeping the existing immigration limits given to the House of Commons less than a fortnight before, the quota for Hungarian refugees was instantly raised to 2,500 persons—and contributing to the anxiety of ordinary people by not receiving guidance on how and where to channel best the donations they were keen to offer. True, the British Red Cross and the organization of Hungarian emigrants living in Britain issued appeals to collect donations—money and clothes— for the refugees and to be sent to Hungary and the students of Oxford University were among the first to open a Hungarian fund. However, it soon became obvious that a nationwide appeal should be launched and a central organization set up for co-ordinating and supervising both the collection of donations—financial and material—and their fair distribution. It could assess and meet the needs of the refugees arriving in Great Britain and of those housed in makeshift camps in Austria and to send aid—mainly food and medicine—to Hungary. The task of setting up

---

[7] Judith Cripps, Roger Cooper, Basil and Christopher Lord. Of their escapade in Hungary László Cs. Szabó reported in detail on the BBC Hungarian broadcast and included it in a short story: A négy fogoly. (The four prisoners.) *Magyar Szó,* 15 Feb. 1957.

[8] *The Times.* 11 Oct. 1956, p.4.

such an all-embracing national organization was readily accepted by Sir Cullum Welch, the newly installed Lord Mayor of London.

What the original subject of the Lord Mayor's speech at the Guildhall banquet on Friday, 9 November 1956 might have been, is not known. His acceptance of launching a national appeal for Hungary cancelled all previous plans, and instead he announced his intention to set up a Hungarian Relief Fund immediately. According to a letter sent by the Principal of London University, Dr D.W. Logan, to the Equerry to Queen Elizabeth the Queen Mother, informing her as the Chancellor of the University of the steps taken by university officials for Hungarian refugee students. The idea of such a fund was first suggested by Dr Bolsover, Director of the School of Slavonic and East European Studies to the City Remembrancer on Tuesday, 6 November, two days after the invasion of Hungary.[9] The following day the Mayor of Deal sent a telegram to the Lord Mayor to the same effect and he was quickly joined by the mayors of Birmingham, Leeds and Wolverhampton, who had already initiated the collection of donations in their cities but felt that the co-ordination of the effort should be nationwide. Sir Cullum Welch was open to the requests and after consulting the Foreign Office, which gave its approval to the scheme, was ready to announce the immediate launch of The Lord Mayor of London's National Hungarian & Central European Relief Fund— shortened to the Lord Mayor's Fund—in his speech at the Friday evening Guildhall banquet.

The following day the newspapers reported it in full and the Lord Mayor himself spoke to the nation on the BBC, asking the people of Britain to be generous in their support of "this most deserving cause". He aimed to collect £1 million by the end of November: "... Every one of you listening tonight will I am sure, have been deeply moved and saddened over the distressing plight of the thousands of refugees and homeless caused by the recent events in Hungary. In this island we have withstood invasion, and we have maintained the standard of freedom for hundreds of years—and without fear. To the Englishman, his home is his castle, and the thoughts of us are daily centred on our families, our children and our friends. We live in peace and freedom, and so we find it difficult easily to picture the stark horror which has overcome another independent-minded people. We therefore feel great sympathy for the citizens of Hungary in their present hour of need, and we admire the brave spirit of those who seek to be free man. We have no exact knowledge at this moment of the

---

[9] Letter by D.W. Logan to Lieutenant-Colonel M.J. Gilliatt. 15 Nov. 1956. University of London Archives. Records of the Hungarian Refugee Students Scheme (hereafter UoLA). CB3/4/12.

help which can most usefully be given, but we are all of us aware of the need, and we do know of the splendid work which is so rapidly being organised by the Red Cross and other voluntary organisations . We know that there are urgent needs for medical assistance, for emergency food supplies, for clothing, for child care, and for transport and resettlement of the homeless. These all cost money in themselves and can only be a small part of the total requirement.

"Many individual friends of freedom and of Hungary, and a number of organisations throughout this country, have felt the need to show early and practical assistance and sympathy with these unhappy people. As a result I have as the Lord Mayor of London, had many countless enquiries as to the best way of organising this relief to enable our natural urge as fortunate free people to take a practical form... Last night at the Guildhall Banquet I announced that I was prepared to launch a National Fund for this relief, and today that Fund has been created... On behalf of those citizens of Hungary, whom we so much admire and who to-day are in distress... I invite you listening to me to-night to subscribe generously to this Fund... All contributions will be welcomed, and they will be acknowledged."[10]

In his letter to *The Times*, published on Monday, 12th November, prompted by the ever increasing number of refugees, he added: "The agonizing course of recent events in Hungary has been followed by the people of this country with growing sorrow and dismay. Thousands of lives and homes have been shattered and a stream of refugees has been pouring across the frontiers. The plight of these refugees is pitiable indeed, as they have no means or prospect of support except from the generosity of those throughout the world whose sympathies have been aroused... It is impossible at this stage to measure the need for help. This need is already immense. No one can be sure how loud will be the cry of distress which will be raised by stricken people in Central Europe. It is certain that the cry will not fall upon deaf ears."[11]

He was also able to announce in his BBC broadcast on Sunday that the first donations had already been received. The Lord Provost of Glasgow telegraphed his support with an immediate contribution of £1,000 and the same sum was made available to the Fund by Sir Winston Churchill, who expressed his keen interest in the cause, through his Birthday Trust. There was no time to waste; the administration of the Fund had to be set up with the utmost speed. Again, he was able to assure the people of Britain that

---

[10] Broadcast by the Lord Mayor of London on BBC radio. 10 Nov. 1956. In: The Lord Mayor of London's National Hungarian & Central European Relief Fund. *Report of the Fund November 1956 – September 1958.* [London, 1958], pp.3-4.
[11] *The Times*, 12 Nov. 1956, p.11.

offices had already been allocated for the Fund in the Mansion House and were just being equipped, the necessary skeleton staff had been appointed and the Fund should be fully operational by the following Monday. The Bank of England offered to supervise the administration of the financial transactions. Notifications were sent to all mayors, provosts and other municipal heads in the country requesting their support and an Advisory Committee was to be established to include the mayors of major cities to assist and guide the Lord Mayor of London, who would take the chair of the Committee. The largest national charities had been mobilized—among them the British Council for Aid to Refugees (BCAR), the British Red Cross, the Women's Voluntary Service, the YMCA and YWCA, the St. John Ambulance Brigade and the Save the Children Fund—to co-ordinate their activities for the greatest effectiveness and efficiency under the aegis of the Lord Mayor's Fund.

At the peak of the campaign over a hundred people – most of them volunteers – worked in the Fund's offices twelve hours a day. All helping hands were needed: during the time the Fund was open, over 116,000 separate donations were sent directly to the Mansion House in the form of cheques, postal orders or cash. Each donor received a receipt and a letter of thanks. (It is remarkable that after the Fund was closed and the accounts audited and presented to the Committee, the total sum spent on administration, including printing and postal charges, amounted to a mere £16,410, or, if only the cost of manpower is taken in to account, the total cost spent on staff was the incredibly low figure of £2,537, that is, less than 0.095% the total collection.) Most of the equipment was lent and stationery given free or at a nominal cost: typewriters were on loan from the Imperial, Oliver and Remington companies, Roneo Ltd. provided the filing cabinets and Biro Swan Ltd. made a gift of pens. Printing of the receipts, letters and other necessary forms was done at a much reduced cost and expert advice provided free. Newspapers reproduced a specially designed appeal poster and reported on the state of the Fund almost daily.

Practically all companies, firms, financial and other institutions in the City wished to participate in the campaign—the largest of them contributing thousands of pounds. The Lloyds Corporation donated £25,000, members of the Stock Exchange £18,250 and members of the Baltic Exchange £16,760. The major banks, led by the Bank of England, donated well over a thousand pounds each. The Houlton Press brought out a picture book: *Cry, Hungary*, depicting the scenes of the revolution and refugees crossing the border, and offered the total proceeds from its sale, more that £6,000, to the Fund. To reach the target of collecting one million pounds in a very short period of time, a truly national effort was needed and the country rose magnificently to the challenge. Reading the reports it seems that everyone was collecting donations, or making contributions in some way or other throughout the land.

Christmas was approaching and even the preparations for the festivities were intertwined with the Hungarian cause. Children were going round in the streets from house to house singing Christmas carols and asking for pennies not for themselves but as contribution to the Lord Mayor's Fund. Or, they were making stocking fillers—toys or tiny presents—and selling them to raise money for the same purpose. All schools and youth organizations were engaged in collecting and parents were asked to give freely at school plays and concerts. A "gift sale" organized by the Committee of Farmers in Central Scotland raised £2,736 and a farmer in Wiltshire offered 1,000 Christmas trees to be sold at the Borough Market in Southwark, realising nearly £200.

The Italian portrait painter, Pietro Annigoni—well known for his magnificently austere portrait of the Queen—designed a special Christmas card with the text: "At Christmas we will remember them". 200,000 cards were sold and the total income from the sale, over £10,000, was transferred to the Fund. Theatres and concert halls gave special performances in aid of the Fund, raising substantial sums from the price of the tickets; the Royal Festival Hall, for example, held a concert "An evening for Hungary" and collected £5,409. Cinemas also put on special shows: The Cinematograph Exhibitors Association arranged for a short film to be shown in cinemas all over the country for a whole week and raised more than £150,000, an exceptionally large sum. Children sent in their pocket money and pensioners their few spare shillings, often with letters and gifts; jewellery, even wedding rings were donated anonymously to be sold and the money raised to be added to the Fund. Individual donations were received from the Queen and members of the royal family. One of the largest individual gifts—£10,000 (a huge sum of money for the time) was donated by Lord Nuffield. The final Report of the Lord Mayor's Fund describes in detail its operation and provides a list of donors: first the towns and municipalities, then companies, institutions and individual members of the public; the names and the amount of donations, printed in double columns, fill twelve and a half A4 pages. [12]

Within a fortnight of the first announcement of setting up the Fund the target of collecting one million pound—a very ambitious aim—had to be doubled, because the number of refugees leaving Hungary was well over

---

[12] The Lord Mayor of London's National Hungarian & Central European Relief Fund. *Report Nov. 1956 – Sept. 1958.* [1958.] pp.68-80.

the original estimates and still growing. The government raised the quota again, from the 2,500 Hungarian immigrants, whose reception in the United Kingdom had been agreed only in early November, to 12,000. It was easier to placate the public outcry about the number of Hungarian refugees allowed to enter the country than quell the unrest about the Suez crisis. Because as soon as the new limits were announced, fresh criticism was levelled against the government's stinginess. On 17th November, the very same day as the aeroplane with the first refugees touched down in England, a letter by A.L. Price was published in *The Times*: "It has been announced that that this country will take 2,500 refugees from Hungary. Why only 2,500? I have asked this question several times in the last two days. It worries me. Can there be any convincing answer to it? These refugees are the victims of a tyranny as cruel and devilish as any in recorded history. Belgium will take 4,000. This nation of 50 million prosperous people will take no more than 2,500. Surely, someone in authority should explain to the nation exactly why we can take only 2,500? Let the reasons be stated quickly, clearly, and without evasion or concealment. And, Sir, if the reasons are unconvincing, many people will be very angry."[13]

The government was, indeed, truly grateful to the Lord Mayor for setting up his Fund and organizing the nationwide collection as the Foreign Secretary, Selwyn Lloyd, expressed it in his letter: "In the adjournment debate in the House of Commons on December 19, I referred to the response that had been made to your Fund for Hungarian Relief, but I would like to convey to you in a more personal way the gratitude of HM's Government for all that you yourself have done to bring the Fund up to the figure which it has now reached."[14]

On Christmas Eve, the Lord Mayor wrote a letter to the Vice-President of the United States, Richard Nixon, because they were unable to meet on his return from Austria as planned. He informed Nixon about the Fund's new target and why it was necessary to amend the original in such a short time: "When I first opened, on 9 November, my National Appeal for Hungarian and Central European refugees, the struggle in Budapest was but young, and the number of refugees visualised as entrants to this country was but 2,500. Since then the terror has increased, driving over 130,000 refugees into Austria of whom this country to date has taken 12,000. With these new facts before me I doubled my target to £2,000,000. The first million was collected from the public and largely from small

---

[13] *The Times,* 17 Nov. 1956.
[14] Letter by Selwyn Lloyd to the Lord Mayor of London. 28 Dec. 1956. Corporation of London Records Office. Ref.No. PD.145.8.

subscribers in the first four weeks: today, Christmas Eve, the total stands at £1,705,000. Of that sum I have already had to spend, earmark, or have urgent requests for £1,689,600."[15]

The target figure of two million pounds was reached exactly two months after the Lord Mayor's Guildhall speech, on 9th January 1957. Although the enthusiasm for the Hungarian cause slowly began to wane, contributions continued to arrive for a considerable time. The final amount reached £2,609,434, or if the interest earned is added to the sum, the final figure was £2,649,428, much higher than even the doubled target. Considering the economic constraints the people of Britain had to endure even a decade after the war, it was a real sacrifice on the part of many to spare some of their meagre income for donating it to the Lord Mayor's Fund. The collection of such a large sum in such a short time surpassed all expectations. It can only be ascribed to a mass outpouring of sentiment, very rarely experienced in Britain, which moved all hearts and minds, and to the common effort to offer sympathy and help. People wished to mitigate the impotence of the politicians and to exonerate the ordinary men and women of the country. Ordinary citizens also opened their doors to the refugees: short or longer term accommodation was offered by many, the refugees were invited to tea, often enlivened by teaching the newcomers English, and to share the Christmas festivities with the family. Friendships were born, many still alive today, after more than fifty years, although kept alive now mostly by the children of both the hosts and their guests. The magnificent effort displayed in those extraordinary days of the winter of 1956 was perhaps best summarized in the letter written by the Council of the Institute of Directors to *The Times*: "When the complete story of British aid for Hungary is known, it will, we are sure, prove an astonishing chapter in the long history of charitable help which over the years this country provided."[16]

It is not surprising, therefore, that the Lord Mayor's Fund also gave to the majority of more than 500 Hungarian refugee students the opportunity to complete their studies in Great Britain. When announcing his intention to set up the Fund, Sir Cullum Welch outlined the way he wished to distribute the monies collected through the existing major charitable organizations: about one third, through the Red Cross, would be used to send what might be most needed to Hungary and financial help to Austria for the reception, accommodation and maintenance of the refugees, and about two thirds would be used by the BCAR for taking charge of the

---

[15] Letter by the Lord Mayor of London to the Vice-president [of the USA]. 24. Dec. 1956. Ibid.
[16] *The Times*, 28 Nov. 1956, p.9.

refugees coming to the United Kingdom. They placed them in suitable camps, taught them English and gave them training and advise on how to settle down speedily, and to start a new life successfully. However, within a short space of time it became apparent that among the refugees there were thousands of students and a fair number of them might opt for coming to Britain where they would be seeking an opportunity to continue their higher education.

In his broadcast on the BBC on 17 November, the Lord Mayor mentioned the appeals launched by the universities for the provision of scholarship for these students.[17] The university appeal funds had high targets, but the authorities doubted whether they would be able to raise such a large amount from the contributions. In addition, when the true number of students arriving in the United Kingdom, many of them with the general influx of ordinary refugees became apparent, it seemed to exceed all previous assessments. The universities realized that they would need substantial additional financial aid to cover their expenses. Although the Lord Mayor did not specifically include the funding of scholarships for students from the national appeal at that time, the Committee of Vice-Chancellors and Principals (CVCP) decided to seek his help at the earliest opportunity. The university authorities were convinced that without a large grant transferred from the Lord Mayor's Fund, they would not be able to carry out their commitment, undertaken so readily and with such enthusiasm, to give all deserving Hungarian students a chance to complete their studies and to obtain qualifications in Britain.

---

[17] In: The Lord Mayor of London's National Hungarian & Central European Relief Fund. *Report Nov. 1956 – Sept. 1958.* [1958.] p.6.

CHAPTER III

THE UNIVERSITIES' ACTION

The British public, including the staff and students of the universities, were aware of the decisive role the Hungarian students played in the revolution, as they were kept well informed about it, almost on a daily basis, by the media. *The Daily Telegraph* for example, published an article by a "Hungarian student" on 26th October entitled: "Hungary's plain warning to Communist rulers", in which the anonymous author regaled the readers with the ever increasing demands and brave action of the Budapest students.[1] It might have been this report which induced the students of Oxford to set up a general Hungarian relief fund, named the Balliol Fund, after the college of the initiators. They issued a call to everyone to donate as much money as they could afford in order to offer immediate help to Hungary. The overflowing enthusiasm with which the public regarded the uprising, resulted in a rapid response; within a few days enough monies were collected to enable two undergraduates, Ian Rankin and Robert Scott, to leave at once for Vienna, taking with them essential medical supplies to be forwarded to Budapest.[2] Ian Rankin sent reports to the newspapers on their journey and experiences,[3] and in an article written for *The Observer*, he singled out the students' participation in the events in Hungary.[4]

It was, however, a letter by the Rector of Szeged University, Dezső Baróti, signed by seventeen of the university's professors and published by *The Manchester Guardian* on 5th November, which must have made the biggest impact.[5] In the letter, the Rector and his fellow professors turned to the universities of the world, asking for their support in building a new, democratic Hungary: "to rally to our side with their moral authority".[6] The

---

[1] *The Daily Telegraph,* 26 Oct. 1956, p.8.
[2] *The Oxford Mail,* 29 Oct. 1956.
[3] For example: *The News Chronicle,* 20 Oct. 1956.
[4] *The Observer,* 4 Nov. 1956.
[5] Appeal by university. *The Manchester Guardian,* 5 Nov. 1956.
[6] The Hungarian version of the letter exists in a copy, made for the Police Force of County Csongrád on 1 May 1957, to be used as evidence in the trial of Baróti and his "accomplices" for their participation in the "counter-revolution". Published by

letter was drawn up on 3rd November, when there was no indication that the Soviet Army was ready to crush the revolution; it was full of hope in the future. The next day, the fatal 4th November, when the Red Army invaded Budapest, it was published in the local paper and broadcast in English, French and German translation on the Free Széchenyi Radio—seemingly no one at Szeged had yet realized early that Sunday morning, what was happening in the capital. The text was telegraphed to large number of universities and other academic institutions in the West, where, by that time it could be read only as a desperate cry for help. Among the recipients of the appeal was the International Committee of Science and Freedom, whose chairman, Professor Michael Polányi—an eminent scholar of Hungarian origin, professor of chemistry and natural philosophy and Head of the Department of Social Sciences at Manchester University—immediately sent it to *The Manchester Guardian* for publication while he himself, on behalf of the Committee, dispatched a telegram to the Soviet Embassy in London, expressing his protestation and voicing his anxiety about the fate of his university colleagues. As might have been expected, it was to no avail: Baróti was put on trial and sentenced to several years in prison. He then languished in second-rate jobs until his retirement and many of the professors who had signed the letter, were dismissed, demoted, or severely reprimanded.

After the Soviet invasion the British newspapers continued to carry reports about the situation in Hungary, including the call for a general strike by university students[7], or the deportation, especially of young people, from Hungary to the Soviet Union.[8] The desperate fight against the Red Army and against the re-grouping Hungarian Secret Police still continued; many of those who had taken up arms were students. However, it soon transpired that among the refugees leaving Hungary, there was also a considerable number of university students, who wished to continue their studies in the West. Understandably, the overriding interest of British students and the authorities of higher education institutions in the United Kingdom, turned their attention to these refugee students and their renewed effort was redirected to help them—arranging for their selection in Austria and their transfer to England and, first and foremost, raising monies for scholarships, to provide the financial support they would need while completing their studies in this country. On 10th November the

---

Bálint, László: *A megtorlás Szegeden.* (Reprisals in Szeged.) Szeged, 2004, p.227.
[7] 13,000 students call strike. *The Daily Telegraph*, 6 Nov. 1956, p.12.
[8] Mass deportation of young Hungarians. Round-up begins: hostile students. Ibid. 14 Nov. 1956, p.1.

students at Oxford voted to dissolve the Communist Club. Within a couple of days, they decided to close the Balliol Fund, which by that time had collected over £5,000, and to set up a special scholarship fund for Hungarian students with immediate effect. In no time, by 14th November, £400 was raised for this fund also, mainly by undergraduates.[9] They used every means at their disposal: the President of the Merton College Junior Common Room, E. B. Mullins for example, informed *The Manchester Guardian*, that by 115 votes to none, the members had each decided to donate £1 to the fund to support Hungarian students coming to Oxford.[10] The students of Cambridge and the University of London soon followed suit. The University of London Union also had opened a general Hungarian fund in October. By mid-November this also stood at £1,000, when ULU, learning about the action of students at Oxford, closed it and opened a scholarship fund for Hungarian students coming to London University.

The much quoted letter by John D. Bu'Lock in *The Times* on Wednesday, 14th November therefore, pushed open doors when urging the universities "acting individually or in concert, to provide places for Hungarian students and to ensure that they will be adequately supported [...] Action of this kind, though limited in scope, would at least be an expression of our deep sympathy for the Hungarian people, and perhaps a more practical one than the composition of letters of protest and counter-protest which seems to have been the main activity of Britain's intellectuals in the past week." [11] In his response, published two days later[12], the Vice-Chancellor of London University, Dr John F. Lockwood, assured the public that plans had already been made by the universities to open their doors to students from Hungary. The day before, three university teachers left for Vienna (F. W. D. Deakin, Warden of St. Antony's College, Oxford, Professor C. A. Macartney, also from Oxford but representing Edinburgh University and Professor F. H. N. Seton-Watson from the School of Slavonic and East-European Studies, University of London[13]) to assess the situation at first hand, to report back

---

[9] The Oxford students' action was reported daily by the national newspapers and in more detail by *The Oxford Mail*, 14 Nov. 1956.

[10] *The Manchester Guardian*, 15 Nov. 1956.

[11] *The Times*, 14 Nov. 1956, p.11.

[12] Ibid. 16 Nov. 1956, p.11.

[13] All three representatives were historians interested in and had extensive knowledge of Eastern-Europe: Deakin (1913-2005) assisted Churchill in writing his memoir of World War II., and as the first Warden of St. Antony's it was he who actively helped to create its profile concentrating on the analysis of current

to the CVCP on the size of the problem and to suggest ways to resolve it; furthermore, Dr Lockwood agreed to liaise between the CVCP and the Lord Mayor's Fund regarding the financing of any action. Individual universities had opened funds for Hungarian student scholarships and he, himself, had issued such an appeal to all staff and students of the University of London with the aim of raising £20,000.

On the very same page, Lindsay Keir, Master of Balliol College, A. L. P. Norrington, President of Trinity College and Janet Vaughan, Principal of Somerville College, informed readers on behalf of the newly established Oxford Hungarian Committee about the action taken by the undergraduates: "We would be glad if we might draw the attention of your readers to a fund set up by junior members of Oxford University to provide scholarship at British universities and technical colleges for Hungarian refugee students. Great enthusiasm has been shown by undergraduates, who have already raised a substantial sum of money, but it will obviously be beyond their resources to meet the whole need. The committee of this fund which hopes to set up a joint organisation with similar bodies in other universities, has the backing of many senior members of this university, and several colleges have already expressed their willingness to receive Hungarian students."[14] At the end of the letter they asked readers to contribute to the fund and gave the details of the bank account, to which cheques could be sent.

The setting up of the Oxford Hungarian Committee and its subsequent operation refutes all accusations levelled periodically against university committees,[15] that their alleged *raison d'être* is to hinder any decision and to postpone any action. When a pressing problem presents itself, universities are bound to refer it to a committee established specifically to deal with it; the committee then examines it from all possible angles, discusses it at umpteen meetings, writes up a report, preferably with a minority report presenting dissenting views, submits it to a specified body which warmly welcomes it and then—the report is shelved and no action is taken until the re-examination of the same issue by a new committee,

---

events with special reference to Eastern-Europe and the Soviet Union; Macartney (1895-1978) was an expert on the history of Hungary in the first half of the 20th century with a number of outstanding books on this topic to his credit; Hugh Seton-Watson (1916-1984), the son of R. W. Seton-Watson, notorious for advocating the dismemberment of Hungary after World War I., whose research also focused on the recent history of the area.

[14] *The Times*, 16 Nov. 1956, p.11.
[15] See, for example: The Steering Committee for Efficiency Studies in Universities: *Report*. London, 1985.

probably years later. The Hungarian committees, set up by universities all over the county in the winter of 1956, were of a completely different nature: they were borne impulsively out of the deeply felt sympathy for the Hungarian cause and of the need for urgent action. Instead of using the usual delaying mechanism through strictly adhering to formalities, they set out to achieve their purpose as rapidly as possible and the orderly way of carrying out their function (set meetings with properly drawn up agenda, minutes taken and decisions recorded and accountability through solid bookkeeping and auditing) was deemed secondary yet necessary to bring quick but at the same time reliably well-informed results.

The Oxford Hungarian Committee is one of the best examples of these ad hoc committees, created almost instinctively by a strong pressure of emotional need, but run, according to the usual rules, by clear-cut reason. Norrington, the President of Trinity College (still known for the *Norrington Table* published yearly on the performance of the Oxford colleges) and the chairman of the Hungarian Committee (which, on account of his chairmanship is also referred to as the Norrington Committee), summarized, most probably for the University authorities, its establishment, aims, structure and method of operation: "The first initiative, in the matter of relief for Hungary, was taken in Oxford by the undergraduates, and two separate organisations arose more or less spontaneously. There was the Balliol Fund, directed in the first place simply towards helping the Hungarian people while the fighting was going on. Various first-aid supplies etc., were bought and actually taken out to Hungary. When the fighting was over and the flight of refugees began, this fund still had plenty of money in hand, and it could perhaps be used to augment the second fund to which I now come.

"The second organisation, started a bit later than the Balliol Fund, was directed simply to provide money to enable Hungarian students to continue their studies at English universities. When the undergraduates started on this, three or four weeks ago, they had no idea how many students, suitable for British university education might be available, nor whether there would be any financial help from the universities or from H. M. Government, nor whether similar spontaneous efforts to raise money would be made elsewhere in the U. K. The undergraduates, male and female, simply got to work, and they in fact raised about £4,000. Before they had gone very far, they asked a few Senior members of the University to lend their name as sponsors, and in this quite accidental way the Principals of Somerville and St Anne's, the Master of Balliol, the Warden of St Antony's, the Warden of Rhodes House and myself got drawn in.

"But it soon became clear that a Senior Committee had to exist, to watch the developments and maintain some sort of organisation during the vacation, and the sponsors seemed the obvious people. This is the Committee 'approved by Council' [...] Working under the rather loose control of this Senior Committee (which has only held one formal meeting) there are at least three other inter-locking committees, if you could call them that. There is first, and the earliest of this mushroom growth, the Undergraduates' Committee, with its Senior Treasurer, Mrs. Foot. Their function is to collect money. Secondly the Senior Committee set up a Reception Committee to deal with the physical problem of the 34 Hungarian students who arrived in Oxford on 30 November [...] Its secretarial headquarters are in my house [...] The telephone has been in action for roughly eight hours a day. Thirdly, we have a small Finance Sub-Committee of the Senior Committee.[...] I think there are now two main administrative problems: first, these amateur organisations at Oxford must soon be, if not replaced, at any rate harnessed to the machinery of the University [...] Secondly, we have to keep in step with other British universities, and I doubt if we could do this except through the Registry."[16]

Due to the pressing need of receiving the Hungarian students, organizing their accommodation, and setting up the language courses for them, the Oxford Hungarian Committee met once a week during the first few months, then fortnightly while there was still any business raised regarding the students, or even the non-student Hungarian refugees at Oxford. The minutes of the meetings[17] reveal the all-embracing nature of the issues the Committee had to deal with, its thoroughness in resolving the problems and the pastoral care it extended to every single student. The members carried out the often arduous work with a missionary zeal while, at the same time, they did not let sentiment obscure the purpose of their mission.

The universities in Britain approached the welcome of the Hungarian students in many different ways, although the basic tasks they all had to face were the same: first, they had to set up a local appeal fund in order to raise money for scholarships and to cover their own expenses and secondly, they had to receive groups of students arriving in the United Kingdom for both short- and long-term stay and to arrange English lessons for them, preferably starting the day after their arrival. Most but not all universities set up a Hungarian Committee (in Cambridge, for example,

---

[16] Norrington, A. L. P.: *Hungarian students for Oxford.* Typed report, [13 Dec. 1956.] The report is undated, but from other documents in the file, its date could be established. Bodleian Library Archives (henceforth BLA). UR6/OVS/H File 1.
[17] Ibid.

the reception of the students and dealing with all the problems which cropped up was done single-handedly by the Registrary); already on 23rd November the Principal of Glasgow University reported to the CVCP that Scottish universities had established committees comprising staff and students to direct and oversee the reception and distribution of 20 Hungarian students among themselves and to make a co-ordinated fund raising effort.[18] The University of London also wished to launch an appeal centrally, but involving all the schools and institutes of the University in the action.

The University of London was—and still is—a federal higher educational establishment, consisting then of over forty larger and smaller semi-independent schools and institutes. The central administration, housed in the Senate House, was kept at arm's length from the operational management of the constituent colleges of the University, but it formulated and implemented overall rules and guidelines and issued general notices, demands and appeals. So, as indicated in his letter to *The Times* on 16th November, Dr Lockwood, the Vice-Chancellor, issued an appeal addressed to all members of staff and to all students of the University. The letter of appeal, entitled *Relief Fund for Hungarian Students* and signed by him, by T. P. Creed, the Chairman of the Collegiate Council and by R. E. Harris, President of the University of London Union, is undated, but it must have been dispatched within a couple of days and received by the heads of colleges on Monday, 19th November at the latest. It concluded with the rousing words: "We should like to help and maintain many; our power to help will be measured by the size of the Fund which we can raise. We set as our objective a sum of £20,000 which, if we all give liberally, we should easily achieve."[19] The substantial file in the London University Archives, containing letters from a large number of individuals and groups, addressed to the Vice-Chancellor or to the Principal, Dr Logan, and enclosed with the donations, bears witness to the gratitude many felt that the University offered them opportunity to contribute specifically to the cause of the Hungarian students.[20]

There were, however, also those who felt that the University's appeal came too late, a good ten days after the Lord Mayor's Fund had been launched. Staff and students had already sent their donations to this Fund and they would be unlikely to contribute further amounts of money.

---

[18] CVCP: *Minutes*. 23 Nov. 1956. CVCP Archives. Modern Records Centre, Warwick University. (henceforth CVCPA)
[19] Relief Fund for Hungarian Students. [16. Nov. 1956.] UoLA, CB3/4/42.
[20] Ibid. Cheque acknowledgements and offers of help to Dr. Logan.

Indeed, in some instances the university authorities actively encouraged staff and students to participate fully in the national fundraising campaign. Furthermore, some colleges expressed their unease about contributing to a central fund; they would have been happier to spend the money they had collected directly on Hungarian students allocated to their own institution. Imperial College might stand as an example both of the seemingly belated action and of the mixed feelings about the University's central control.

The Rector of the College, Dr Patrick Linstead, sent a circular letter to all Heads of Departments and senior administrators on Monday, 12th November, urging them to organize a collection in their sections and send the result to him in the form of a cheque. He would then pass these on as the College's contribution to the Lord Mayor's Fund. Linstead felt that he was "carrying out the wish of the college by arranging for a contribution to the Fund which had been opened by the Lord Mayor."[21] This call for organized action, though, was seen by some as an already belated response both to the unfolding event in Hungary and to the strengthening student protest on behalf of the Hungarian freedom fighters. A letter by P. Emerson of the Royal College of Science—the Faculty of Science at Imperial College—reveals the depth of disquiet many must have felt. The letter was published in the College's student magazine *Felix*, on 16th November, but it was written on the 10th, two days before the Rector issued his circular. It refers to the student protests of the previous days and to the apparent inaction by members of the College: "During the last few days the Press has given prominence to a number of meetings by the students of the University of London expressing concern over Hungary and Suez. Without exception these meetings have been inadequately publicised on the notice boards of Imperial College and, consequently, poorly supported by members of this College."[22] Emerson had misgivings about demonstrations in Whitehall—presumably against the government's Suez policy—but felt that "It would be unfortunate if this College was thought to be apathetic." The first circular letter sent out by the Rector was, therefore, welcomed with quiet satisfaction by members of the College and the collection of donations began in earnest.

Within a week, however, the Rector received the Vice-Chancellor's letter of appeal and decided to earmark the donations already collected for the University of London's appeal, rather than to send them to the Lord Mayor's Fund as originally intended. In a note to the College Secretary, G C. Lowry, he gives two reasons for diverting the monies to the University:

---

[21] Letter to G. C. Lowry by R. P. Linstead, 12 Nov. 1956. Imperial College Archives (hereafter ICA), Hungarian Relief, SS/1/4.

[22] *Felix*, 16 Nov. 1956, p.2.

firstly—he argues—to provide help specifically to Hungarian students is "a very appropriate cause", and secondly, the target of £20,000 set by the University is very high and would be difficult to realize it without the active support of all the schools and institutes. He asks Lowry's opinion about the proposed new arrangement.[23] His concern about the reception of his new proposals was, indeed, not without foundation. Partly, because the students responded with great vigour to his first appeal by organizing all sorts of events in aid of the collection, including among them the proceeds of the sale of the student magazine *Felix*, a two-day intensive campaign selling Hungarian tricolour lapel emblems supplied by the Polish Society, a successful dance by a coalition of the International Relations Club, the Royal School of Mines and the Polish Society, thus raising over £200 for the Red Cross[24] and were unlikely able to match this amount for a university fund. The Rector also partly feared that staff might wish to send at least a portion of the money they had collected to the Lord Mayor's Fund, because they had reservations about any "college money" flowing directly into central university coffers.

This was borne out by the response he received to his second circular: the Department of Chemistry, for example, requested him to halve the £26 collected, giving £13 to the Lord Mayor's Fund and £13 to the University of London, while the Department of Electrical Engineering sent two separate cheques, £6/12/00 for the university's appeal and £10 to the Lord Mayor's Fund. However, by early December the total of £280 was collected for the University's Hungarian Students Relief Fund. Dr Linstead sent a cheque for this amount to the Vice-Chancellor with a typed covering letter, in which he manually inserted "first" before the word contribution, in order to indicate that further donations might follow from the College, since he wished to extend the appeal for support to former students and staff through the Old Students' Associations, the alumni organizations of the College.[25]

This final appeal was probably modelled on the appeal by the University of London Convocation to its 35,000 members, which was put forward by the chairman of the Convocation, P. Dunsheath, soon after he heard the Vice-Chancellor reporting on the fund-raising effort for a Hungarian Scholarship Scheme at the meeting of the Senate of the

---

[23] Letter to G. C. Lowry by R. P. Linstead. 19 Nov. 1956. ICA, Hungarian Relief, SS/1/4.
[24] Full report in *Felix*, 30 Nov. 1956, p.1.
[25] Letter to J. F. Lockwood by R. P. Linstead. 5 Dec. 1956. ICA, Hungarian Relief, SS/1/4.

University of London on 21st November.[26] This was a massive operation; sending individual letters to each member of the convocation was undertaken mostly by a volunteer force. Even the Imperial College appeal to the alumni, although much smaller in scale, required careful planning. The idea was first floated at the meeting of the College's Governing Body on 14th December, where the Rector emphasized that the Hungarian students, provisionally allocated to Imperial College, would be supported from the contribution to the Vice-Chancellor's fund. It was agreed that an appeal would be made in the New Year, with a target figure of £3,000.[27] Before Christmas, the Rector approached the Presidents of the Old Students' Associations to act in conjunction with him, the Chairman of the Governing Body and the President of the Student Union as sponsors of the appeal. A leaflet was drawn up and posted to alumni in January 1957.[28] On 15th March the Rector informed the Governors of the result: £654 8s 0d had been collected up to that date.[29]

This figure, compared with the target must have been seen as very low and, at the end of May, it was agreed that an appropriate sum should be released from the Beit Reserve Fund to top up the collection. A manuscript note by the Rector records: "I think the College should do this. It is a good thing in itself and I understand that other institutions have done it; we should not want to be left behind."[30] So, Linstead was able to send a second cheque for £900 to the Vice-Chancellor at the end of May with the promise of a further contribution in July.[31]

The appeal fund was kept open well beyond the end of the academic year and the final cheque of £324 was dispatched to the University in December 1957, raising the total of the money collected to just over £1,500.[32] It is not surprising that the ambitious target of £3,000 was not reached: many potential contributors had already given often large sums to

---

[26] His letter, informing the Vice-Chancellor about the Convocation's appeal was then included in the Statements for the next meeting of the Senate on 19 December. In: University of London Senate: *Minutes of 21 November and 19 December 1956.* UoLA ST2/2/81.

[27] Imperial College. Governing Body meeting 14. Dec. 1956. ICA.

[28] Imperial College of Science and Technology. *Hungarian Student Scholarship Fund.* January, 1957. ICA, Hungarian Relief, SS/1/4.

[29] Imperial College. Governing Body meeting 15 March. 1957. ICA.

[30] Memorandum on the Governors' donation to the appeal. ICA, Hungarian Relief, SS/1/4.

[31] Letter to J. F. Lockwood by R. P. Linstead. 29 May 1957. ICA, Hungarian Relief, SS/1/4.

[32] Imperial College. Governing Body meeting 13 Dec. 1957. The Governors took note of the final analysis of the results of the appeal.

the Red Cross or to the Lord Mayor's Fund in mid-November 1956, before
the university's appeal was launched. By the spring of 1957 interest in
Hungarian refugees had waned and the appeal had to compete with other
charities. Some people were, in any case, hostile to the Hungarian refugee
student cause as letters addressed to the Rector by a couple of alumni
testify. One of them wished to draw attention to the plight of British
subjects expelled from Egypt who deserved similar support and another
asked that at a time when British universities are "crying out for financial
help to improve educational facilities for the benefit of our fellow
countrymen, is it sensible to sponsor an action to help Hungarian refugees
during their initial start in a new land?" The Rector in his reply assured
them that the College's Hungarian appeal did not preclude that members
of the College would be unsympathetic to other deserving causes, and that
the money was well spent as "our Hungarian refugee students seem to us
to be of high calibre in every sense of the word, and show signs of
becoming valuable members of our community."[33] Overall however, as in
other universities, the Imperial College appeal can be regarded as a
success; it actively engaged a large number of present and past members
of the College and channelled their wish to help in a direction close to
their heart—to sponsor students studying in the College. And, although the
appeal reached only half of its original target, it was one of the biggest
donations made by a School to the London University Hungarian Student
Scholarship Fund.

Looking back half a century on, it would be easy to deduce that the
exaggerated expectations the universities seemingly harboured about the
fundraising potential of their Hungarian relief appeals were no more than a
somewhat naive belief in the boundless generosity and inexhaustible
financial resources of their staff and students. This would be, however, a
misreading of their intentions. Although the university authorities
occasionally expressed their confidence in raising enough money for the
scholarships of the students allocated to their institution, that is, for
educating and sustaining them fully during their years of study, at the
same time they also voiced their concern about requiring additional
support both for organizing the reception of the students and arranging
full-time, intensive English classes for them, and for covering fully the
expenses of their university courses. One can only assume that the very
high targets set for the appeals were to serve more as inspiration for
offering help freely and as inducement for donating as generously as

---

[33] Letters by Russell Patterson and A. R. McKechnie to R. P. Listead and his reply
to them, 12 and 22 Feb. 1957. ICA, Hungarian Relief, SS/1/3.

anyone could afford, than aims based on proper financial assessments. To obtain this extra support they needed to look no further than the newly established Lord Mayor's Fund, which might also provide grants also for educational purposes.

True, the Lord Mayor in his broadcast on 17th November alluded to the Hungarian refugee students, but only in the context of the universities' schemes to raise money for scholarships and studentships for them.[34] The information about the universities' action most probably reached him via the Vice-chancellor or the Principal of London University. The Principal, Dr Logan, on the other hand, also spoke in his previously mentioned letter to the Equerry to Queen Elizabeth, the Queen Mother, about "the education of the refugees" as one of the basic requirements to be met by the Lord Mayor's Fund – without specifically mentioning the students.[35] The two strands, financial support for the education of the refugees in general, and financial support for the education of university students in particular—both from the Lord Mayor's Fund—soon became intertwined. The agenda for the meeting of the CVCP on 23rd November already included an item for official confirmation: the delegation of the Vice-Chancellor, Dr Lockwood by the Chairman to act as intermediary between the CVCP and the Lord Mayor and his various committees.[36] This authorized Lockwood to represent the universities' case for financial aid where ever it could usefully be discussed and where it might receive high-level support. Lockwood wasted no time to present his case as widely as possible.

The World University Service (henceforth WUS) was entrusted by the BCAR to co-ordinate the identification and registration of Hungarian students arriving in England with the mass of refugees. To assess the magnitude and requirements of the task and to set up workable procedures, WUS called a meeting of all interested parties, the British Council, the Ministry of Education and the Foreign Office, the relevant Trade Unions and the National Union Students and, of course, representatives of the universities: Lockwood from the CVCP and delegates from the Oxford and Cambridge Hungarian Students Scholarship Funds. The meeting took place on 26th November, and after a lengthy discussion it was Lockwood again who was authorized to speak on behalf of this group as well (soon to become a WUS Committee) with the Lord Mayor. Presenting the case for

---

[34] The Lord Mayor of London's National Hungarian & Central European Relief Fund: *Report Nov. 1956-Sept. 1958.* [London, 1958.] p.6.
[35] Letter by D. W. Logan to Lieutenant-Colonel M. J. Gilliatt. 15 Nov. 1956. UoLA, CB3/4/12.
[36] CVCP. *Minutes.* 23 Nov. 1956. CVCPA.

the students, he was to give the Lord Mayor an indication of the approximate cost of their education and how much of it the universities might be expected to raise and what immediate financial help the CVCP would need for selecting and interviewing potential students in Austria, transporting them to Britain and providing temporary accommodation for them. The following day Lockwood met the Lord Mayor and the meeting proved to be very fruitful: the Lord Mayor agreed to transfer £10,000 with immediate effect to the CVCP to cover the cost of bringing the selected students to England and of placing them at designated universities.

The next WUS Committee was scheduled for 4th December and was attended by the Principal, Logan. The question of the ever increasing number of students arriving in England and the financial provisions for their education was again among the main topics discussed. The next day Lockwood sent a letter to Sir Gilbert Flemming, the Permanent Secretary of the Ministry of Education, summarising the views expressed at the meeting and reported to him by Logan: that by now over 300 Hungarian students were expected to take refuge in Great Britain, about half of them of university standard, the other half probably more suitable for pursuing studies at technical colleges. The universities expressed themselves willing and able to place 150 students, although they would need additional financial support to educate them fully, the cost of which was estimated between £200,000 and £250,000. The maintenance of students designated to technical colleges would, of course, be the responsibility of the Ministry through the Local Education Authorities.[37] Lockwood sent a copy of the letter to WUS, asking for a supporting letter "to reach Sir Gilbert Flemming as soon as possible."[38]

The universities' plea for additional funding was much strengthened by similar claims coming from diverse quarters; at the inaugural meeting of the Advisory Council of the Lord Mayor's Fund for example, the Mayor of Birmingham voiced his concern about Birmingham University being unable to accept as many refugee students as it would like to have, due to lack of funding. The city received 200 Hungarian refugees and could accommodate a further 300. The University indicated that it would take 40 students if some additional funds were made available for their support. The Lord Mayor—who was already aware of the possibility of directing suitable students to technical colleges as well as to university degree courses—suggested that he would explore all possibilities and seek guidance from the Ministry of Education. The Advisory Council accepted

---

[37] Letter by F. W. Lockwood to Sir Gilbert Flemming. 5 Dec. 1956. UoLA. CB3/4/37.
[38] Letter by F. W. Lockwood to Miss E. Rudinger. 5 Dec. 1956. Ibid.

his proposal but agreed that grants released for various purposes, among them to the universities for the education of students, should be transferred to designated bodies like the CVCP and/or the WUS, which would be accountable to the Lord Mayor's Fund.[39] Thus, the pressure both on government resources and on the Lord Mayor's Fund to provide for the Hungarian students increased day-by-day, although no one expected the final decision to be reached with undue haste. However, the transfer of an emergency grant for the immediate needs of the CVCP at the very beginning of December[40] enabled the Committee to bring 150 selected students by specially chartered flights to Britain between 26th November and 11th December and to place them in hastily prepared temporary accommodation.

The incredibly tight schedule of securing some money to cover the costs and of interviewing, selecting and transferring students from Vienna to England and distributing them to reception centres meant that the normal decision-making procedures were largely bypassed. Lockwood, Logan and leading members of the Oxford Hungarian Committee embarked on the implementation of a scheme, of which only the vaguest outlines had been formulated. These were not presented to, let alone approved by the CVCP. Lockwood of course, consulted the Chairman who gave his verbal agreement to some of the action—for example sending three academics to Vienna to assess the situation in situ and report back on their findings to the CVCP—but most of the details must have been decided ad hoc, as dictated by the events. The Norrington Committee in any case felt that the money they had already collected would cover the cost of bringing a few students to Oxford at once, and similarly, although with less firm financial backing, Lockwood and Logan also decided on a unilateral course of action and took matters into their own hands. The CVCP was scheduled to meet on 23rd November when the question of the Hungarian students would first be discussed, the report on the situation in Austria received, and decisions taken on the numbers the universities would accept and how the students would be selected and brought to Britain. Since the first group of students arrived by air on 26th November, it is inconceivable that the interviews could have been conducted, the suitable students selected and the flight arranged only after 23rd

---

[39] The Lord Mayor of London's National & Central European Relief Fund. Advisory Council: *Minutes of the inaugural meeting.* 15. Dec. 1956. Corporation of London Records Office. Ref. No. PD.145.8.
[40] Lockwood received the official notice of the transfer of £10,000 from the Lord Mayor's Fund in a letter by D. Morley-Fletcher, Honorary Secretary of the Fund, dated 1 Dec. 1956. UoLA, CB3/1/1/1.

November, that is with the full consent of the CVCP. The rest of the flights must also have been booked in advance and one can only deduce that Lockwood, Logan and the Oxford group went ahead with their own agenda in the hope—or perhaps even in the firm belief—that the CVCP would endorse their action.

And that is precisely what happened at the CVCP's meeting. The minutes speak about a "considerable discussion" on the topic of the refugee students and the notes taken record in unusual detail the points raised. Page after page reveals the sheer enthusiasm of the leaders of British universities in committing themselves to participate in a national scheme which would enable the students to complete their studies.[41] The report by the dons who travelled to Vienna was tabled by Lockwood and presented by Hugh Seton-Watson who highlighted the most relevant passages.[42] The report was divided into three main sections. The first, entitled *Numbers*, gave a summary of the situation as at 17th November. Among the refugees there were approximately 1,400 students, almost all of them male, some of university calibre, while a large proportion of them were probably more suited to follow courses in technical colleges. 600 students were from the Faculties of Mining and Forestry of the University of Sopron, located near the Austrian border; they left Hungary en masse, together with their teachers and the teachers' families. They were currently housed in St. Wolfgang, near Salzburg and had expressed the desire to stay together.[43] Another 600 students were in various camps set up for the refugees and about 50 had found accommodation with friends and relatives (the report assumed that these students were more of a "university type"). About 120 students had already been separated from the mass of refugees and transferred to two special residences near the town of Graz. It was noted that the number of refugees pouring into Austria including the students was rapidly increasing on a daily basis.

---

[41] CVCP: *Minutes.* 23 Nov. 1956. CVCPA.

[42] Seton-Watson, H.: *Students among Hungarian refugees in Austria.* Ibid.

[43] The faculty of Forestry happily achieved their aim: they were accepted by the University of British Columbia, Canada. The language of instruction remained Hungarian but the degree they received was fully acknowledged as equivalent to Canadian university qualification by the government. On the history of the faculty and students, see: Hidas, I. Péter: Menekült magyar egyetemisták Kanadában. (Hungarian refugee students in Canada.) In: *Az 1956-os Magyar Forradalom Történetének Dokumentációs és Kutatóintézete. Évkönyv III.* Budapest, 1994, pp.125-136. Some students from the Faculty of Mining studied in Britain, supported by the National Coal Board.

The next section, simply called *Machinery*, dealt with organizational matters. The initial sorting out of students and their registration had been undertaken by the Austrian Student Union in Vienna and in Graz and it seemed they had been very quick and thorough. There were some students from Cambridge who were helping mainly with teaching the refugee students English. Mr Hitchcock from the British Council in Vienna concentrated on the students who had expressed a wish to go to England to complete their studies there; he was assessing each case in some detail and compiling lists of the ones deserving further consideration. The final section is devoted to the *Recommendation*. It was worth noting – says the report – that the German and French governments had already offered places to 150 and 100 Hungarian students respectively – while the Free University of Berlin would accept 200. Considering these figures, members of the British delegation recommended that the universities of Great Britain should open their doors to 150 students to give them a chance to complete their studies. However, the majority of these students might be more suited to courses at technical colleges and polytechnics, leaving only a small minority who might be deemed fit to enter degree courses. Of this group, about twenty students, with whom the members of the delegation had met in Vienna, could be brought to England without delay. Regarding the formulation of any plans however, it should be taken into account that were the situation in Hungary to greatly improve and if any of the students wished to go back, they should not be barred from doing so; moreover, the monies collected in Britain could be used for their benefit in Hungary as well.

Seton-Watson brought the report up-to-date by adding that in the meantime the number of refugees had dramatically increased and that the proportion of students amongst them seemed to be larger than before. In light of this, they would recommend that the number of students to be received in Britain should be increased from 150 to 200. After a lengthy debate however, the CVCP decided to retain the original figure of 150 places. Seton-Watson also suggested that the CVCP should send a suitable person to Vienna to help the British Council in the task of interviewing and selecting the students, and that the groups thus selected should be transferred to Britain as soon as possible, as life in the refugee camps was demoralizing the young people, who felt incarcerated there and were rapidly losing hope. Finally, he drew attention to the possibility that the mass of refugees being admitted to the United Kingdom might include many students of university standard and they should not be forgotten; they were just as much deserving of a place at a higher educational institution as the 150 students brought directly over from Vienna.

Members of the CVCP agreed that although the universities had launched their own appeal, all individual efforts and action should be tightly co-ordinated. As Lockwood had already accepted the task of liaising on behalf of the CVCP with the Lord Mayor's Fund, it was agreed that he should continue his good work and represent the universities at the meeting called by WUS for 26th November. To furnish him with relevant information the universities were to supply him with facts and figures about their action and, at the same time, they were also to let him know how many students they would be able to accept at short notice. The assessment of places immediately available was of utmost importance as the student flights would be arriving within days and the accommodation organized as an urgent measure by the University of London would certainly not be enough to house 150 incoming students. The universities might also wish to indicate the number of students for whom they were offering places on the degree courses. Lockwood agreed to summarize the findings and circulate it to all members together with the notes taken at the WUS meeting. It should reach the vice-chancellors well before the next meeting of the CVCP.

The most appropriate way of handling the money collected by the universities was also raised and it was agreed that the donations should not be merged with the Lord Mayor's Fund. The universities' appeal was specifically made for scholarships for Hungarian students and the university authorities would know best how to use it for this purpose. Finally, it was stressed that the English language courses for the students should also be organized as of the highest priority. To continue the discussion beyond the time allocated for the meeting, the Chairman suggested that members, who were interested in the cause of refugee students, should stay after lunch for an informal chat amongst themselves on the many issues still to be raised, debated and resolved. It is of no surprise that the vice-chancellors and principals who devoted the afternoon to further discussion were also the ones who accepted the responsibility to serve on the committees established by the CVCP on the same day: the Sub-Committee for Hungarian Students and the Sub-Committee for the Selection of Hungarian Students. The terms of reference of the first committee were to support Lockwood and Logan in co-ordinating every aspect of a nationwide scheme for the education of the Hungarian students and to liaise with the second committee, which was entrusted with selecting the students (first those in Vienna, then those who arrived with the refugees in Britain) and then with allocating them to individual universities. The distinct roles of the two committees were clearly defined but it soon became evident that the problems they had to deal with overlapped a great deal. From January 1957 onwards, at the suggestion of the Registrary of Cambridge University, R. M. Rattenbury, they had joint meetings, whilst retaining their separate names in the heading of the minutes. (For the sake of brevity, in this text the joint committees are referred to as the CVCP Hungarian Committee.)

The membership of the committees was, indeed, illustrious; being composed of the most eminent leaders of British universities. It included the then Chairman of the CVCP, Sir Edward Appleton, Vice-Chancellor of the University of Bristol, who wished to make a personal contribution to the cause; Rattenbury, the Registrary of Cambridge, mentioned above, who from mid-December onwards, when the first Hungarian students arrived at Cambridge, single-handedly dealt with all the problems associated with their reception and education; F. W. D. Deakin, Warden of St. Antony's College, Oxford, who travelled to Vienna on behalf of the CVCP and was the organizing force behind the transfer of the first group of students to England and accepted the responsibility to chair the Selection Committee, and the Vice-Chancellors and Principals of the universities of Birmingham, Durham, Edinburgh, Leeds and Leicester. London University was, of course, represented by the Vice-Chancellor, Lockwood and the Principal, Logan, who many times stood in for each other. They jointly oversaw the running of the whole, complicated, time-consuming but immensely exciting operation, not missing a day or a detail.

Logan, in his Report to the University for the academic year of 1956-57 paid special tribute to Lockwood for the demanding work he had willingly embraced: "But above all, we are indebted to the Vice-Chancellor who, in addition to his many burdens, is carrying the heavy responsibility of directing the whole operation and dealing personally with the great financial problems involved."[44] J. F. Lockwood (1903-1965) was a cultured arts man, Master of Birkbeck College, who was accessible and, at the same time, an excellent organizer in the best academic tradition. As the *Dictionary of National Biography* notes: "[...] he was renowned for certain qualities displayed everywhere at home and abroad, and, some thought, shown at their best in the team-work of committees: stamina, courage, persistence, gentleness, sympathy, bonhomie; objectivity, thoroughness, conciseness; skill, diplomacy and leadership of a new kind." Logan himself (1910-1987), is remembered for his outstanding administrative capability: "A prodigious worker"—summarises his

---

[44] University of London: *Report by the Principal for the year 1956-57.* 1 Apr. 1957, pp.60-61.

contribution to university administration the obituary in *The Times*—"he had impressive organizing ability and was a consummate draughtsman. He was impatient with inadequacy and with opposition based on ignorance or vested interest."[45]

It is not the fact that the leaders of the universities also came under the spell of the boundless enthusiasm felt by almost everyone in Britain for Hungary and the Hungarian refugees, and that they personally wished to participate in the action which was, first and foremost, the universities' own concern, that one finds even after half a century truly astounding, but their willingness to accept the considerable extra burden in addition to their already heavy duties. As the existing records testify, though sparing in emotive words, they carried out their task over the years with exemplary thoroughness. One can only guess what prompted them to offer their time and energy so unstintingly to the Hungarian cause; the former refugee students however, can only remember them and their deeds with deeply felt gratitude.

---

[45] *The Times*, 20 Oct. 1987.

CHAPTER IV

THE FIRST HUNDRED AND FIFTY STUDENTS

Surely, there must exist a psychological explanation of the rather curious fact that while every person who escaped from Hungary in 1956 recalls every single detail of how he or she left the country, crossed the border and arrived in Austria, the memories of the days spent in various refugee camps or in other make-shift, temporary accommodation have become somewhat blurred and the sequence of events rather muddled. Pictures might emerge from the swirling mass of recollections, sharp and vivid as if the things they recorded had only happened yesterday. I can still clearly see myself standing at the window on the corridor of a train in my shabby loden winter coat, my stockings, shredded to bits during the flight, twisted around my ankles. I am motionless, unaware of what is going on around me, spellbound by the sight of the panorama opening up before my eyes. What was the destination of the train, no one knew; most probably a camp somewhere in Southern Austria. In the small town of Jennersdorf, busloads of refugees—including us—were offered lunch in a factory, then we boarded the special railway carriages arranged for us. It was snowing heavily; the dancing snowflakes, driven by fierce winds, obliterated any view. During the afternoon the snow eased off, then as daylight faded, it stopped altogether. The sky cleared and in the bluish moonlight the bare rock-face of the mountains, high above us, shimmered with unreal intensity. The train was rushing alongside a bubbling stream, the ravine was surrounded by dark pine forests. The valley then widened to accommodate large lakes; their water must have been warm, because in the coldness of the night thick mist formed on their surface and rose steadily upwards.

We arrived at the camp, called Pfeffernitz, late at night. At the end of the Second World War the British Army had been stationed there. Many years later, the husband of a friend of mine told me in London that he had served there as the army's interpreter. Later, it became the home for some Swabian families—ethnic German people who had lived in Hungary for centuries but were, nevertheless, deported after the war as suspected Nazi sympathisers. I cannot recall what we did in the camp, how we spent our time, except, that driven by boredom, and to ease the feeling of melancholy which slowly engulfed us, we occasionally left the camp and explored the neighbourhood. We even embarked on a journey to discover the nearest town, Spittal, but after walking only a few hundred metres on the snow-covered road we stopped entranced at sight of the strip-lighting of a petrol station. We had never seen such dazzling illumination, such a display of visual delight before! One summer some twenty years later we decided to revisit the stations of our refugee life in Austria, including the camp at Pfeffernitz. Nothing seemed to have changed, the pictures stored in our memory closely corresponded to reality. Only the lights of the petrol station had faded to become the everyday lights of an ordinary service station.

What most of us still recall of our life in the Austrian refugee camps is the compulsion to ceaselessly collect news; we felt that at all times we had to know all options available for planning our future life in order to make best use of the opportunities. That the news was meagre and the options limited did not matter as long as we were able to acquire them; pondering over them gave us the illusion of having at least some control over our destiny. The Austrians, although unprepared for the sudden influx of thousands of refugees, did their best to accommodate, feed, clothe and process them. First they made use of the potential refugee quarters near the Hungarian border and around Vienna by opening up the barracks occupied by the Russian Army until their departure in early 1956 when Austria gained full independence. The authorities however, soon had to set up camps all over the country; there were refugee groups for example, which found themselves within days after crossing the border as far away from Hungary as was possible within Austria. One of the students related that his group had been transported to a small town called Götzis near the Swiss border. He had relatives waiting for him in Vienna and had to find his way back by himself, travelling along the whole length of the country.[1]

The well-briefed, especially the students, made their way to Vienna, if necessary by standing at the roadside and soliciting lifts in passing cars, as Vienna was perceived to be the place which offered the greatest opportunities. Even if they encountered detours by being shunted around the country, they hoped to get there eventually. Iván Zmertych had at first no idea where his group had been taken but soon learned that the camp, high up in the Alps, was near Mariazell, one of the best known places of pilgrimage in Austria, especially revered by Hungarians, since Louis I, King of Hungary, attributed his victory over the Turks in 1377 to the

---

[1] Interview with Sándor Váci. 23 Feb. 2006.

Virgin Mary of Mariazell. Zmertych recalled that his family members had vowed that if they were ever able to leave Hungary, they would go to Mariazell to express their gratitude for their deliverance. He and some friends whom he had convinced of the beneficial effects that such a pious deed might bestow on them, made the journey of over eight miles to the votive church in the most inclement weather – bitterly cold and snowing hard. Their pilgrimage however, was not in vain: Zmertych was soon transferred to a student hostel in Vienna. He read on a piece of paper pinned to the notice board, that the British Council was recruiting students to give them a chance to continue their studies in England. He contacted the British Council officials, was interviewed and offered a place on the second chartered aircraft, which landed at Blackbushe on 30 November.[2]

The Austrian authorities soon realized that it would aid the quick and smooth registration of university students if they separated them from the general mass of refugees and housed them separately both in Vienna and elsewhere in the country. The task was most effectively carried out by the local student organizations and many of the refugee students found themselves in rather grand accommodation, including castles and imposing stately homes. The main advantage of the scheme for the students was the immediate information they obtained on available grants and the countries offering them. Everybody, of course, listened to Radio Free Europe, read the notices which changed daily and listened to hearsay which spread among the students like wildfire. Their knowledge and assessment of the situation was more or less up to date and this, in turn, helped those officials who were dispatched to Austria to select the most promising students for their country, among them the three professors sent by the CVCP to gather information and report back as soon as possible. Soon after their arrival in Vienna on 15th November, they were able to meet about three dozen students, specially lined up for them by the British Council's representative, Mr. Hitchcock. Not only were they briefed by the students about the current situation, but during the meeting the professors gained enough insight into the potential of each individual to enable them to compile a short list of those who should be transferred to Britain at once. Although the professors had no specific mandate from the CVCP to select and send refugee students to British universities before the Committee passed a formal resolution, they wanted to assemble a group of some 30 people to be flown to England before the end of November. More precisely, the students' destination was to be Oxford as two of the three professors—Deakin and Macartney (the latter representing the Scottish

---

[2] Interview with Iván Zmertych. 3 March 2005.

universities but a member of All Souls College)—were from Oxford University and, in addition, the Balliol Fund and the collection started by the Oxford Hungarian Committee covered at least some of the initial costs.

Memories of the interviews by the students are somewhat patchy, but according to the details recalled,[3] the proceedings were rather peculiar, especially for those coming from behind the Iron Curtain. Most of the students had no knowledge of English. There was an interpreter to assist them, a Hungarian émigré journalist called Tasziló Daróczy, who had been living in Vienna for some time. (Tasziló is the name given to a hapless figure featuring in the staple jokes about the Hungarian aristocracy and it was thought to be comical to meet a flesh and blood Tasziló so soon after leaving the Communist environment, where Taszilós existed only in jokes.) He asked the questions and translated the answers. In the background a man sat in silence, occasionally nodding with approval. That meant that the student was accepted. The man might have been Deakin who was most eager to assemble the first group of students to be brought to England and certainly not Macartney who would not have needed the help of an interpreter. It is not clear why Professor Macartney did not play a more prominent part in the selection procedure. Macartney knew Hungarian well. He had spent some time in Hungary, was an expert of Hungarian history and, last but not least, he regularly broadcast during the Second World War on the BBC External Services Hungarian programme.

Others recall[4] that Max Hayward also participated in the interviews; he was urging some of the applicants to make the right decision and to choose Oxford and it was he who escorted the students during the flight to England. Although the documents do not mention Max Hayward's presence in the investigative group sent by the CVCP to Austria, it must have been obvious for Deakin, the Warden of St. Antony's College to include the young researcher on his staff in the team. Hayward was an expert in Soviet and East European politics: he had spent several years at the British Embassy in Moscow and spoke Russian, had studied at the Charles University in Prague and at the outbreak of the revolution in Hungary began to study Hungarian as well. (Former Oxford Hungarian students fondly remember Hayward's indignant riposte to their doubts that he had been able to understand and interpret the obscure layers of meaning in the poem *The black piano* by the Hungarian poet, Endre Ady: "What is it that cannot be understood in that poem?"). Nevertheless, the fact that the first group of students selected in Vienna by academics with strong Oxford

---

[3] See, for example, Gömöri, György: Op. cit., p.28.
[4] Interview with András Sándor. 31 Oct. 2004.

connections and that people on the first flight were transferred to Oxford soon after their arrival in Britain, gave them the impression—still current today—that it was the Oxford Hungarian Committee, that independently organized the whole selection procedure, looked after them during the coming months and finally, financed their study in England out of their own resources.[5] It should, however, be stated clearly that although Oxford University played a major role in the Hungarian refugee student scheme, the responsibility for all relevant arrangements rested, via the CVCP, with the leaders of all the universities of the United Kingdom.

In the selection of the first group of students the nature of their studies in Hungary did not matter much. Later, however, it was easier for students who had followed courses in sciences or engineering to be accepted for continuing their studies in British universities. Nevertheless, even during the first interviews students received helpful advice if they expressed a wish to change subjects. To the question which university he would like to go, László Jámbor for example gave the answer promptly: "To Oxford". Not because he had weighed up the advantages or disadvantages of studying at other universities, but because, being under pressure, simply no other university's name came into his mind. Before his imprisonment in Hungary Jámbor had been a medical student, since he wanted to become a doctor. But with a new life ahead of him, he contemplated pursuing a new field of interest, that of politics, which the years he spent in prison as a political prisoner had awoken in him. He expressed the wish to read PPE. This was more than readily accepted by the interviewing professors, since a three-year course, even at Oxford University, would cost considerably less than sponsoring a five to six year course in medicine. Jámbor's wife Kati attended the interview with her husband. She had also been a student, at the Arts Faculty of Budapest University and also wished to change subjects, her first choice being medicine. Having listened however to the discussion between her husband and the panel about the difficulties of enrolling for a medical degree in England, Kati did not dare to voice her wish, but thinking quickly, named psychology as a possible alternative. This was instantly approved and both of them were included in the list of students compiled for the first flight, but for some reason or other, they missed it. They were flown to England on the next plane and moved temporarily to Leeds University; useful perhaps for them to learn that large and well-established higher education institutions could also be found elsewhere in England. Eventually they

---

[5] For example in Várallyay, Gyula: Op. cit., pp.47-48.

were transferred to Oxford and gained their qualifications in 1960 in PPE and PPP respectively.[6]

To assemble the first planeload of students to be brought to England caused some difficulties. Lockwood, in his report to the CVCP described the composition of the group as "rather unusual". It contained students of great potential with first-rate minds, some of them already with a first degree. There were however individuals in the group who were seemingly not suited for higher education or those who had probably never attended university courses in Hungary. In addition, among the 34 passengers there were no fewer than seven musicians and five students of the dramatic arts. Lockwood offered an explanation: a number of people selected had missed the flight—which had actually happened in the case of the Jámbors— others had decided at the last minute to stay in Austria or choose another country. In the end, the numbers had to be made up from those who for whatever reason wanted to come to England. There was even a person only willing to board the plane if the 16 year old boy in his custody was also allowed to travel with him.[7]

H. W. R. Walters, Secretary of the University of London Appointments Board, flew to Vienna at the request of the CVCP on November 28th, entrusted with the task of interviewing and selecting students for further charter flights; they were planning at that stage four flights altogether. Walters, on account of his extensive interviewing experience and of his intimate knowledge of the employment market in the United Kingdom— he had overseen during many years the placement of thousands of freshly qualified graduates—was acutely aware that what the country needed were well-qualified scientists and engineers and that students studying for degrees in these subjects would have an excellent chance to find well-suited employment with good prospects. They would not encounter the problems with which arts students might have to grapple. Bald, or nearly bald, and in spite of a girth reminiscent of Mr. Pickwick, Walters was full of energy. His enthusiasm knew no bounds. He turned up occasionally amongst those of us already at London University and tried to explain something important, loudly, perhaps in the belief that we would understand the message better. From the exertion, beads of perspiration appeared on his forehead, which he tried occasionally wipe away with an oversize handkerchief. Of course, we knew that he was full of goodwill towards us, that he wanted to provide the best for our future and that we depended a great deal on the help of the Hungarian Office which he

[6] Interview with Katalin Jámbor. 26 Jan. 2005.
[7] Lockwood, J.F.: *Second memorandum of the Vice-Chancellor of the University of London*. 3 Dec. 1956. UoLA.CB3/2/1/2.

managed - yet, instead of listening to him and trying to understand what he said, we looked at him, like naughty children, with barely concealed merriment. He might have lacked Mr Pickwick's humour, but embodied for us that humorous but lovable figure. I am sure that the situation in Vienna was the reverse: there the students, perhaps also perspiring, had to convince Walters that they had the right background and attitude to be able to continue their studies successfully at the higher education institutions in Britain.

The "right background" did not, of course, have the same meaning as Péter Rényi implied in his notorious book about the 1956 refugees, whom he described with ill- concealed hatred and venom: "In any case"—he wrote—"there had been a great deal of political screening of the refugee students. The English, for example, had enquired into all aspects of the background of the applicants and continued to do so during the further selection procedures in England. The universities had come to the conclusion that 'it would not help anyone if they would accept also those students who could not compete with the others'. I am convinced many students remembered the times when in Hungary we had fervently debated how to help students with working class or peasant background and some people, ready to wield the weapon of criticism, had still protested that there should be no room for the consideration of social arguments for the admission to higher education. Surely, it must have bitterly disappointed many students that the authorities in the West were inclined to treat favourably those with a bourgeois background rather than students with working class or peasant parents."[8]

During the interviews in Vienna no one, of course, investigated the social background of the students. Quizzing them about their background simply involved asking questions to ascertain, in many cases without any documents the students were able to produce, that they had indeed attended courses at a university in Hungary, how many semesters they had completed, what subject they had studied, whether they had any knowledge of English and where and what they would like to read if admitted to a British university. The students were never asked about their origin or to which social class their family belonged. Although Walters had first been instructed that he should consider only those applicants who could be identified as bona fide students after sifting through the available evidence, this requirement was soon abandoned, in order to also give

---

[8] Rényi, Péter: „Szabad földről üzenik..." (disszidálókról, hazatérőkről) .(„They send their message form the free world"... On the ones who left and on the ones who returned.) Budapest, 1957. pp.83-84.

chance to those potential students who, for political reasons, had been barred from higher education in Hungary.[9]

Lockwood issued five memoranda to the CVCP in less than a month (between 28th November and 21st December 1956)[10], in which he gave a detailed report on all relevant developments regarding the refugee students, including the composition of each group brought to England by chartered flight under the aegis of the CVCP. It is interesting to note that while most of the students arriving with the first flight had studied or gained qualifications in arts or social sciences—not surprisingly, since the selectors were all historians—with the selection passing to Walters, the composition of the groups significantly changed. Most probably following instructions and relying on his own instincts, Walters included more students with a scientific or engineering background. So much so, that in the tables analysing the composition of the groups, engineering students were not lumped together any more, but listed under the type of engineering courses they had followed. According to a table drawn up much later, which also summarized the placement and the grants awarded to the so-called CVCP students, the proportion of the students accepted for university courses was much higher in groups 2 to 5 than in group 1. This also seems to confirm Walters's reliable insight and sound judgement, although he openly complained in the thank-you notes he wrote to his friends that the task he had to carry out in Vienna, especially the refusals he also had to issue, represented "a rather sadder aspect of my job", or "the less pleasant side of selection".[11]

In the end, the CVCP organized the transfer of a total of 154 persons on five, rather than the anticipated four chartered aircrafts, landing in England on the following dates: November 26th and 30th, December 5th, 10th and 11th respectively. The number given to the flight and the serial number allocated to the passengers on each plane provided the identification code for individual students, in use throughout their university studies. (The Hungarian Office referred to the students by this code, for example, in the yearly Progress Reports; the students, however, were not aware of it.) There were not only potential students in the groups, but also craftsmen, skilled and unskilled labourers and an assortment of

---

[9] Lockwood, in his report to the Hungarian Students Committee of the CVCP referred to the earlier decision as a "mistake". In: CVCP. Sub-Committee on Hungarian Students: *Note by the vice-Chancellor of the University of London.* 5 Dec. 1956. UoLA CB3/1/1/1.

[10] Lockwood, J. F.: *Memorandum of the Vice-Chancellor of the University of London.* UoLA CB3/2/1/1-5.

[11] UoLA CB 3/4/59.

relatives: wives, fiancées, brothers, sisters and a number of dependent children. In addition, some of the persons who had claimed to be university students were found to be unsuitable to enter higher education in Britain. A few of those brought over decided to return to Austria and some of them used England as a springboard to emigrate to other countries like Canada, Australia or the United States. For those, who had already obtained their qualification in Hungary and thus were excluded from the refugee students scheme, which awarded grants only for undergraduate studies, the university authorities tried to find suitable employment, or, if they wished to study for a higher degree, to support them with grants from their own resources. At the end of the repeated selection procedures, out of the 154 persons 94 students were awarded CVCP grants to study for a first degree, and a further 26 students received other grants. The CVCP regarded the proportion of 120 persons out of 154 being found suitable to receive support for their education as exceptionally high. Walters returned to London on 10th December. The CVCP recorded its thanks to him at the next meeting of the Committee on 14th December and invited him to join the members for lunch and to give them an account of his experiences.

Thus ended the first, and perhaps the most exciting, but by no means the last, chapter of Walters's participation in the recruitment and selection of suitable Hungarian students for studying in British universities. He was asked again to fly to Vienna in the spring of 1957 to interview those applicants for a Ford grant who wanted to study in Britain. And, throughout the period between December 1956 and late spring 1957, he actively helped in the identification, registration and selection of Hungarian students who had arrived to Britain with the mass of ordinary refugees. His most important activity was, however, to supervise the smooth operation of the Hungarian Office, established under the aegis of the CVCP in London University's Appointments Board. This Office looked after all the Hungarian students for six years: it sought information about their progress, recorded their achievements, listened to the problems they had encountered and gave good advice to solve them. It helped the students to find suitable jobs, or encouraged them to study for higher degrees, and if they chose to do the latter, the Office secured grants to support them for as long as it was required. Walters summarized the conception, operation and achievements of the Hungarian refugee students' scheme several times (for the CVCP, the Lord Mayor's Fund and for other parties). He wrote eloquently of the stirring events of late 1956 and of the huge organizational and administrative requirements of 1957, when the students were allocated to universities and prepared for their courses, first of all by arranging English language tuition for them. He underlined how close the cause of helping the students was to the hearts of the leaders of the universities and how committed they were to translate the plans, formulated by the CVCP, almost immediately into action. It was typical of the modesty of Walters that he rarely signed the reports; his authorship can only be established from the numerous drafts existing in the archives of the Hungarian Office. He described the author, for example, in one of the briefest—only just over two pages long—but one of the best articles on this topic as "contributed by a colleague who was a member of the administrative staff of the University [of London] in 1956 and was closely involved in the events related."[12]

The greatest and most pressing problem the CVCP faced during December 1956 was the placement of the students in temporary accommodation. Although the first term was drawing to its end, there were few vacant rooms available in student hostels or in the colleges. In any case, it would not have been wise—thought the organizers—to scatter the students widely, since they were bewildered in the strange environment and most of them spoke no English. In the first few weeks they might find greater reassurance if their groups were to be allowed to stay together. Lockwood had been well aware of the problem from the start and begun to make arrangements on two fronts well before the first group arrived. On the one hand, he asked a number of major universities to receive a planeload of students and to look after them at least until the beginning of the New Year. The universities of Birmingham, Leeds, Oxford and later Cambridge rose to the challenge. The reception of the first group posed, in any case, no problem. From Blackbushe airfield in Hampshire the BCAR transferred the students by coach to the Lancaster Gate Hotel in London, where they were to spend a few days, during which members of the selection team could observe them and decide, at least tentatively, on their allocation to various universities. After that, they travelled to Oxford under the guidance of Christopher Seton-Watson, the brother of Hugh, who shared in the work of the Oxford Hungarian Committee.

On the other hand, Lockwood also had to provide for each group, accommodation in London for a short stay, so that the students could be interviewed by the designated members of the CVCP Selection Committee. They would then be transferred to the respective reception centre, where they would spend the Christmas break. Lockwood had already obtained the approval of the Senate of London University on 21st November to use £1000 allocated from the university's general budget for

---

[12] Hungarian refugee students 1956-1957. *University of London Bulletin,* No.43, October 1977, pp.4-6.

setting up a temporary hostel for Hungarian students at 41 Tavistock Square. It was one of the properties of London University, an elegant house in a still existing Georgian terrace, which in its hey-day must have been the residence of a well-to-do family. It was, therefore, less suited to the role of a student hostel: students housed in the grand rooms on the ground and first floors felt that they lived in stately apartments, while those, accommodated in the former servant quarters at the top of the building, often sharing the rooms, grumbled about their lot. Not surprisingly, because a few of the lucky ones, quite amusingly, began to play "upstairs/downstairs" to the dismay of the others.

The University of London Union (ULU) enthusiastically offered its help to make the building habitable and the London Hostels Association provided the furniture. The hostel accommodated about 40 students at a time, but because the flights followed each other in quick succession and the groups had to be kept in London for a few days, Lockwood realized that another temporary hostel was needed. He turned to the Rector of Imperial College, Sir Patrick Linstead, who, in a telephone conversation with the Vice-Chancellor on Sunday, 25th November, offered to house some Hungarian students on a temporary basis. This was confirmed in a letter the following day: at 24 hours' notice the College could provide accommodation for fifteen students in dormitories and in double rooms as well as provide them with meals. If any of these students were to be allocated eventually to study at Imperial, they could stay in the hostel at least to the end of the academic year. Otherwise, it would serve as a transit hostel; an annex to Tavistock Square. In addition, Imperial could offer two rooms immediately—at one hour's notice—albeit these would only be available temporarily.[13] The offer was gratefully accepted by the University and earmarked for fifteen students coming by the second flight which was to arrive in Britain on 30th November. The other twenty students would be going to Leeds.

There was no time to waste. Linstead began to make the arrangements for the reception of the students at once. He had a list of potential interpreters in College compiled—two Hungarian speaking dons, Drs Gábor and Kálmán, both from the Department of Electrical Engineering— were put on the list. The Rector set up a Working Party to deal with all aspects of the tasks ahead, which he himself chaired. Key members of the team included Mr Cutcliffe, the Registrar (academic matters), C. C. Seaford, Domestic Bursar (accommodation and financial matters) and the Rector's wife (welfare of the students). He wrote to Westminster Council

---

[13] Letter by R. P. Linstead to J. F. Lockwood. 26 Nov. 1956. UoLA, CB3/4/31/

asking it to derequisition three flats at 12 Princes Gardens—also in an elegant, in this case an early Victorian, house in South Kensington—which would be converted to a hostel. On his instruction the Domestic Bursar produced a detailed work plan for the cleaning, painting and decorating of the hostel, which would be furnished and equipped by the London Hostels Association at 24 hours' notice, if necessary. Imperial College students would take part in the preparations: they would "scrub out the pantry and the bathrooms." Amenities and recreation were not forgotten: two sitting rooms were to be provided, one of them in the hostel. Gifts of books, cushions and other items were to be collected by the Wives' Club of the College. The final touches were scheduled for Friday, so that the hostel would be ready to receive the students on Monday, 3rd December.[14]

The fifteen students from Flight II duly arrived at Imperial College on this date. They were interviewed and assessed at once; the questionnaire they were asked to fill in had been devised by the Hungarian Dennis Gabor, then Reader in Electrical Engineering, later one of the Nobel Laureates of the College.[15] Three of the students in the group had been studying at the Technical University of Budapest, the *alma mater* of Dennis Gabor, and the College was keen to accept them immediately. Because they spoke no English, group tickets were purchased for them so that they could travel to Bloomsbury, where the English lessons for the Hungarian students commenced on 5th December. The College also provided temporary employment to one of the students who already had a degree in architecture; he worked for months in the Bursar's office until he found a suitable job with a leading architectural firm. The other students enjoyed the hospitality of Imperial until early January, when, in the context of the nation-wide change-over named "Operation Switch", they travelled to the universities to which they had been allocated, or acted as the regional centres for the English courses.

The four universities besides London—Birmingham, Cambridge, Leeds and Oxford—which had volunteered to offer immediate accommodation to the students when they arrived in England, also faced considerable difficulties in arranging their reception, especially in finding suitable rooms for them at very short notice. Moreover, these were the universities, joined by the University of Edinburgh in January 1957, which were responsible for organizing the long-term language courses for large

---

[14] Seaford, C. C.: *Accommodation for Hungarian students.* 28 Nov. 1956. ICA, Hungarian Relief, SS/1/4.

[15] Both manuscript and the typed version of the questionnaire exist in the College Archives. They are unsigned, but the stylistic evidence strongly suggest the had of Dennis Gabor. ICA, Hungarian Relief, SS/1/4.

groups of students, so their commitment was not for a few weeks, but for a minimum of six, and in most cases, of nine months.

The group first to arrive was destined for Oxford University and it was transferred from London to Oxford on 30th November. To find a suitable place for the students was the most urgent task of the newly established Oxford Hungarian Committee. As no other hostel was available, the Committee decided to put up the whole group in the Marston Youth Hostel, at the northern edge of the town. Youth Hostels in the 1950s were rather austere establishments: they offered simple dormitory arrangements, shared bathroom facilities and a communal kitchen with sparse equipment to be used by those impecunious young travellers who were willing to accept the harsh conditions as the price of seeing the wonders of the world. Moreover, the winter months in England were cold and damp and the luxury of central heating almost unknown. No wonder that the Committee regarded the Marston accommodation as an emergency measure and even before the arrival of the group it had turned with a request first to the University Chest, then on 26th November to the Hebdomadal Council to requisition Wytham Abbey, a grade one listed manor house about three miles out of Oxford, built in the reign of Henry VII, to be turned into lodgings for the Hungarian students. The request was readily granted and Wytham Abbey would, indeed, have offered a splendid, although somewhat isolated accommodation after refurbishment. In the meantime however, a number of Oxford families also expressed their willingness to offer hospitality for students, and not just over the imminent Christmas period, but for several months, if necessary. The Committee decided to accept the latter solution and the problem of housing the students could be shelved for the time being.

Some of the colleges were also keen to take refugee students. The Hungarian Committee, however, tried to resist placing the students into Colleges, fearing that the college authorities would regard them as "their special Hungarian students" and, because the allocation of the students to universities all over Britain proceeded at a much slower speed, they would be reluctant to release them to take up their places elsewhere. Norrington actually sent a letter to the Heads of Colleges to assess their willingness to accept Hungarian students entering degree courses—that is from October 1957—when the final list of the Oxford refugee students could, with some precision, be compiled. Nevertheless, some colleges, as reported to Committee on 14th December, already "had their eyes on individuals" and two colleges, namely Balliol and Merton were even vying with each other to get the promising George Radda, as their student.[16]

In January 1957 some of the students from Flight I left Oxford for other universities, but others arrived to take their place. In addition, students, who would be placed at the universities of South West England or in the Colleges of the University of Wales, joined the Oxford group for the English courses. Accommodation for these students were often in "digs"—rooms rented for the duration of an academic year—which provided them with a semblance of independence, while the community of the language classes sheltered them from the despondency of being left alone, even lost in an alien environment. One could say it was a perfect balance to ease the difficulties of settling down. Stories of the life of the refugee student days at Oxford still abound. How they staved off their hunger on pennies, cooking what they called "sticky rice"—pudding rice boiled to a gluey mass, perhaps with some fried streaky bacon on top to make it more palatable—or, eating cereals for breakfast, lunch and dinner, for days on end. Good coffee, however, was a priority; it was available at the Italian coffee house *La Roma*, which served the only authentic Continental espresso in town, and this was where Hungarian students assembled daily for a chat, for exchanging experiences and for seeking comfort in each other's company.

Leeds University began the preparation for the reception of the students in similar fashion by setting up a Hungarian Committee towards the end of November under the chairmanship of S. E. Toulmin, Professor of Philosophy. It was, however, Stephen Ullmann, the Hungarian born Professor of French and Romance Languages and Literature, also a member of the Committee and his wife, who looked after all the Hungarian students throughout their years of study at Leeds. At one stage he had taken over the chairmanship of the Committee and it was he who drew up the final summary of the events taking place between December 1956 and the spring of 1962.[17] The arrangements for the reception of the students, as listed in the programme, were quite elaborate and extended to the smallest detail. A small group of dons and Mrs Ullmann were

---

[16] Oxford Hungarian Committee: *Minutes.* 14 Dec. 1956. BLA UR6/OVS/H File 1. Radda, of course, has fulfilled all expectations: as Sir George Radda, formerly Executive Director of the Medical Research Council, he still works as an eminent researcher at Oxford.

[17] University of Leeds. Committee on Hungarian Students: *Hungarian Students' Appeal Fund.* 12 April 1962. Professor Ullmann (1914-1976) lived in the United Kingdom since 1939 and taught at the Universities of Glasgow, Leeds and finally Oxford.

dispatched to London; they were to escort the students, travelling by train, from London to Leeds. A higher ranking university team received them at Leeds railway station and transferred them by coach to Devonshire Hall, one of the hostels allocated for housing the students, where the Vice-Chancellor, Sir Charles Morris, greeted them, flanked by the chief officers of Leeds University. After the ceremony they all repaired to the banquet, specially laid on for the occasion. The programme also mentioned the discreet task entrusted to Commander Evans: he was to hand quietly £2 in an envelope to each student. The events of the day did not conclude with the dinner as the students had to undergo a medical examination before they were allowed to go to sleep.

The next day was devoted to shopping. More precisely, to the selection and collection of items of clothing which had been offered free to the students by the leading shops and department stores at the request of the university. Preliminary lists had been drawn up of the requirements, of the shops able and willing to supply them and of the teams of university people who would accompany the students on the shopping spree. In addition to basics—underwear, shirts, blouses, skirts, suits, pullovers and a winter coat—the male students would also get sports jackets and matching coloured waistcoats, and the female students—but not the males—slippers. Messrs Brill of Bond Street, then regarded as the most elegant of outfitters in town, also gave each man a set of boxed handkerchiefs. The Hungarian Committee issued a statement formally thanking the shops for their magnanimity.[18]

The university was more than conscious of the need both to inform the public about the efforts it was making for the Hungarian cause and to promote it widely. Thus one of the key elements of the programme was the involvement of the press in the proceedings. The Assistant Registrar, L. R. Kay, also a member of the Hungarian Committee for example, wrote to the news editor of the *Manchester Guardian*, advising him about the details of the press conferences, on how the press might be represented at the reception of the students at the railway station and how appropriate it would be to give publicity in the papers to the generosity of the shops and department stores. However, Mr Kay warned the newspapers about the danger of questioning the students too closely: "My Committee are sure that your reporters can be relied on to use the utmost tact and discretion in dealing with these students who have had such harrowing experiences and who have probably been subject to a continuous barrage of press

---

[18] The consultation of the papers relating to the reception of the Hungarian refugee students at Leeds University was kindly made available for me by the University's Central Records Office.

interrogation ever since they left Vienna. We feel sure that you will do
your utmost to respect their feelings."[19] Finally, it should also be
mentioned that the Hungarian Committee made arrangements for the
students to spend the Christmas break with a family and to receive a small
personal gift. A special appeal was launched for this purpose, which raised
£36 and 13 shillings, quite a considerable sum in those days, mainly
collected by the pupils of the Middleton Boys' School. The small parcel
for each student contained "something useful", £2 to spend on what they
wanted and a Christmas card. And a box of chocolate was placed for them
in the two hostels they occupied.

At every university it had been the student body which first held
demonstrations for the Hungarian cause, hailed the revolution and then,
when it was crushed, championed support for the refugee students. The
only exception was the University of Birmingham, where student opinion
was, at least initially, divided. True, the student newspaper, called the
Guild News, published a letter written by third year history student at the
beginning of November, advocating the launch of an appeal for the relief
of Hungarian students. The officers of the Student Union rejected the call,
because—as reported in the paper—"such an action could be capable of
political interpretation and it has been the policy of the Executive, by
precedent, not to interfere with politics."[20] This statement provoked a
debate, concentrating on public versus private views and action. The
strictly apolitical view of the Union was understandable; the Chancellor of
the University was none other than the Prime Minister, Sir Anthony Eden,
and both the staff and the students were aware that the public, and voicing
their views, the media, already had linked the government's reluctance to
help Hungary and the deepening Suez crisis together. The best policy
seemed to be to keep silent about both.

By mid-November the outrage, felt by most students about the
treatment of a country desperately fighting for its freedom, radically
altered the opinion of those hitherto sticking resolutely to neutrality and
the editorial of the 15th November issue of the paper was entitled: "The
slaughter of people wanting freedom is above politics". It continued: "This
is supposed to be an impartial and independent newspaper, but it is about
time that humanitarian principles were raised above the level of politics,
international, or otherwise. This is not a question of policy in which one
organization or country is blamed. It is a matter of grave concern for
Western civilisation. A Red Cross tin is but a superficial appeasement of

---

[19] Letter by L. R. Kay to the News Editor, *The Manchester Guardian*, 30 Nov.
1956.
[20] *Guild News*, 1 Nov. 1956.

the conscience of us all."[21] A week later the first result of the collection for a Hungarian Fund were reported and the following week an appeal was made to all students to volunteer for work in setting up a house for the reception of the first group of refugee students coming to Birmingham. They arrived on 8th December. The *Guild News* greeted them with a headline in Hungarian: "Isten hozta!" – "Welcome!"

At the meeting of the Senate on 7th July 1957, R. T. Jones, Permanent Secretary to the Guild of Undergraduates, presented an account of the reception of Hungarian students by the University. He had summarized the momentous events on a two page typescript which was then attached to the minutes. "It was towards the end of November 1956," he wrote, "when the almost derelict residence on University property at the corner of Somerset Road and Edgbaston Park Road and known as 'Park Grange' assumed a new lease of life [...] Birmingham had offered to provide temporary accommodation for 20-25 students. A Hungarian Student Committee was appointed with Professor F. K. Bannister as its Chairman and containing representatives of the Council, the Academic staff and the Guild of Undergraduates which had for some time expressed a desire to assist their less fortunate Hungarian counterparts. The first task of this Committee was to prepare the 'Park Grange' for the reception of the refugees, thirty of whom arrived on Saturday, 8th December. This work of resuscitating 'Park Grange' was achieved by a truly 'combined operation' involving members of staff, the University Maintenance Department, members of the Guild of Undergraduates, the City Welfare Department and the WVS, as well as members of the general public [...] The greatest transformation was, however, brought about by the many undergraduates who almost completely redecorated the house in an incredibly short time."[22] The report also mentioned the help provided by the Hungarian Dr. Horne and his friends. They acted as interpreters and set up an English language course for the students at once. This course was to function during the first half of 1957 as the main regional course for Hungarian students placed at universities in the Midlands. The students enjoyed the hospitality of local families who invited them for Christmas; some of them still recall with great affection the warm welcome they had received.[23]

When Flights IV and V landed on 10th and 11th December respectively, it transpired that the house at Tavistock Square could not provide even

---

[21] Ibid. 15 November 1956.
[22] Jones, R. T.: An account from the Secretary of the Committee of the help given to Hungarian refugee students in the University. In: University of Birmingham. Senate: *Annex to the minutes.* 2 July 1957. Birmingham University Archives.
[23] Interview with Marietta Záhonyi. 24 May 2005.

temporary accommodation for the 56 students who had just arrived, although each previous group had been transferred to other university reception centres after a few days spent in London. Logan approached Cambridge University and it was agreed that the group would be divided into two; some of the students were to stay in London and the others would go to Cambridge. The timing was just right: the first term was about to end and two of the most prestigious colleges, Trinity and King's College offered to take 25 Hungarian students: ten places were made available at King's and fifteen at Trinity. Dr. Rattenbury, the all-powerful Registrary of Cambridge University – who personally took responsibility for the refugee students – asked the Hungarian born Dr. Robert Bolgár to escort the students from London. (Almost all higher education institution in Britain seemed to have some members of staff who were of Hungarian origin and who were more than willing to help.) The relationship forged between Dr. Bolgár and the Hungarian students at Cambridge was much more than that of providing and accepting help. He invited the newly arrived students to his own home where they also met his mother, a cultured and kind elderly lady who had retained the refined forms of social intercourse she had grown up with at the beginning of the century. The parents of Dr. Bolgár had been members of the diplomatic corps and, in a sense, time came to stand still for them; their whole attitude, the atmosphere of their home still reflected the highly sophisticated conduct of life of their youth. The students, coming from the drab and dispiriting circumstances of Communist Hungary, where sheer survival demanded the rejection of civilized behaviour deemed "reactionary", and where deceit and lies became de rigueur, marvelled at and readily imbued the spirit of the Bolgárs' home.

The rooms provided for the students in the Colleges also elicited astonishment. In Hungary it was not unusual to cram ten, even twelve university students into a miserable looking dormitory. They had to sleep on bunk beds and space was so confined that apart from a table in the middle, where the students were supposed to eat, read and write their essays, there was no room for other furniture, even the rickety metal lockers, holding all their possessions, were lined up in the corridor outside. Yet, it was not the unbelievable comfort, even splendour of the accommodation[24] which made the greatest impression on the students, but the carol service in the King's College chapel on Christmas Eve. They still cherish the memory of the concert, where the Hungarian refugee students

---

[24] See, for example, the description of his accommodation at Trinity Hall, Cambridge, for the benefit of his former school friends: Pálffy, Stephen: *Pályám emlékezete – My path recollected.* 2004, p.12. www.ersekicicero.org

were treated as guests of honour. The beauty of the building—there is nothing to compare the intricate delicacy of the English perpendicular in Hungary—enchanted them, the songs lulled their anxiety and filled them with peace and hope. The warmth of the occasion and the feeling of unity by the congregation in praying together, embraced them too. They felt that they too belonged and that they were accepted as part of the community.[25]

Many of the first group of Hungarian students at Cambridge were soon dispersed and moved to other universities. Their place was taken by others coming early in the New Year for the English language course for which Cambridge also acted as a regional centre. Uniquely, however, all refugee students were housed in Colleges, including term-time, when it must have been more difficult to allocate rooms to them. The arrangement speeded up their settlement in the new environment. Although they were not yet formally accepted as Cambridge students, they shared the college life with other undergraduates, and the upheaval they had endured was slowly replaced by normality.

Besides London, five universities were entrusted by the CVCP with organizing English tuition for the Hungarian students: Birmingham, Cambridge, Leeds, Oxford and finally Edinburgh, which was to take the 20 students who would study at Scottish universities and an additional two, who would go to the Queen's University at Belfast. It did not act as a temporary reception centre, so the first group of students only arrived on 7th January 1957. The delay did not dim the enthusiasm of the crowd waiting for their arrival at Waverley Station. They were photographed alighting from the train and the pictures were spread across the pages of the newspapers the following day. They were carried across town as if in a triumphal procession to the hostel where they were to be housed. The hostel was prepared for them as at the other universities, by the huge effort of the student body and of the university staff and completed in record time. And while Leeds University clothed the students in normal garb, Edinburgh University had to provide protection for them against the inclement Scottish winter. R. M. Young, Deputy Registrar of the University, who often represented it at the CVCP meetings, described the stirring event of that January in an article, written for the *University of Edinburgh Gazette* some months later: "The first batch of twenty-five students—or, more accurately, twenty-four students and one apprentice upholsterer—arrived on 7 January. Fortunately all were males, so there was no need to seek for a second hostel. There were small preliminary difficulties, but, in general, the students settled in without delay. It was at

---

[25] Interview with András Szabó. 19 Jan. 2006.

once obvious that something would have to be done to provide suitable clothing. Most of the students had little more than what they stood up in, and none were equipped to face the east winds of an Edinburgh winter. A minimum scale of clothing was agreed to and thereafter the students were individually interviewed, and a very substantial list of 'deficiencies' was drawn up. After some enquiries, a well-known firm of tailors and boot makers offered to give very reasonable terms for the supply of the necessary items. The other Universities were consulted and their consents were obtained to the necessary expenditure for the immediate equipment of the students. In a few days new suits began to appear, morale improved immensely, and, from being an isolated party of strangers, the Hungarians began to become part of the general body of students."[26]

Once the reception of the 150 so-called CVCP students had been settled, the Sub-Committees had to tackle the task of allocating them to their respective universities, since the language courses, to begin as soon as possible in January 1957, were to be organized on a regional basis. Each regional centre would be responsible for the students allocated to them and for the students allocated to other universities for which, under the scheme, they would also provide the language course. Therefore, during the so-called "Operation Switch", planned for early January, a large proportion of the students were to be moved from their temporary accommodation to the designated centres.

The Selection Committee set up a small team of three for interviewing the students in London, immediately after their arrival. They were entrusted to ascertain the background of the students: what subjects they had studied at which university, did they wish to continue to study the same or related subjects in Britain, or—for whatever reason—did they want to change subjects, and finally, were there any personal requirements which should be taken into account when considering their placement. The team could, of course, suggest that according to their opinion the candidate was not up to university standard and should be referred to a technical college or polytechnic, or in the worst case scenario, rejected outright.

The students, on the other hand, must have felt that they were being quizzed at every turn: first by Walters in Vienna, then by the CVCP team in London and finally by the authorities at the university they were sent to, in the first instance. The students, most probably, could not judge which one of these interviews determined their future. Walters selected them for admission to Britain, the CVCP team allocated them to universities as

---

[26] Young, R. M.: The Hungarian students. *University of Edinburgh Gazette*, No. 16, Oct. 1957, pp.21-22.

their future undergraduates and the university authorities at the temporary reception centres were obviously looking at them as their own potential students, although they were supposed to regard them as short-term guests staying with them for only a few weeks. Nevertheless, they often made it clear to Lockwood or Logan that they wished to retain some of them – a decision which often also reflected the view of the student in question, who had formed a very favourable opinion of the institution during his short stay. So, for the students it was essential to give a good impression at every session with the relevant interviewing group, although they may not have realized this. The CVCP team began its arduous work as soon as the flights touched down: on 3rd December Lockwood was able to advise the CVCP not only about the establishment of the team, but also report that to that date it had already interviewed 69 potential students.[27] The team consisted of Dr. G. F. Cushing, lecturer of Hungarian Language and Literature in the School of Slavonic and East European Studies, University of London, W. J. Dey, Secretary of the University's Entrance Requirements Department and, especially for the assessment of the science and technology students, Professor J. Greig of the Department of Electrical Engineering, King's College, London.

The key person in the interviewing group was Dr. Cushing, a Hungarian-speaking don. Cushing had been a classics student at Cambridge University when, towards the end of the Second World War, he was picked, with some others, to be trained for being parachuted into Hungary on a secret mission. He had to learn Hungarian and, although nothing came of the planned action, he remained a devoted student of Hungarian language and literature for the rest of his life. After the war, between 1947 and 1949, Cushing secured a scholarship and found employment in Budapest: he was the English language lector at the Eötvös József College, an institution reserved for the education of an elite corps of students and thus, he became thoroughly acquainted with the Hungarian higher education system. (In 1949, the so-called "year of changeover", when the Communists seized power and total control of the country, Cushing was accused of being a spy of the Western imperialists, or at least, a person with the secret mission to undermine the new People's Democracy, and was expelled.) His knowledge of the structure of Hungarian universities and their curricula, proved very useful for the interviewing team. The team had to interview over 150 students within a fortnight but even within this limited time, Cushing was able to find out

---

[27] Lockwood, J. F.: *Second memorandum of the Vice-Chancellor of the University of London.* 3 Dec. 1956. UoLA, CB3/2/1/2.

with some certainty, even without supporting documentation, whether the candidate was telling the truth. On behalf of the team he was also expected to discuss with the students their future: what and where they might study in Britain to complete their education and then find suitable employment.

Not being among the 150 selected CVCP students, it was somewhat later, on the afternoon of 31st December, that I was called to Senate House for an interview. I still would like to think that it was my new coiffure—paid for from the first week's salary I earned in the Seidler household—and my strikingly multicoloured but gently moulting rabbit fur coat which I had obtained in the camp that attracted the attention of Cushing. I must have presented, indeed, a rather an odd sight. He offered me a place at Westfield College, University of London. Unfortunately, it was to study German for an Honours degree, a great mistake, since my knowledge of German, that Cushing had no time to gauge, was so slight that I was destined to fail my exams. Cushing, although a good ten years older than his interviewees, was regarded by the students as one of them, as their friend. He might have spoken Hungarian with a marked English accent and his remarks, often unintentionally funny, contradicted the rather reserved manner in which he uttered them. He surveyed us from behind his glasses with a teasing smile, as if he were our playmate in this extraordinary adventure. And we felt that Cushing understood us, that he fully knew what had happened to us and shared in our experiences. That he was able to judge our potential and comprehend our aspirations. Little were we aware that amidst the camaraderie our career was silently mapped out, and that the decisions taken then shaped our future in England.

Even after the first few months when Cushing's expertise had been constantly called upon, he kept an eye on the students. He was often present in the Hungarian Office, quietly observing whatever was going on and which problems were bothering the students. Hovering in the background, he seemed to guard the Office or, as it sometimes seemed to us, he acted as a guard to the Secretary of the Office, Miss Marshall herself. The Hungarian Office was formally set up at the University of London in March 1957, or, more precisely, it was then that the Senate formally approved the activities that the staff of the University of London's Appointments Board had been carrying out on behalf of the CVCP since mid-November 1956.[28] The Office was under the general guidance of Walters, Secretary to the Appointments Board, while Miss Marshall was the full-time officer allocated to run the Hungarian student scheme. And while we impishly laughed at Walters's slightly comic figure

---

[28] University of London. Senate: *Minutes.* 27 March 1957. UoLA, CB3/1/4/1.

and regarded Cushing as our pal, Miss Marshall enjoyed our greatest respect. We felt that she was, without exaggeration, our fairy godmother, a God-given substitute parent, provided for our much needed support. She knew all about us and our needs. We could turn to her in confidence and in the knowledge that she would offer us help and good advice. She was a typical Englishwoman—or what we imagined a typical English woman should look like—tall and slim with upright, almost military bearing, her hair, upswept from her brow, revealed a firmly boned but kindly face. She displayed immense authority, she was solid and reliable; she was our rock. The innumerable complaints, with which we burdened her during the years she was looking after us, did not diminish her initial romantic disposition towards the anxious, ambitious, loud and somewhat unruly crowd we must have presented. Her correspondence reveals the hard line she occasionally had to take, but her strictness, almost invariably, served our interests. Even today, when I pass the building in Gordon Square where the Hungarian Office was located, I seem to see for a fleeting moment Miss Marshall's smiling face behind the large, ground floor window pane.

Cushing and his team must have drawn up a brief report on each student they had interviewed, possibly including recommendations about allocating the students to a particular higher education institution.[29] This was passed on to the CVCP Hungarian Students Selection Committee to help it with the distribution of the students among British universities. The Committee held its first meeting on 10th December 1956. Under the second agenda point Lockwood outlined the principles which should be observed and illustrated them with appropriate examples.[30] The simplest and most evident was the case of those students who had followed a particular course in Hungary which was taught only in a single institution in Britain—for example the study of Turkish and Persian languages at the School of Oriental and African Studies at London University—they should be allocated to that institution. A change of subject should be avoided without good cause, especially if it would result in starting a university course from the beginning rather than the continuation of the study of a particular subject. Students should be dissuaded from entering courses for qualifications in medicine, since medical education would require support

---

[29] The main collection in the University of London Archives CB3: *Records of the Hungarian Refugee Students Scheme*, contains a substantial amount of personal details and information on the students, including the notes on their interview, allocation, progress, qualifications and finally, employment. These files in the Archive are, however, closed until almost to the middle of this century.

[30] CVCP. Hungarian Refugee Students. Selection Committee: *Minutes.* 10 Dec. 1956. UoLA, CB3/1/4/1.

for a minimum of five years and, at that time, financial support even for a three year course was not at all secure. The Committee must consider the family ties of the students: husbands and wives, sisters and brothers and engaged couples should be placed at the same institution even if they were to follow different courses.

Finally, Lockwood stressed that universities, acting as reception centres, should, on no account engage in the pre-selection of the most promising candidates: "Another problem should be faced from the start. The Selection Committee consists in effect of representatives of universities which have provided the initial reception centres. They have therefore had the advantage of seeing groups of the students personally and getting to know them individually. It would be fatal to allow any impression to arise in other universities that those providing the initial reception centres had taken the cream of the students."[31] Nevertheless— he admitted—it would be foolish to completely disregard the request already submitted by some universities to retain one or two students whom they had received and after talking to them, found eminently suitable to enter a degree course there and then. He quoted amongst others the case of Imperial College. The Rector of the College had sent him a list of five engineering students whom he would like to take as his students. If agreed, they could start their courses immediately, that is, in the second term of the current academic year. Three of the five students arrived with Flight II and were housed at Lockwood's request at Imperial. The other two, however, did not come to England on the CVCP chartered flights; they came with a general refugee group and were moved to a camp for refugees. Although registered as students, they were anxious that the authorities would not learn of their existence in time and they would miss securing a place for themselves at a university in Britain. They decided not to wait, but took responsibility for their own destiny. They were not alone.

---

[31] Ibid.

CHAPTER V

THE REST OF THE STUDENTS

Although Lockwood and Logan kept stressing whenever and wherever they spoke about the Hungarian refugee students scheme, that the universities would not be able to provide grants to more students than the 150 brought to Britain by the CVCP, both of them were aware right from the start that there would be many more students arriving with the general mass of refugees. They thought that these students should also be considered for entry into the British higher education system just as the students hand-picked in Vienna. In his report to the CVCP Seton-Watson corroborated this view. He had received similar information about Hungarian students being distributed to various camps in Austria, who would be likely to miss the news about the recruitment carried out by the British Council and, even if they decided to come to England, would be transported with the other Hungarian refugees coming to this country.[1] When sending Walters to Vienna to select students for the next three or four special flights, the CVCP therefore agreed to instruct him to help the British Council in Vienna to locate these students, as well as arrange their transport to Britain if possible, or at least, to register them so that on arrival the officials of the Home Office would be able to separate them from the rest of the refugees and pass their details straight on to WUS. In the meantime WUS had set up a Committee for the registration of about 300 students whom they then thought were likely to be sent to various camps in Britain. The membership of the Committee included the representatives of the University of London, the Ministry of Education, the Local Educational Authorities (LEA) and the British Council.[2]

Walters soon reported from Vienna that some non-CVCP students had also been interviewed—although without his participation. To his knowledge the BCAR was organizing two groups, containing twenty and

---

[1] Seton-Watson, H.: Students among Hungarian refugees in Austria. CVCP: *Minutes.* 23 Nov. 1956. CVCPA.
[2] CVCP. Sub-Committee on Hungarian Students: *Agenda. Note by the Vice-Chancellor of the University of London.* 7 Dec. 1956. UoLA, CB3/1/1/1.

seventeen students respectively, who would be dispatched to Britain.[3] Oddly, there is no mention of these groups of students and their fate in any documents. Logan, in his *Memorandum* of the 7th of December however, was able to give a fairly full report to the Hungarian Sub-Committee on the current situation regarding the students coming to Britain as part of the general influx of refugees. To date—reported Logan—about 8000 Hungarian refugees had arrived to Great Britain and WUS had registered 176 students among them. According to WUS estimates, this number would easily reach the figure of 350 by the time they had finished separating the students from the other refugees. Furthermore, since the government had agreed to receive 11,000 Hungarian refugees, another 3000 were expected to arrive within a few weeks and the proportion of students was expected to be much higher in this group than in the earlier ones.

While the estimates changed from week to week, a large number of students had indeed arrived by various means and had been distributed to camps—mainly in the temporarily empty army barracks—made available for the refugees. It is quite possible that the Home Office had received lists of students from the British Council in Vienna and after registering the students for an ID card, the officials had notified WUS. However, before WUS would have been able to send them the forms they were requested to fill in, let alone, arrange their interviews, some of the students, being anxious about their future, left the camp and travelled to London, to present themselves at the University of London. In his report, the Principal of the University mentioned eleven such students who, by the 7th of November, turned up in his office at the Senate House. Logan was known for always adhering strictly to the official line—in this case a written notification submitted by WUS before receiving the students—but he could not conceal his admiration for their ingenuity and bravery, as so soon after their arrival in a strange country and most likely without any knowledge of English, they instinctively knew who to turn to and found their way from the camps to Senate House without any mishaps. As he wrote in letter to Rattenbury, the Registrary of Cambridge University: "Those [students] that I have met are really very good indeed and I am full of admiration for their intelligence and their persistence. Two students who had come in through normal British Council for Aid to Refugees channels and were in a hostel at Leighton Buzzard managed to get from there to the Senate House with the sole aid of a dictionary!"[4]

---

[3] Ibid. *Memorandum by the Principal of the University of London.*
[4] Letter by W. D. Logan to R. M. Rattenbury. 8 Dec. 1956. Cambridge University Archives (hereafter CUA), UA Registry file R3445/56.

Another two students, László Keresztury and Gyula Székely, took a similar course. They left the Osterley refugee camp with the aim of travelling to London and, being engineering students, of visiting Imperial College, apparently in order to meet the students studying there. They turned up at the end of November when great preparations were underway to make a hostel habitable for the Hungarian students expected to arrive on 3rd December. So there was a noticeable "Hungarian fever" gripping the students and staff at Imperial. Since they spoke good English, they not only met the students, but were also introduced to the academic staff. Finally, they ended up in the Rector's office and were received and interviewed by Patrick Linstead himself.

The Rector's impression of the two students had been so favourable that on the very same day he spoke to Logan about the College's intention of accepting them. Logan was not amused by the proposal, which he deemed to be rather irregular. There followed a correspondence, the polite tone of which barely disguised the growing tension as to who should be entitled to make the final decision about the placement of the refugee students.[5] Logan was, of course, right to insist that the overriding interest of the CVCP scheme was to find places first of all for the 150 students they were just bringing to England and that Keresztury and Székely should wait patiently for their turn, that is, for the call by WUS to be interviewed for places, if any were still vacant. In the meantime, the students from Flight II arrived and, of those housed at Imperial, three engineering students seemed also to be eminently acceptable for undergraduate courses. So, Linstead was now speaking of a short list of five students he was ready to accept. Finally, Logan consented to the Rector's request and at the beginning of January 1957 he sent a letter to this effect to Linstead. (However, one should not forget that, as mentioned earlier, Logan used the case of Imperial in his early December address to the Selection Committee as an illustration of the right of individual universities to make the final decision regarding their own students!)

Imperial College's own students used the incident for voicing their misgivings of the University's central administration. The students' paper *Felix*, under the heading: 'Red tape ignored', gleefully related the 'victory' of the College over university bureaucrats: "Two Hungarian engineering students, face to face with laborious British administrative procedure for entry to a university and tired of kicking their heels for a week, came to Imperial College to meet the students. As a result of introductions to members of staff they were invited to attend academic courses, on an

---

[5] ICA, Hungarian Relief. SS/1/4.

unofficial basis, immediately, while the Hostel and Union provided them
with the necessities of life. This stung the bureaucrats of the University of
London to action and almost immediately the unofficial Hungarians
became official Hungarians."[6]

The students were, of course, wrong to accuse the Vice-Chancellor and
the Principal of London University, both of them acting on behalf of the
CVCP, of being faceless bureaucrats; the task of interviewing, sorting and
allocating the incoming refugee students was huge and complex,
demanding heroic efforts. The CVCP officials rightly viewed the partisan
action by individual Colleges and universities with alarm as this seriously
impeded the strict procedures adopted for the speedy completion of the
work in hand. And, in addition, they had to deal with other problems, like
tracing the students who had simply disappeared.

We, the three students from the University of Szeged, were among
them. After our arrival with a group of refugees, we were quartered in the
army barracks at Crookham, where we were photographed and issued with
ID cards. As we claimed to be students, we were also told about WUS, the
body which, in due course, would arrange our registration and interview
with the university authorities. Depending on the interview, we might be
offered a university place. This sounded very promising, but days passed
and nothing happened. We whiled away the time by exploring the nearby
village, Fleet, marvelling at the luxurious, deep green lawn in the middle
of December and, because as Hungarian refugees we were given free
access to the cinema, we decided to see Bill Haley's new film, *Rock
around the clock*. We were amazed by the behaviour of the audience:
when the music turned really loud, everybody jumped up, they clapped
their hands to the rhythm and shouted the songs along with the musicians
on the screen. Since in Hungary we had never heard of Haley, Elvis
Presley or of rock and roll, we thought that the English were rather
peculiar movie goers and had a quaint habit of appreciating films. On most
afternoons we attended a tea party to which a local family had kindly
invited us and, and together with tea and cakes gave us English lessons by
pointing to various objects in the room and naming them. And we were
waiting, with ever-growing anxiety, for the notification from WUS.

After a week or so, we could wait no longer. If WUS was not sending
us the application forms to the camp—we reasoned—we should go to the
WUS office in London to pick them up and fill them in. Our pocket money
covered the cost of a railway ticket to Waterloo and, with the kind help we
received from anyone we asked, we first found Baker Street underground

---

[6] *Felix*, Christmas number, Dec. 1956, p.9.

station and then the WUS office at 59 Gloucester Place. While we were busy completing the forms, the people working at WUS pondered what to do with us. They did not wish to send us back to the camp, so some sort of accommodation needed to be found for us in London on that very day. We were redirected to Cumberland House, where a charity was dealing with the problems of the Hungarian refugees. The lady in charge, Mrs. Webster, after making a number of telephone calls, triumphantly informed us that she had found not only places for us but also temporary employment. It would not be amiss to earn a few pounds before we were admitted to university.

The two boys—she said—would go to a family of modest means but generous heart and I would be employed as a general help—with the children, in the house and in the kitchen—in the household of Mr and Mrs Seidler. The elegant Georgian house of the Seidler family was located at the corner of a deceptively quiet, leafy square in Knightsbridge, moments away from the bustling Brompton Road and its big stores. Seidler was the London correspondent of *Newsweek,* so little wonder that I was ceremoniously introduced to their many guests as "their Hungarian". Mrs Seidler taught me English, showed me the local shops and last but not least, she felt compelled to take me at the earliest opportunity to her own hairdresser. She also invited my two fellow students for the Christmas dinner *en famille.* It was a real feast with a huge turkey, all the trimmings and a whisky-soaked Christmas pudding. We could not say much, our vocabulary was too limited even for forming basic sentences, but we pulled the crackers, put on the paper hats on and learnt to sing *Jingle bells.* Curiously, I accepted all that happened to me or surrounded me—the beautiful antique furniture, the blazing logs in the fireplace, my own comfortable room under the eaves and the effort by everyone to make me feel at home—as something natural and self evident. This was now the reality and there was no other reality to which I could compare my present circumstances. Reality, as I had known it, was left behind in Hungary. What I experienced in England was nothing but dream and I did not question dreams.

I was not alone accepting without question or even surprise the life opening up before me that Christmas. A Hungarian woman student, who had been temporarily moved to Birmingham University, was invited for the festivities by a branch of the chocolate manufacturing Cadbury family. She was enchanted by the magnificent panelling of the entrance hall and the superb carvings on the staircase railing in their large, but otherwise not ostentatious mansion. Nevertheless, she regarded the decoration as nothing unusual, to be found most probably in many similar houses in England.

Decades later, passing through the newly reorganized English furniture galleries at the Victoria & Albert Museum, she was startled to recognize the same panelling and carvings, donated by the family to the museum, as an outstanding example of the applied arts of its period.[7]

After Christmas we received an invitation to attend an interview at the University of London and soon after that, in the first half of January 1957, the notification that we had been accepted as students. My fellow students from Szeged had been allocated to the University of Oxford, while I was to be a student at Westfield College, part of the University of London, in line with the suggestion made by Dr. Cushing at my interview. Looking back at the events of that winter, I have to confess my wholehearted admiration for the incredibly well-organized manner with which WUS handled the registration of the Hungarian refugee students. We had left the camp without telling anyone, found new accommodation in London, again without notifying anyone of our new addresses, yet WUS not only registered us, but arranged the interviews and sent us a letter about the arrangements. We were among the first groups of students for which WUS took responsibility. Our code numbers: U.28, U.30 and U.31—which I discovered during the research for this book—simply meant that we were the 28th, 30th and 31st students registered by WUS among the mass of refugees arriving in England. The letter "U" stood for "Unattached", a rather odd word chosen to signify our status, since we did not come alone, all of us were actually attached to a particular group of refugees. Initially, WUS's task was to find these "Unattached" students, register them, pass the details to the CVCP interviewing team, arrange the interviews and notify the students of when and where they should present themselves and, presumably, to keep records of the whole process, including the acceptance of the students by a particular higher education institution. The registration of the students finished at the end of April 1957, when, a list, containing 270 names, concluded with the words: "[The] Academic Registrar and Mr Day reported on 30. iv.1957 that there were no more suitable forms left at WUS."[8] Giving this as a reason for ending to identify and select the students is quite extraordinary; although well before the dawn of the photocopying age, it would have been easy enough to produce the required number of stencilled forms on demand. The list in question was seemingly compiled in batches, registering the students as they arrived, giving beside their names the name of the camp where they were located. After U.35, however, the subjects the students had studied also

---

[7] Interview with Marietta Záhonyi. 24 May 2005.
[8] Unattached Students. UoLA, CB3/6/1/1/7.

appeared together with the number of semesters they had completed. Another much more finalized list of the very same 270 "U" students, compiled sometime in the autumn of 1957[9], gave the placement against the names and the source of the grant the students received. Or, it simply stated that the student was found not suitable to receive higher education. Therefore, it seems that with filling in the last available registration form, that is, no.270, and processing the registered students, WUS had completed its task.

This was, certainly, very far from what happened. WUS registered a few additional students, presumably without asking them to fill in the standard form: a year later it supplied information about 289 WUS students to Dare and Hollander for their survey.[10] Of the 270 WUS registered "U"students 57 were transferred to the sponsorship of the CVCP, in order to bring the number of CVCP students up again to the agreed 150 undergraduates, since the original 150 students, brought over by the chartered flights had been depleted to 94. This had been achieved by weeding out the non-students, those unsuitable for university studies or those who were more suited to studying at art schools or other colleges, and last but not least, the postgraduates for whom other sources of financial support were sought. The group of 150 students, now under the aegis of the CVCP were hence labelled the "Quota", or "Q" students and referred to under this designation in the Progress Reports and in other documentation.

There remained, however, slightly more than 200 students on the WUS list who had been judged in the interviews as "university standard" but for whom the CVCP could not accept responsibility. The universities were actually willing to enrol these students as well, but were not able to provide grants for them, and could not waive the tuition and other fees to be incurred during their studies. It was left for WUS to seek a solution to the problem. WUS decided to apply to the Lord Mayor's Fund for help. The request for additional grants was not in vain: in the summer of 1957 WUS also received the very substantial sum of £141 000, from the Fund to be used for the education of those Hungarian students who, through no fault of their own, remained excluded from the CVCP scheme. The sum was deemed to be adequate for the support of about 100 students on a three year course. It is now well-nigh impossible to establish with certainty the number of WUS sponsored students. While the Hungarian Office meticulously compiled data and regularly issued reports on the "Quota"

---

[9] Unattached Students. UoLA, CB3/6/1/1/9. The list is undated. However, it lists me under my married name and I got married at the end of September 1957.

[10] Dare, Alan and Hollander, Paul: Op.cit., Appendix III, p.XLVI.

and the Ford students—the latter also came under the responsibility of the Office—it did not keep records of the WUS students, apart from including some, but by no means all of them, in the comprehensive lists of Hungarian refugee students it occasionally produced. From the correspondence with the WUS Office, which is still in the possession of some of the former WUS students, it can be deduced that WUS also kept detailed records of the students and their progress, but alas, due to a reorganization of the activities and administration of the WUS Office, including the transfer of its archives, all the documents relating to the period before 1973 have either been mislaid or lost, or even destroyed.[11] According to various estimates the number of students under WUS's care ranged between 80-100 persons. This figure is corroborated by the list of students and their addresses provided by WUS to Dare and Hollander for their survey. According to this list, in the academic year 1957-58, 65 WUS students entered university courses in Britain, joined by another 24 newly enrolled students in 1958-59. Finally, WUS also accepted responsibility for 7 students, formerly supported by the National Coal Board, bringing the total up to 96 persons.[12]

To apply for and especially to be awarded a WUS scholarship was, at least initially, fraught with difficulties. The number-one criterion set by WUS, from which it would on no account deviate, was the submission of a written proof that the applicant had been accepted for an undergraduate course by a British university. Universities, on the other hand, would only accept additional students if they were able to present a letter from WUS stating that it was willing to support them during their studies. This Catch 22 situation existed well into the summer of 1957[13], when, after a long wait, WUS received the necessary financial back-up from the Lord Mayor's Fund. Until then, WUS's understandable refusal to encourage the students, let alone to promise them grants, resulted in the growing frustration felt by the affected students, that no one was willing to

---

[11] Information supplied by Isabelle Emcke, Administration Assistant of Education Action International, Refugee Education & Training Service, formerly WUS. 2 Dec. 2005.

[12] Dare, Alan and Hollander, Paul: Op.cit., Appendix III, p.XLV.

[13] Several students who remained stuck in a refugee camp for months, sent letters directly to the university authorities asking for their help. The universities however, could only advise the students to turn to WUS in the first instance. See, for example, the correspondence between the Rector of Imperial College and some Hungarian students at the Hednesford refugee camp. ICA, Hungarian Relief, SS/1/4.

champion their just cause. The two examples quoted below illustrate their commendable efforts or even ingenuity, to overcome the difficulties.

László Huszár seemed to be among the "first ones" in the many stages of his escape from Hungary and his arrival in England. On 4th November, that ill-fated Sunday when the Soviet tanks overran Budapest, he happened to be in the Hungarian border town of Sopron and after listening to the news on the radio and hearing the desperate final plea by the Prime Minister of the country to the West for immediate help, he realized that there was no future for him in his native land and he had to flee. On the very same day, together with some others, he crossed the border to Austria. Pictures taken of these first groups of refugees were released for the international press. Huszár soon found himself in Vienna and, being a qualified architect, was offered a good position in a leading architectural practice. However, his aim was to emigrate to England, a country visited by his parents in the 1930s, who had subsequently kept alive the links with their English friends, even during the war and its aftermath. They told him about the solid, dependable, tolerant way of life in Britain, the best example of a true democracy. Huszár shared this view; he was convinced that in a long-established democracy, extremist opinions and movements like Communism, although enjoying protection due to the strict observation of the doctrine of free speech and free assembly, would not take root or have any following. He learnt English in the hope that one day he too would be able to visit England. When he heard about the recruitment of refugees to be settled in Great Britain, he immediately applied and was on the first aeroplane to touch down at Blackbushe airfield on 17th November, bringing the first group of Hungarians over from Austria. Again, in no time, he was offered a job, appropriate to his training and qualifications: he started work in the architectural department of the London County Council on 3rd December. It seemed that he had achieved his aims and that his future was truly settled.

Huszár, however, had other ideas. He had only enrolled at the Faculty of Architecture at the Technical University of Budapest, because no other options were available to him, and he regarded his architectural studies as a sort of safe haven in the storm of political upheaval where he could quietly take refuge. His main interest was politics, inflated by the events of 1956. In London he met and sought the friendship of Hungarian émigré writers, because he still believed that not all was lost, but that the West would, in some way or other, throw a lifeline to Hungary. Their duty was to keep public interest in the Hungarian cause alive. In order to understand the nature of politics better, he decided to immerse himself in the study of political thought; he wanted to enrol in a university course for a second degree. An American girl, whom he met at a Christmas party, compiled for him a list of the universities offering relevant courses and Huszár chose the course at the London School of Economic as the most suitable option. He applied to the LSE for a place. The LSE would have accepted his application, but could offer no maintenance grant. Huszár then decided to turn to WUS. He was refused again: as he had a first degree and appropriate employment with excellent prospects, WUS could not consider him for a grant. It had to reserve the awards for impecunious students already enrolled at higher education institutions.

Taking these refusals into consideration Huszár concluded that he would need to have some savings to enrol at the LSE and thereafter he should give up his job. As an unemployed student, already at university, he might be given a grant. Hazarding everything, he started the course at LSE in October 1957 and within a month, resigned from his post at the London County Council. Then he reapplied to WUS for financial support as an unemployed student. A week later he received a letter: his application had been accepted and he would receive the necessary support until he obtained his degree.[14] In concluding the story, it would be fair to point out, that when Huszár first applied for a grant in the late spring of 1957, WUS was not in the position to promise grants, as it had not yet received the funding for scholarships from the Lord Mayor's Fund. Furthermore, by late November it was clear that the funding it received would be more than adequate to cater for everyone's needs and WUS was therefore in the happy position of being able to award scholarships even in slightly debatable cases. That, however does not detract from Huszár's efforts and his willingness to take risks in order to relentlessly pursue his desire to study politics in Britain.[15]

In order to fully understand and appreciate the story of András Zsigmond[16], the action of the National Coal Board (NCB) regarding the Hungarian refugees should also be taken into account. Almost as soon as the huge influx of Hungarian refugees into Austria had begun, the NCB realized that the chronic shortage of skilled miners, with which the industry was not able to cope, could be resolved at a stroke. They needed about 4250 miners and hoped that among the refugees they would easily find and recruit enough young, strong males, who, after learning some English and receiving training, could be sent down the mines, as early as the late spring of 1957. The NCB consulted the unions and no objection was raised to the plan. So, the NCB immediately set up several recruitment

---

[14] Interview with László Huszár. 7 Feb. 2005.
[15] See also his obituary in *The Times*, 14 July 2007.
[16] Interview with András Zsigmond. 17 Feb. 2006.

centres in Austria. In the small town of Jennersdorf, for example, near the Hungarian border, they positioned a red double-decker bus to serve as the NCB office. It was run by a Hungarian émigré living in England, József Tótfalusy. It was he who received also the two medical students—András Zsigmond and his friend, László Antal—who arrived at Jennersdorf after several weeks of being on the run, in early January 1957. Zsigmond and Antal had just started their third year studying medicine at the University of Pécs and had been deeply involved in the revolution: both of them had served on the University's Revolutionary Committee, edited the new student paper entitled *The Free University of Pécs*, and played an active role in the search for and arrest of the local Communists, including members of the secret police, the ÁVH. By mid-December they were convinced that if they stayed at Pécs, they would be caught, arrested, put on trial and severely punished by a long prison sentence, if not worse. They decided to leave the country, but escaping became increasingly difficult, because the government began to close the border with Austria again. Having seen the red bus on the market place at Jennersdorf and having heard the enticing words of Mr Tótfalusy about the excellent prospects the NCB offered, they put their names down for the next group of potential miners leaving for England. They thought that once there, they would be able to get a place at a university. Their train, specially chartered by the NCB, arrived at Blackpool on 13th January. They were to start their English courses immediately and parallel with that the training to join the British miners. The English lessons proved to be very useful indeed, but Zsigmond and Antal became more and more concerned about their chances of becoming qualified doctors in Britain. They were not alone. Peter Rényi, in his notorious book mentioned earlier, referred to an article published in *The Yorkshire Post*, which talked about the plight of Hungarian refugee students who languished in the camps set up for the miners with little or no hope of entering university education in England. At the end—Rényi added—they might not even be allowed to go down the mines and work at the coalface.[17] Rényi, of course, used this example to illustrate the disinterested or even dismissive attitude of the British to the refugees. Nevertheless, it was true that among the refugees there was a distinct group of Hungarian mining engineering students.

These students had been studying in the Faculty of Mining Engineering at the University of Sopron. The students and staff of the University's other faculty, the Faculty of Forestry, left Hungary *en bloc*, and were re-housed at the University of British Columbia, Canada. A substantial

---

[17] Rényi, Péter: Op.cit., p.81.

number of mining students, however, came to England, under the
sponsorship of the NCB. At the meeting of the NCB on 4th January 1957,
Dr. Reid, a member of the Board reported under the item on the
recruitment of Hungarians that "38 mining students had been brought into
the country, some with practical experience. They were now being taught
English and would soon be available for employment. The demand from
Divisions for their services exceeded the numbers which could at present
be provided."[18] The minutes of the meetings of the NCB for 1957 contain
no further reference to these students. At the 22nd February meeting of the
CVCP however, the Vice-Chancellor of the University of Durham
mentioned that at the request of the NCB they had accepted 32 Hungarian
students to study mining engineering at King's College, on the Newcastle
campus of the University. Fees and grants for the students would be paid
by the NCB.[19] After consulting with other universities offering relevant
courses, ten students continued their studies at Newcastle, three at the
University of Nottingham and Sheffield respectively, while Birmingham
University accepted two students. Their final acceptance depended—as in
the case of all other students—on the successful English language exam in
the summer of 1957. Furthermore, they were required to attend courses for
two full academic years, irrespective of the number of semesters they had
completed in Hungary.[20]

While these figures account for 18 students only instead of the 38
mentioned in the minutes of the NCB meeting, it might be assumed that no
special records were kept on these students at other universities. The
figures provided by the Hungarian Office to Dare and Hollander mention
the NCB sponsored students[21], but the files in the archives of the Office,
currently accessible for research, do not refer to them at all. It is only by
chance that new information has come to light; at the University College
of Cardiff for example - then part of the University of Wales – a further
four mining students were studying in the company of the "Quota"

---

[18] National Coal Board. *Minutes.* 4 Jan. 1957. National Archives, NCB COAL
21/9.
[19] CVCP. *Minutes.* 22 Feb. 1957. CVCPA
[20] Photocopies of the relevant correspondence of the Academic Registrars of the
Universities of Durham and Nottingham and of the draft proposal on the
admittance of Hungarian students prepared for the Senate of Durham University
were kindly made available for me by the Archives of the University of Newcastle.
[21] Dare and Hollander mention 28 NCB sponsored students, of which seven were
transferred to WUS at the beginning of the academic year of 1956-59. Op.cit.,
Appendix III, p.XLV.

students also allocated to Cardiff.[22] (It might be worth mentioning that the employment of the several thousand men brought to Britain by the NCB as potential miners never materialized. Although the unions agreed to the scheme and the government, especially the Home Office and R. A. Butler, the Home Secretary, lent its full support,[23] the miners themselves were not willing to accept "the foreigners" as their workmates. This was less due to an aversion to the Hungarians than a fear that the rights of the miners to resist the employment of immigrant workers by the NCB, fought for and successfully gained during the bitter years of the recession in the 1930s, might be rescinded using the case of the Hungarian refugee miners as a precedent. According to the report issued by the NCB in September 1957, to date only 529 Hungarian miners had joined the British labour force, only slightly above 10 per cent of the original estimate. Soon afterwards the whole scheme was abandoned.)

The case of the Hungarian miners is only relevant to the story of Antal and Zsigmond in that their apprehension of being rapidly trained for working in a coal-mine, eased as the months passed. Their anxiety, however, of missing the chance of being considered for the continuation of their medical studies in England was, indeed, not without foundation. Since in the camp, reserved mainly for the future miners, they had not been approached by anybody concerned with the separation of the students from the other refugees, at the middle of February they decided to turn to the local representative of the NCB, Mr. Potts, for information and advice about whom they should approach with their enquiries about the possibility of enrolling at a university. Mr. Potts suggested that they should write to WUS. The reply to their letter came by return of post. They received the standard registration form and a warning that because of the limited number of places available for medical students, it might be difficult to allocate them to a medical school. They should consider switching to study related subjects – dentistry, for example. The WUS secretary, who wrote the letter, told them that they should continue to attend the English language course diligently and, if the NCB would be willing to sponsor their studies or at least to contribute to their financial support, they should immediately let WUS know.

Two months passed and nothing happened. The two young men received no communication from anyone. In the meantime, they had been transferred to the Barnsley camp—also a miners' camp—and at the

---

[22] Information kindly supplied by István Selmeczi.
[23] The problems with the employment of the Hungarian refugees as miners were reported almost weekly in the Hungarian newsletter, *Heti Hírek,* published by the Home Office for the information of the refugees.

beginning of May they wrote to Mr. Potts again, pleading with him to explore all possibilities with the NCB. The response came from WUS: it was highly unlikely that they would be able to start a university course in the coming academic year, so they should urgently seek employment. They should save as much money as they could and enrol at a university in October 1958. They might be awarded a grant, or some form of financial support from a Local Education Authority; this should be supplemented by the savings they had made, which could be used for the purchase of textbooks and any other necessary equipment. That WUS might provide a grant for them was not even mentioned.

Antal and Zsigmond were devastated by the proposal. They were adamant not to miss another year and determined to study medicine. There was no other choice for them but to act on their own. It was Antal who first had a stroke of luck: by chance he made the acquaintance of a student from Keble College, Oxford, who mentioned to him the plan of the College's undergraduates to fully support a Hungarian refugee student during his years of study. They had already collected adequate funds for the scholarship and were at the point of inviting applicants for an interview. Antal applied for the place, was interviewed and offered the scholarship.[24] He obtained his medical qualifications as an Oxford student, via the University of London External Degrees Department.

In the meantime Zsigmond requested an interview at Liverpool University and to his surprise, he was asked to attend a hearing on 29th July. He must have impressed the professors beyond any expectation. He was provided by the Dean of the Faculty of Medicine not only with a letter stating that the University would be happy to admit him, but that it would also take into consideration the two years Zsigmond had completed at the University of Pécs. He would start in October as a third year medical student. The University, however, was not in the position to offer him a grant; he would be required to find support from other sources. Zsigmond immediately informed WUS, attaching to his letter a copy of the Dean's note. Within days he received a reply from WUS telling him that a letter was to be dispatched to the University of Liverpool advising the Dean that WUS would make an award to Zsigmond to cover fees and maintenance over a period of four years. Of course, WUS was by then able to play the role of the magnanimous donor as it had received generous funding for Hungarian scholarships from the Lord Mayor's Fund a couple of days before. The letter from WUS concluded with heartfelt congratulations

---

[24] For a detailed account see Antal, L.: 50 years on – Hungarian uprising 1956. In: *the brick: the newsletter for Keble alumni.* No.38, Michaelmas term 2006.

which were, indeed, due to both Antal and Zsigmond. Had they not pursued with relentless determination, often seemingly against all odds, their aim to be admitted as students to a medical school, they might never have been discovered among the refugees, registered by WUS and advised about the course of action they should take. They would, most probably have missed a year and by then, discouraged by the slowly growing indifference to the Hungarian cause, they might even have given up trying. Their success is a personal success; but their gain has also been a gain for Liverpool, where they still practise as family doctors. WUS said farewell to András Zsigmond with a charming letter of congratulations when he completed his university studies in 1962. Written by the Welfare Secretary, Margaret Putnam, it is addressed to Dr. A. Zsigmond and begins: "I am very happy indeed to be able to address you in this way. Many congratulations on your success which only your hard work has made possible. It gives us great pleasure here to know that we have been able to assist you to become qualified."[25] To complete the story, it should be added that he received during his student years additional funding from Barnsley Council, the town which had hoped to have him trained and employed as a miner.

The contribution by the Local Education Authorities (LEA) to the Hungarian refugee students' scheme should not be underestimated either. Under the guidance of the Ministry of Education, which extended the rules governing the award of grants to British students studying in polytechnics and technical colleges to cover Hungarian students as well, LEAs played a substantial role in financing their higher education. The preparation of the directive about the financial arrangements, however, took a long time, more than four months rather than weeks as initially envisaged. The question regarding the students arriving with groups of refugees - as opposed to the CVCP special flights – had already been raised at the first meeting called by the BCAR at the end of November 1956, although in general terms, simply to flag up the problem for discussion at the next meeting, scheduled for 4th December. That a far-reaching discussion had taken place at the next meeting on 4th December, is evident from the extensive correspondence immediately following the meeting between Lockwood and Logan from the CVCP and several high-ranking officials of the Ministry of Education.

---

[25] I am very grateful to Dr. A. Zsigmond for providing me with photocopies of the extensive documentation he has on his student years and subsequent career and for the permission to quote from them. He is currently acting as an Honorary Consul for the Republic of Hungary in Great Britain.

The opening letter of 5th December was written by O. J. Roach, one of the representatives of the Ministry. Referring to the debate, he advanced two lines of argument. First, there should be no distinction made between the two groups of students – the 150 students who had arrived by the CVCP chartered flights and the students coming with the general mass of refugees, the only criterion for admission to a university should be their suitability based on the assessment of their knowledge and potential. It is highly likely that among the CVCP students there would be some unsuitable for university education, but among these there might be some who could successfully follow a course at a technical college. Secondly, if it were assumed that 150 places would be made available to Hungarian students at the polytechnics and technical colleges in addition to the 150 places already offered by the universities, then of the total of 300 students the best 150 would continue their studies at university level and another 150 would study for a technical college diploma, irrespectively of the way they had arrived in England. Finally, Roach exhorted the universities not to encourage the students to believe that their admission would be automatic; their entry would be determined by passing their English exams and their respective placement by agreement among the institutions themselves.[26]

Lockwood, to whom Logan must have shown Roach's letter, wrote a letter to Sir Gilbert Flemming, Secretary of State at the Ministry of Education, in which he expounded the matter further. He was very pleased—he said—that through the LEAs the Ministry committed itself to claim a share in the financing of the education of the refugee students. From the interviews conducted to date however, it was evident that more than 150 Hungarian students should be admitted to university courses. Therefore, the number of university places should also be increased. The universities would be willing to accept more students, but they would not be able to finance more from their own resources than the original 150 they had already agreed to.[27] On the very same day, by return of post, Flemming replied to Lockwood. He sent to Lockwood what he termed as "preliminary comments", which should not be taken as actual decision on the part of the Ministry. He readily agreed that there might be more than 150 students judged to be suitable for university education and, in an oblique way, encouraged the universities to explore how they would be able to take increase the number of places: "…It would certainly be wrong for the universities even not to ask themselves the question whether places

---

[26] Letter by O. J. Roach to D. W. Logan. 5 Dec. 1956. UoLA, CB3/4/37.
[27] Letter by J. F. Lockwood to Sir Gilbert Flemming. 5 Dec. 1956. Ibid.

could be found for them from the point of view of teaching resources and so on, because they could not see their way to increase their financial liabilities." He vaguely hinted that the extra financial liability might be met from public funds, but would not commit himself to a more definite proposition. As for creating places at technical colleges he defused Roach's rather positive statement by giving a typically evasive answer: "It is quite true that we are exploring the suggestion which he [i.e. Roach] mentioned, and you are therefore right in taking this as a pointer to the possibility of some form of help for these students from public sources, but nothing is settled yet."[28]

During the following fortnight Lockwood twice raised the question of LEA grants for Hungarian students studying at technical colleges, since resolving it became rather urgent. The CVCP interviewing team had already produced a shortlist of 17 students who, although they had arrived on the charter flights, had been found more suitable to study at a technical college rather than at a university. Lockwood wished to know whether a decision about financing them had been reached or not. In the name of Flemming, Lockwood received a reply from R. N. Heaton on 18th December. According to him "it should be only a matter of days before we get the decision of Ministers."[29] A decision had indeed been timely, as the handling of the issue of the Hungarian students by the Ministry was tabled at the House of Commons on 20th December. To Dr. Stross's question on whether the Minister of Education could give an assurance that facilities will be offered to the students to continue their education Sir David Eccles replied that the arrangements to be made for the students, including those at technical colleges, were being considered and that he hoped that they would be given a new start in life.[30]

The wheels of the administration turned, as usual, very slowly. The directive sent at last to the Local Authorities by the Ministry of Education is actually dated 25th April 1957.[31] Still, it arrived in time to regulate the entry of the Hungarian students into the technical colleges and their financing through the LEA grants for the academic year commencing in October 1957. The directive opened the doors to a large number of Hungarian refugee students to study for a diploma which, if the student so wished and was willing to persevere with further studies and exams, could be converted into a University of London external degree. The preamble

---

[28] Letter by Sir Gilbert Flemming to J. F. Lockwood. 5 Dec. 1956. Ibid.
[29] Letter by R. N. Heaton to J. F. Lockwood. 18 Dec. 1956. Ibid.
[30] *Hansard.* House of Commons. 20 Dec. 1956.
[31] Ministry of Education: *To Local Education Authorities. Administrative Memorandum No. 550.* 25 Apr. 1957.

made it clear that the Minister had considered the necessity of introducing special arrangements for financing the scheme. However, when the potential size of the commitment had been more clearly established, and after consultation with the association of local authorities and education committees, he came to the conclusion that normal arrangements, at least in the first year, should apply. Then a survey should be carried out in order to evaluate how the systems worked and whether any adjustments should be made. This meant that the Hungarian refugee students – and those expelled from Egypt, who were always bracketed with them – would be treated the same way as British students: the same rules would apply for their admission and they would enjoy the same rights for receiving grants from the appropriate LEAs.

It is just as difficult to estimate the number of Hungarian students benefiting from this scheme as the number receiving WUS scholarships. The structure of local authorities has changed over the years; some of them have merged, while others have ceased to exist. The same applies to the former technical colleges and polytechnics, especially during the fundamental reorganization of the higher education institutions at the beginning of the 1990s. Furthermore, an investigation into the existence of archives pertaining to the years between 1956 and 1962 in the new "mega-universities" in London and in the neighbouring area - created by merger of the former polytechnics and technical colleges - revealed that no records have survived which would shed light on the number of Hungarian students studying and obtaining diplomas at these institutions. Collating the currently available information, including those gained from the recollection of former students, the figure of about 100 students enrolled in the polytechnics and technical colleges in greater London alone can be established with some certainty. A few of the Progress Reports compiled by the Hungarian Office for the "Quota" and Ford students[32], occasionally contain references to students who had been referred to technical colleges. More revealing are the lists and reports in the London County Council Education Committee's files at the London Metropolitan Archives[33]: these contain the names of Hungarian students who received Major County Awards both for preliminary studies – presumably language and/or foundation courses - and for further education courses in sessions of 1957-58 and 1960-61. The combined list contains 57 names; 11 of them

---

[32] CVCP: *Progress reports of Hungarian refugee students: Quota students.* UoLA, CB3/5/1.; *Ford Foundation supported students.* UoLA CB3/5/2.
[33] London County Council Education Committee: *Hungarian and Egyptian refugees. Hungarian students obtaining Major County Awards.* London Metropolitan Archives. File EO/HFE/3/22.

received grants in both academic years and it can be assumed that these students progressed with their studies satisfactorily. Other students might have graduated at the end of the previous academic year.

The LCC files also include the correspondence between Professor Scott, Head of the Department of Architecture at the Northern Polytechnic, and the officials of the LCC Education Committee regarding those architecture students who were sponsored – at least partially - by the Royal Institute of British Architects. The action taken by RIBA serves as yet another example of the extraordinary efforts by British institutions to provide help to the Hungarian refugees. Early in the spring of 1957, RIBA approached Professor Scott with a request to assemble a small group of about ten to twelve Hungarian students who expressed an interest in studying architecture. His department should organize English language courses for them, introduce them to the basic tenets of architectural studies, give them lessons in drawing, mensuration and elementary construction and, during these exercises, evaluate their aptitude as potential students of architecture. Professor Scott submitted two lists of these students to the LCC Education Committee containing nine names altogether. Although RIBA contributed to the cost of maintaining the students, the involvement of the LCC suggests that additional funding was needed from the Council. Yet, none of these students appear on the list of Major County Awards and they may, therefore, be regarded as additions to the previously mentioned 57 students. Furthermore, a former architecture student at the Northern Polytechnic recalls a number of students in the group who do not appear on any list or in any correspondence, strongly suggesting that the number of students in technical colleges and polytechnics should be generously rounded up rather than pared down. The student in question was actually supported by the Middlesex County Council. Today he still remembers fondly of Professor Scott and the years he spent at the Northern Polytechnic. The friendly atmosphere, the care taken by the teaching staff and the encouragement the students received, created for them something like a second home, helped them to find their feet in their new environment and gave them a solid professional foundation for their future careers.[34]

Another source of information on Hungarian students in technical colleges is provided by the minutes of the Sub-Committee for Hungarian Students of the University of London External Council.[35] The Sub-Committee approved over 50 applications for obtaining an external degree

---

[34] Interview with Sándor Váci. 23 Feb. 2006.
[35] University of London. Council for External Students. Sub-Committee on Hungarian Refugee Students: *Minutes.* 1957-62. UoLA, CB3/1/5.

between 1957 and 1962. About half a dozen of the applicants were "Quota" students – placed mainly at Oxford University - but the rest of them studied at polytechnics and technical colleges in London and all over the country. If any of the technical college students who had completed their studies, wished to take exams for a BA or BSc, they could do so at the University of London only as external students. It is noteworthy that the greatest number of applicants from a single institution were the Hungarian students at the Regent Street Polytechnic (now the University of Westminster). It is surprising that in spite of the fairly large London contingent, there is only one name which appears both on the LCC Major Country Awards list and in the minutes of the Sub-Committee. This again corroborates the notion that the existing lists cover a proportion of students only and their number in reality was much higher than recorded in the documents. This is borne out by the statistics on student numbers given in the survey of Dare and Hollander. They register 73 students enrolled at technical colleges in the academic year 1957-58, to which 28 new students are added in 1958-59.[36] They do not indicate where and at which institution these students were studying.

Due to the lack of records, it is only by chance that any information about their success or failure has surfaced, either by coming across the names of former technical college students as postgraduates in various universities or through the reminiscences of those who have kindly consented to be interviewed. For the former, the list drawn up of postgraduates at Imperial College provides a good example: scrutinizing the 11 students studying for a PhD in the 1960s, two students were found who had started their higher education courses in London, one at the Northern, the other at the Woolwich Polytechnic. After gaining their BSc external degrees from London University—one of them obtained a first class degree in mathematics—they embarked on their research projects which they successfully completed.

For the former students who were willing to commit their stories to paper, thus providing a glimpse into the experiences of those who studied at the technical colleges, the story of the Kruppa brothers might serve as an interesting example. Both Mihály and Miklós Kruppa were engineering students in Hungary. They left the country on 25th November 1956, and two days after their arrival in Austria, they were, together with 600 other refugees, transferred to England and placed in a camp near Swindon. Although lists of the students located in the camp had been prepared, noting their future intentions, no officials from any institution contacted

---

[36] Dare, Alan and Hollander, Paul: Op.cit., Appendix III, p. XLVI.

them before Christmas. They had, however, received an invitation from an English family to spend Christmas with them in London. Initially they were reluctant to accept it, since they knew little English and did not wish to be a burden on their hosts, but then, with encouragement from their hostess-to-be—an American woman—they arrived at the family's house on Christmas Eve. To use Miklós Kruppa's words they "had an interesting Christmas although communication without English was difficult and tiring". In January, back again in the camp, they received a letter from the family offering them help with sorting out their future and suggesting that in the meantime, they stay with them. The Kruppa brothers moved to London on 14th January and, as they state in their reminiscences, they "detached themselves from the student groupings and organized assistance". It should, however, be mentioned, that in spite of being apparently registered as students in December, their names do not appear on any student list compiled either by the CVCP Committees or by WUS.

The family did everything possible to seek advice and help on behalf of the brothers. First, they found a place for them at the City of London College, Moorgate, to learn English, then, in early May, the Dean of the College arranged an interview for them with the Head of the Engineering Department at the Northampton College of Advanced Technology. As a result of the interview, they were both offered a place. Their chance to continue their studies therefore, came not through an organized approach, but through concern and help of individuals. Their grants, however, came through the normal channels for technical college students: they received Major County Awards and their names appear—for the first time—on the LCC Education Committee's lists. Both Mihály and Miklós Kruppa obtained their University of London BSc degrees in 1961 and then embarked on postgraduate studies: Miklós received an MSc from Birmingham University in 1965 and Mihály, also an MSc, from Bristol University in 1967. Both of them carved out for themselves successful and most satisfying careers as engineers. And they still stay in touch with the family who had invited them to share Christmas with them more than 50 years ago. Mihály Kruppa ends the summary of his life in Britain with a tribute to them: "I wish to express my thanks to all the people who helped me, especially in the early and difficult days, to resume and complete my engineering studies. Some of the people who made it easier for me to start a new life in this country became good friends."[37]

As mentioned above, both the CVCP and WUS received substantial sums from the Lord Mayor's Fund for the education of Hungarian

---

[37] Written statements kindly given by Mihály and Miklós Kruppa.

students, but the confirmation of the grant and the transfer of the monies came rather late in the year - towards the end of the academic year 1956-57 for the CVCP and as late as the end of July for WUS. This delay caused a lot of anxiety, for no promises given to the students could be substantiated and, in many cases, no promises could be given at all. Lockwood and Logan therefore, on behalf of the CVCP, decided to approach several foundations requesting contributions to the scheme by establishing grants for an agreed number of students. As early as the middle of December 1956, for example, Logan sent a letter to Dean Rusk of the Rockefeller Foundation, because he had heard from a friend who had just returned from Paris that the Foundation had made $600,000 available in connection with Hungarian refugees. He enquired whether this fund was already earmarked, or could the CVCP apply for some money to be released for providing much needed help with the financing the education of 150 students who had been, "by a piece of remarkable private enterprise", already brought to Britain. Dean Rusk travelled to Vienna to review the situation and to report to the Trustees by the end of the month. The Rockefeller Foundation indeed decided to use the whole grant for the education of the refugee students, but only for those who had remained in Austria.[38] Logan received a similar refusal from the Nuffield Foundation, although this was more understandable, since he had asked for help with the financial support for students training as dentists. The Trustees considered the request but agreed that it was outside their remit to release monies for this purpose.[39]

    Much more successful was the approach made by the CVCP to the Ford Foundation, although the end result was quite different what the CVCP had expected. The first tentative letter was written by the Deputy Vice-Chancellor of London University on 18th January 1957, addressed to Dr. Henry T. Heald of the Ford Foundation. After a brief introduction summarizing the current situation regarding the Hungarian refugee students already in Britain, he distinguished three distinct groups and the problems associated with each one. Most of the 150 students under the care of the CVCP had places allocated for them, but the fundraising for their maintenance undertaken by the universities had not reached its target and their maintenance over three or more years of study remained a pressing question. The second group contained the students who had been found unsuitable for university studies, but who could still do well on

---

[38] Letter by D. W. Logan to Dean Rusk. 13 Dec. 1956 and ensuing exchange of telegrams. UoLA, CB3/4/47.
[39] Correspodence between D. W. Logan and W. A. Sanderson. 21 Feb. - 28 March 1957. UoLA, CB3/4/38.

courses at technical colleges. The CVCP had no funds at all to draw on to guarantee their education. And finally, there were student in the third group, many of them very deserving, who had come in among the ten or eleven thousand Hungarian refugees and whose status was only just being established. Their number might reach the order of 100. There were no funds available for sponsoring them. The Deputy Vice-Chancellor asked Heald if there were any sources of money which could be applied to the education of Hungarian students already in Britain where there was a well systematized organization in existence for the most efficient use of any additional funding.[40]

The Ford Foundation responded to the letter by return of post. However, it made it clear that the Foundation intended to widen the circle of students whom it would support: it contemplated setting up a system of awarding grants to over 500 refugee students located in West European countries. To explore the best way to achieve this, the Foundation would send its representative, Shepard Stone, to Vienna and invite representatives of six European countries to attend a meeting to discuss the possibilities open for Hungarian students in their higher education institutions. The conference took place between 4th and 6th February 1957 and, in the end, it was attended by experts not from six but from nine countries. The Ford Foundation offered $1 million for supporting the students; after deducting the cost of administration, $890 000 was available for grants; these would cover all the costs of the students' education over two years. The catch was – at least for the CVCP – that only Hungarian refugee students still in Austria would be eligible for grants. It could not, therefore, be used for the support of the students already in Britain, but would provide the opportunity for an additional 75 students to come to this country and to continue their studies here. In addition, the Ford grant would be available for postgraduates as well, giving them a chance to complete their research for higher degrees. The Foundation urged the countries to organize the selection of the students at the earliest opportunity and to speed up the procedures, it requested the British Council in Vienna to co-ordinate the whole effort. The British Council in turn asked the CVCP to send Walters to Austria again, so that he, together with the other delegate, Professor Greig from King's College, London, could interview and select the British contingent of the Ford Students.[41]

---

[40] Letter by the Deputy Vice-Chancellor of the University of London to Dr. Henry T. Heald. 18 Jan. 1957. UoLA, CB3/4/37.
[41] For the best summary of the preliminaries and the organization of the selection for the Ford grants see the report by Lockwood to the CVCP: CVCP. *Refugee*

They found that to fill the 75 places offered by the Foundation, was by no means an easy task. At the end, they listed 68 students whom they felt they could safely recommend to the CVCP for acceptance. By the time the transport for the group was arranged, the numbers had further dwindled; eight students decided to go to other countries, two stayed in Vienna, and a note against the names of the remaining four simply stated that they had "disappeared". The 54 remaining students were rapidly allocated by the CVCP Hungarian Committee to universities and, where they found it more appropriate, to technical colleges. The largest number of Ford students— 16 of them in all—was, for example, accepted by the then Royal College of Science and Technology, Glasgow (now the University of Strathclyde) to study engineering.[42] The English language courses began for the Ford students in the summer of 1957 and in most cases continued until the end of the year or, if deemed necessary, even longer. Their administration was entrusted to the Hungarian Office, which regularly produced detailed statistics on their progress.

From time to time, it was possible to switch from one type of grant to another. Géza Fehérvári, for example, had begun to write up his dissertation on Islamic art in German; at the recommendation of his erstwhile teacher, Ervin Baktay, a well known and respected expert in the field, Fehérvári received support from the Rockefeller Foundation in Vienna. But when he learned about the British Council's recruitment of Ford students for England, he immediately applied for a place. By the summer he was a postgraduate student at the School of Oriental and African Studies in London, and started to re-write his thesis in English. He was awarded his PhD in 1961.[43] Because the Ford grant covered the expenses of his research only for the first for two years only, he, like most of the Hungarian students, was also helped by the Lord Mayor's Fund to complete his studies and to obtain his qualifications in Britain.

The Free Europe University in Exile, which had its European headquarters in Paris, also offered a number of scholarships, mostly for arts students. It was understandable that Free Europe wished to support first and foremost students interested in humanities and/or social sciences, since the main aim of the Foundation was to foster the emergence of dissident views in Eastern Europe. The bureaucratic and over-complicated

---

students from Hungary. Agendum 10: Report by the Vice-Chancellor of the University of London. 22 Feb. 1957. UoLA, CB3/1/3/3.
[42] CVCP. Joint meeting of the Committee on Hungarian Students and the Sub-Committee dealing with the allocation of the Students: *Minutes.* 16 July 1957. UoLA, CB31/3/3.
[43] Information kindly provided by Professor Géza Fehérvári.

method of applications however, often deterred even the most dedicated students from submitting an application. The four copies of the application form were to be supported by a detailed CV, including—as the guidelines stated—"all useful information on [the applicant's] life, studies and various activities. The curriculum vitae must include a chapter on aspirations where the candidate will note his/her general ideas on life, his/her [as applicable] present or future aims on professional, intellectual, social, family, political, philosophical, etc. grounds". The Hungarian Office handled the applications, provided help with the translation and corresponded on behalf of the students with the Paris headquarters. When after submitting the written applications four 2"x2" photographs of the candidates were also requested, one of the applicants wrote a desperate note in halting English to the Hungarian Office: "…or if any new wish would come up from the 'Free University', please don't endeavour further. I will rather give up."

The Free Europe University in Exile awarded grants to ten students studying at British universities, although initially they had been talking about supporting 50 to 60 students. This was, however, the lesser problem. The problem, which could have had serious consequences for students studying with a Free Europe grant, was that the Free Europe University in Exile forgot to notify the Hungarian Office of the fact that the scholarships were to be given only for a limited time. When the rumours about this reached the Hungarian Office in November 1958, the Secretary sent a letter to the Paris office, enquiring about the length of the time the grants were supposed to cover. She received the astounding reply: the support for the Hungarian students came under the so-called 'Emergency Program', initiated at the end of 1956. It has now been decided to maintain it for the period of a further year as from 1st July 1958, therefore, it would terminate at the end of June 1959 instead of 1958.[44] It was fortunate that the curtailment of the programme – hailed as a generous extension by Free Europe – did not cause a serious problem. The funds available in the coffers of the CVCP were considered adequate for the full support of the Free Europe students as well as the Ford students as from the academic year 1959-60.

It should, however, be acknowledged, that Free Europe regarded as the highest priority, the provision of grants to those students who had been persecuted in the Communist regime, expelled from universities and incarcerated as political prisoners. It was also willing to consider unusual

---

[44] For the correspondence between the CVCP Hungarian Office and the Free Europe University in Exile see the file at UoLA, BC3/4/25.

cases when seemingly all efforts to obtain a grant had failed. This enabled, for example, Felix Allender to complete his studies at Imperial College. Felix Allender had a most unusual background. His family had English roots; his great-grandfather had been a mechanical engineer working in the metallurgical industry in the Midlands at the middle of the nineteenth century. This was the age of industrialization on a grand scale and his innovations—he obtained six patents between 1859 and 1865—greatly contributed to the rapid development of manufacturing equipment. Since he was dismayed by the attitude of the factory owners who employed him and made extensive use of his innovations without giving credit to the inventor, he decided to try his luck on the Continent. He moved from country to country, designing machinery and helping to set up factories. Marrying a German girl in the town of Brünn, he settled down in what was then the Austro-Hungarian Empire. His son, Henrik Allender, Felix's grandfather, followed in his father's footsteps: as a leading engineer he filled several important posts in the Monarchy; between 1911 and the end of World War I, he was the director of the National Iron Foundries of Hungary. Felix's father was the first to break the family mould: instead of engineering, he studied economics and became a financial adviser in the Hungarian National Bank. He spent a year in England, which he greatly enjoyed, called Britain a "paradise" and was determined to keep the family's tradition of strong English identity alive. He married a Hungarian woman but made sure that she and his two children learned English. He built up good relationship with the British Embassy in Budapest and obtained an English passport.

At the end of World War II, after spending the siege of Budapest in the Bank's cellars, he returned to the headquarters, hoping to participate in the rebuilding of the country. In a short time he became totally disillusioned by the new regime: the Communists, who had no financial know-how, took over the control of the Bank, his superior was brought to trial and executed. He felt that he was under constant threat and was finally dismissed in 1952. The only way out of this intolerable situation was—he thought—to relocate to England. He took action and paid a large sum of money to a person in the secret police working in the Ministry of Interior, who had promised him a Hungarian passport with which he and his family could leave the country. The plan failed: the person was unmasked and put on trial. Allender never got his passport and lost not only the money he had paid out for it, but all their valuables, even their home. The family was forced to do manual labour but the sons managed, against all odds, to enter higher education. Felix Allender, the older brother, obtained the best possible result at the final examinations in a well-regarded grammar school and was, according to the rules, automatically accepted by the university. (Otherwise he would never have gained admission because of his family background.) In the first two years he studied mathematics, then switched to chemistry.

The big break for the family came in the summer of 1956. They were issued with Hungarian passports and allowed to leave. Arriving at Victoria station in early September, with a few bags containing all their possessions, they were met by an official. With this organized reception however, the official support ended. The family was soon dispersed and all of them were encouraged to get jobs; any job. Felix's mother had to work as a domestic servant. Felix found employment in a laboratory, but what he wanted was to resume his university studies. His enquiries about university places and grants were rebuffed: all efforts by that time – late November – were being directed towards finding places for incoming Hungarian refugee students. As he was British, and not a refugee student, he was told to use the normal channels of application for entry into higher education open to British youth. The only prompt action taken by the British Government was to try to conscript him into the army; this, through the timely intervention of Colonel Lambert at the Recruitment Board, was to be deferred until he obtained his degree. (But, of course, the greatest obstacle for him was to enrol in any British higher education institution!) Felix showered all possible organizations, committees and individuals with petitions for places and grants, but to no avail. It was already late spring 1957 and he became more and more desperate, when his friends, two Ford students who were to study at Imperial College, advised him to see Professor Roberts in the College's Chemistry Department. After the interview Allender was offered a place on condition that he would get a grant from some source. After many more applications, he was finally awarded a grant by Free Europe. The grant was perhaps the greatest gift Felix Allender ever received. It corrected the injustice meted out to him for having arrived in England a few weeks earlier than the refugee students, as a result of which he had been denied help on the grounds that he was not a Hungarian. The way was now open for him to get a degree, followed by postgraduate studies for an MBA at the prestigious Management School, INSEAD, at Fontainebleau, near Paris. The single tiny flaw in the whole story is that the person who championed his case at the Free Europe – and who was actually responsible for selecting the students for a grant - had been an old and trusted friend of the Allender family.[45]

---

[45] Interview with Felix Allender. 4 Jan. 2006.

Several other foundations and charities contributed to the education of the Hungarian students by offering bursaries and other donations. The United Nations Association, for example, supported ten students with the money collected by the readers of *The News Chronicle*, or the Gulbenkian Foundation which provided grants especially for music students. The extant records, currently accessible for research—lists of students and tables of their allocation, the reports prepared for the CVCP, the Lord Mayor's Fund or any potential grant giving body—provide varying and constantly changing figures and can only be interpreted as a momentary state of affairs. Nevertheless, it can be safely stated that by the summer of 1957 about 500 students had gained provisional places in higher education institutions and were promised the appropriate maintenance grants. The CVCP was responsible for the 154 "Quota" students and looked after the 54 Ford students, WUS supported about 80 students, the NCB 20, Free Europe 10, UNA 10, the Gulbenkian Foundation 6 and LEAs approximately 150. In addition, there were a number of students who received support from other sources, for example, the postgraduates at Oxford University, whose maintenance was paid out of the Oxford appeal fund. Even these figures can only be seen as provisional as some of the students left for other countries and others decided not to pursue their studies. Their places, in turn, were taken up by new applicants. And, it must not be forgotten, that actual enrolment for the courses depended on passing the English language exams. The preparation for these exams filled the lives of almost all the students during the first nine months of 1957.

CHAPTER VI

THE ALLOCATION AND REGISTRATION
OF THE STUDENTS

As early as 23rd November 1956, when the CVCP first discussed the question of the Hungarian students, Lockwood outlined the three most important steps the universities should take in order to ensure their systematic, well co-ordinated action for integrating them into British higher education. He suggested that these steps should be implemented immediately following the selection of the students, bringing them to England and providing temporary accommodation for them. The very first task was the assessment of all available places at the universities and the allocation of the students to these places. Secondly, intensive English language courses should be set up for them before they could pass into the ordinary university stream the following October. The English classes should start at once, or at the latest by the New Year. Thirdly, the whole question of university entrance requirements should be reviewed to accommodate the refugee students; to what extent should the university standard work they already completed in Hungary be recognized?[1]

The Hungarian Committee of the CVCP began to handle these tasks without delay and with great vigour, but, for obvious reasons, the collection of the relevant information and adopting the best solution to each one of the problems had to run parallel, often cancelling each other out. For example, by the time the first lists of students had been drawn up to match the offer of places from the universities – allowing the finalization of their allocation – it was decided that the language courses should be organized on a regional basis. The students, therefore, could not be transferred to the institutions they would be admitted for their courses in October 1957, but had to be moved and housed for six to nine months at the few select universities designated to act as regional language centres. The allocations therefore, almost ready on paper by the beginning of January, were to be regarded as part of a medium to long-term plan,

---

[1] CVCP. *Minutes.* 23 Nov. 1956. CVCPA

shelved for the time being and a new, interim plan, called "Operation Switch" was implemented instead. It was to have taken effect on 31st December 1956, but following the protest by the universities that this date would fall into the Christmas closure period, it was postponed to 7th January 1957. The plan gave precise details of the relocation of the students: their names and numbers, their travelling destinations and railway timetables for their departure and arrival. The Committee for the Selection and Allocation of Hungarian Students, however, continued its work. During the month of January the universities were informed about the students allocated to them for entering courses in the following academic year. Many of them opted to contact these students and sent them, at the suggestion of the CVCP, an informal contract about their conditions of acceptance. This was to be signed and returned to the university authorities.

Following the CVCP's decision to accept 150 refugee students, Lockwood asked the universities to send him information about the number of students they would be willing to take and support from their own resources. He indicated that he would need to have it as soon as possible.[2] According to the table enclosed with his Second Memorandum to the CVCP, dated 3rd December, seven universities had responded to his request by that date, offering 47 places. This number included the 20 places offered by the Scottish universities. A manuscript note on the table—probably a late addition by Lockwood himself—indicated that two more universities had written to him offering seven places for Hungarian students.[3] Both the number of responses and the places offered fell well below his expectations. It must be stressed that it was not the reluctance of the universities to participate in the scheme which delayed their reply to Lockwood, but the very tight deadline for giving their response. It left little or no time at all for the necessary consultations within the universities which were to commit themselves to financing a costly project. The tuition and maintenance of a student over three years—the standard undergraduate course—would require a considerable sum of money.

At the next meeting of the Selection Committee on 10th December, Lockwood presented a new proposal for the allocation of students. Instead of waiting for information on the number of places offered by universities, he decided to base the minimum allocation to each university on the University Grants Committee's statistical returns of student numbers in the

---

[2] Ibid.
[3] Lockwood, J. F.: *Hungarian Refugee Students. Second memorandum of the Vice-Chancellor of the University of London.* 3 Dec. 1956. UoLA, CB3/2/1/2.

academic year 1954-55. The largest student population of more than 18,000 students was registered at London University, therefore it would receive the proportionately largest number, that is 34 Hungarian students. The Scottish universities came next with 20 students, to be distributed amongst themselves, then Cambridge with 15 and Oxford with 13 places. Lockwood allocated altogether 154 places; the extra four students would be going to the Queen's University, Belfast. Small universities would get two or three students, the smallest three only one student each. The table also contained the number of places already offered by the universities, which, during the previous few days had considerably increased and reached 89 offers.[4] The principle of the proportional distribution was accepted by the CVCP and the continuously updated list of confirmed places was tabled at the meetings. By the middle of January the number of firmly confirmed places reached 144, of which 143 also had the name of the student added to each allocated place.[5]

It is interesting to note, that by the end of March the number of places had increased to 162, well above the original 150. These 162 names were given to the Lord Mayor's Fund, which had requested detailed information about the composition of the CVCP- sponsored students, in order to estimate the need for additional support.[6] This list provided the definitive analysis of the distribution of the students who had come to England on the CVCP chartered flights and those WUS registered "Unattached" students, whom the CVCP had taken over, that is, the whole complement of the so-called "Quota" students. (A supplementary table gave information also about the students who might be admitted to universities but would be supported from other sources. Since the applications for and acceptance of students for a Ford or Free Europe grant were still in progress, the numbers were relatively small and tentative. In addition, as the letter written to the Lord Mayor explained, there were a further 119 students registered by WUS, who had not been interviewed yet. It was, however, more than likely that some of them should also follow university courses.)

---

[4] CVCP. Hungarian Refugee Students Selection Committee: *Agenda.* 10 Dec. 1956. UoLA, CB3/1/4/1.
[5] CVCP. Joint meeting of the Committee on Hungarian Students and the Sub-Committee Dealing with the Allocation of the Students: *Document A: Proposed distribution of Hungarian Students. 4th revised list. 15 Jan. 1957.* 24 Jan. 1957. UoLA, CB3/1/3/1.
[6] CVCP. Joint meeting of the Hungarian Committees: *Agenda. Appendix A: Students allocated and accepted by universities.* 26 March 1957. UoLA, CB3/1/3/2.

The lists revealed that the CVCP Selection Committee had completed its task of allocating the students with a remarkable speed—with a few exceptions by the end of January 1957—but they did not reveal how the members of the committee had reached their decision about the placement of the students; on what grounds had they decided to send a student to a particular university? Yet, the location was of paramount importance for the students, in many cases, it was the single most relevant factor in shaping their future. There was a reasonable amount of information available about the students who had arrived on the CVCP's special flights. The committee could refer to the notes taken both at the interviews in Vienna and by the small CVCP interview team in London. Academic staff at the temporary reception centres also asked the students about their plans and assessed their abilities; the opinion they had formed about their potential was often communicated to Lockwood or Logan, mostly with the comment that they wished to retain selected students as their own undergraduates. The students themselves may have expressed their own desire to continue their studies at a particular institution, if they knew enough of the British educational system to judge which would be the best path to follow. Alternatively, if they had been advised by someone else, either in Hungary or in England, they might have applied for a place at particular university. This must have been the reason that a number of students chose the London School of Economics; its reputation must have spread far and wide, even behind the Iron Curtain.

Sometimes, from the hazy recollections of the distant past, hilarious stories have emerged on how particular students might have been by picked by their respective universities or colleges. István Pálffy, a student at Trinity Hall, learned only years later why the college had decided to choose him from the list of Hungarian students presented to Cambridge colleges: "The Fellows had met to pick a Hungarian refugee to admit and support... As the names of candidates were being read out Louis Clarke, one of the oldest Fellows of the college (elected long before a compulsory retiring age was introduced), was, as was his wont, apparently half-dozing near the end of the table. However, when they got to my name he perked up, although generally given to being stone-deaf, and spoke: 'Pálffy? Pálffy, did you say? Went shooting with a Pálffy once – 1910, was it? Or 1911? Can't remember. Excellent shot, though. Must have this one!' So, rather than stick a pin in the list of candidates, the Fellows agreed to my admission, subject to a satisfactory interview with the Senior Tutor."[7]

---

[7] Pagnamenta, Peter, ed.: *The hidden Hall: portrait of a Cambridge College.* 2004, pp.113-114.

The allocation of the science and engineering students caused little problem, although it was usually by chance that they ended up as students in a leading science and technology university in London, in a large red brick university, or at a lesser institution elsewhere. Placing the other students proved to be more difficult. The registration form, distributed by WUS among the "Unattached" students, simply asked the applicants to state whether they would like to continue to study the same subjects as in Hungary, to which most of them were likely to give an affirmative answer, since what else could they say? The key word for them was "continuation". There was no question on the form asking which other courses they might wanted to pursue had they wished to change subjects. The questions on the form were translated into Hungarian and the odd choice of words and the peculiar construction of the sentences might even have amused the students, had they not felt compelled to give the most acceptable reply. Lockwood, in any case, was against the students changing subjects and instructed the Selection Committee to handle such requests with the greatest circumspection; many of the students had completed several semesters and it would have been foolish to start their university education afresh. Of course, it would also make a difference for the CVCP not to have to provide financial support for a number of students for the full three years.[8]

By far the greatest problem the Selection Committee faced concerned the placement of the medical students. Lockwood exhorted the committee members not to consider a request by any student to change subjects in order to study medicine. There were few places available and, because of the overproduction of newly qualified doctors, limited opportunities for finding suitable positions for them after they had obtained their degrees. Not to mention that supporting a large group of students over five to six years' of study was beyond the means of the CVCP. As a top priority, they were to concentrate all their efforts on the allocation of the students who had studied medicine in Hungary. It might also be useful to examine how the length of study could be shortened. Several of the medical students had completed two or three years' study in Hungary, passed the approved examinations and, because of their maturity, they might be exempted from the first and second examinations for medical degrees in Britain. The CVCP commissioned a brief outline of Hungarian medical education as a background paper and asked the University of London External Registrar to assess the situation with special reference to the existing university

---

[8] CVCP. Hungarian Refugee Students Selection Committee: *Agenda.* 10 Dec. 1956. UoLA, CB3/1/4/1.

regulations and precedents and how these could be applied to the case of the Hungarian students. During the Second World War for example, the length of medical studies of the French, Belgian and other European students who sought refuge in Britain, was substantially shortened, if they had studied at a reputable European university at least for four years and successfully sat exams in the foundation subjects of biology, chemistry and physics. Based on these precedents and on the case of some students from the University College of Ibadan, Nigeria, who had recently been allowed to complete their examinations at London University, the External Registrar made the following recommendations: if the Hungarian students in question had completed their third year at a medical university in Hungary, they would be exempt from the 1st M.B. examinations. Furthermore, they would gain exemption from attending some of the preparatory courses for the 2nd M.B. examinations with the exception of anatomy and physiology. Consequently, the length of their education would be reduced to the three clinical years, which would correspond to the length of study undertaken by the non-medical CVCP students.[9]

The acceptance of these proposals somewhat eased but did not eliminate the problem of the education of the medical students, who numbered between an estimated 30 to 50 people in what the CVCP termed as the "medical pool". The allocation of these students proceeded piecemeal over the first six months of 1957 and was not completed until late summer. There were however, some exceptional examples of the welcome extended to the students in medical schools, some of which were willing to offer far more places than they were originally assigned. For example, at St Bartholomew's Hospital Medical School - one of the medical schools within London University - the former Dean, Professor Charles F. Harris, was serving as Deputy Vice-Chancellor of the University in 1957, and in that capacity was well acquainted with the CVCP's Hungarian refugee students scheme and with the associated issues. (He was often consulted on these issues by the University's Academic Registrar and it was he who, on behalf of the Vice-Chancellor, approached the Ford Foundation for financial help.)

When confronted by the problem of the medical students, instead of seeking a solution by referring them elsewhere, he invited a number of them to apply for places in his former institution where he still chaired the College Council. In the academic year 1957-58, there were altogether 136 newly enrolled medical students at Bart's, among them not fewer than

---

[9] University of London: *Memorandum from the External Registrar to the Principal. Hungarian medical students and medical education.* 4 Dec. 1956. UoLA, CB3/9/1/2.

eleven Hungarian refugee students: six designated "Quota" students, three with grants from WUS and two enjoying support from UNA.[10] The "Quota" students paid no entrance, tuition or examination fees, not even fees for the use of the laboratories as all of this expenditure was paid for by the School. (The Hungarian Refugee Student appeal had raised in the School just over £261, but this sum was transferred into the University of London's Hungarian Fund.) The remittance of the fees caused some concern and was discussed first by the Executive Committee then by the College Council. "It was agreed—as recorded in the minutes of the Council's meeting—that it would be right to continue to support such student as had been accepted, but not to accept any further applicants on these same conditions."[11] There were, of course, no more Hungarian student applicants for places in the autumn of 1958, and the progress of the students already there was exemplary. According to the records, eight of them received their diplomas on time, two of them with special distinction: one was awarded the Willett Medal for excellence in operative surgery and the other the Roxborough Prize of 14 guineas for excellence in dermatological studies.[12]

Even with hindsight, it is now quite difficult, or well-nigh impossible, to discern how the Selection Committee reached certain decisions on the allocation of the students. For example, one medical student who had arrived on Flight I and had been housed "temporarily" in Oxford, was retained there, while another medical student on the same flight, was quickly sent to Newcastle. Not surprisingly, of the students who had been encouraged, against their wishes to study dentistry, quite a few changed their minds and requested transfers to study something else. One student, for example, who was allocated to the Royal Dental School in London applied to change his subject and was consequently moved to the University of Sheffield – to study economics. For the record, he successfully obtained his degree there. A few of the universities notified

---

[10] St Bartholomew's Hospital Medical School: *Annual Report of the College Council for the year ended July 31, 1958.* St Bartholomew's Hospital Archives.
[11] St Bartholomew's Hospital Medical School: *Minutes of the College Council.* 18 June 1958. St Bartholomew's Hospital Archives.
[12] Information kindly provided by the St Bartholomew's Hospital Archives. The prices earned by the Bart's Hungarian medical students were, by no means unique examples. András Barabás, a medical student at Manchester University won two essay competitions organized annually for medical students by the BMA and the Royal College of General Practitioners. It is also notable that he and his brother György Barabás were awarded their doctorate (MD) on the same day in 1967 by Manchester University. (Based on information provided by András Barabás.)

the Selection Committee of their inability to accept a particular student—
in most cases they were not offering courses which the student was
supposed to take—or, as was their right, they could refuse to accept any
student without giving a reason for their rejection. It was perhaps most
difficult to assess the potential of arts students, some of whom were,
indeed, compelled to change their subjects. In some cases it transpired
only much later that this was not the best advice they had received.

When I had my interview with Dr Cushing and told him that I had
studied Hungarian language and literature and history at the University of
Szeged, he immediately replied that I should start thinking about other
subjects which I could read with more profit; what would I do with a
degree in Hungarian literature in Britain, what jobs, if any, would require
the knowledge of Hungarian? Taken aback, my mind was a complete
blank, I asked him for suggestions. (With hindsight, I wish I had said that I
wanted to study history.) "What other languages have you learned?" he
asked. "Russian", I said, but like my contemporaries, I had a mental block
about learning the language of the oppressors; what I learned one day—
and earned the best marks for it—I forgot by the next. So, to study Russian
was out of the question.

I had started to learn German at least three times during my school
years, and this meant that while I was well acquainted with the basic
grammar, my vocabulary was less than limited, it was practically non-
existent. The last effort I had made was, in fact, in the autumn of 1956; the
newly-acquired freedom about the choice of subjects we could study drove
me to pick up my German studies again, this time more seriously. I had
even invested in a book; I bought an old paperback edition of Heine's
Buch der Lieder in a second hand bookshop and, on the afternoon of the
23rd October I was sitting on the top of my bunk-bed, alone in the
normally busy room of the student hostel trying, with the help of a
dictionary, to read at least the shorter poems in the volume. I did not get
far, as the call to join the demonstration reached me through the open
windows. Putting the book down, I raced downstairs and marched with the
crowd through the streets, singing and shouting. The revolution had
started. It was, therefore, with an easy mind, that I accepted Cushing's
suggestion to study for a German Honours degree at Westfield College,
University of London. I could make up lost ground in England. Cushing
was also satisfied with the deal we struck: he sorted out my future studies
and, at the same time, was finally able to allocate a Hungarian student to
Westfield College, which had been asking for its "own refugee student"
for some time.

Westfield College was the so-called "ladies' college" of the University: small, exclusive, catering for the educational needs of about 300 young women. The courses offered included English, history, modern languages and mathematics. It was the middle of January 1957 when I was able to move into the college, sharing a room with a first year student, Anne Lois Evans, who was studying English literature. With great enthusiasm, Anne tried to teach me English, naming the objects in the room and explaining that the thick, red, steaming drink we were given as our "supper tray" on Saturdays, was none other than tomato soup, which was to help us to overcome our shivering in the damp cold of a winter evening. I accepted her help without any questions, without the due appreciation her kindness deserved. Just as I accepted the offer of Professor Mary Beare – she was called invariably Miss Beare – Head of the Department of German, to supplement the University's teaching programme by giving me personal tuition in English. The classes consisted of reading Bernard Shaw's *Candida* – why she picked this play for my instruction, I could never fathom. She tried to explain the words to me, sometimes through German, which, of course, was also beyond my grasp. The most exasperating moment came when she, blushing with embarrassment, could not demonstrate what the word *pissoir,* found in Shaw's text, meant.

I also diligently attended the official language course, organized for us by the University in Tavistock Square and by late spring I had learned enough English to realize that my position was utterly hopeless. The knowledge of the students, entering the first year for an Honours degree in German surpassed my knowledge at least three times over, and even if I devoted all my waking hours between April and October to catching up with them, it would still be to no avail. And my task was not to immerse myself in the mysteries of the German language, but to prepare for the English exams which I had to pass to gain admittance to the university course. And to learn a foreign language through another foreign language seemed to pose for me at this stage insurmountable difficulties. There was one thing I could be certain of: I would fail all the exams and never get a degree.

I turned first to Miss Beare with my problem. She sent me to Miss Chesney, the Principal of the College, who explained to me that the allocation of the "Quota" students had been completed and if I wished to follow a university course, I had to stay at Westfield. My suggestion that I might study history—which I had studied at Szeged—was turned down by the Head of the History Department; she queried my ability to be able to cope with mediaeval English which formed part of the second year curriculum. What did she know of the punishment meted out for those who had to learn Old- and Middle-High German for three years! After considering the avenues open to me, Miss Chesney found a near-perfect solution: I should enrol for a General degree rather than an Honours degree. I have to study three subjects instead of one, but at a lower level. One of them should remain German, which I have to take as a student at Westfield, the other could be history of art, which I could study as an inter-collegiate student at Birkbeck College and the third could be Hungarian at the School of Slavonic and East European Studies, which would, of course, be a child's play, enabling me to concentrate on the other subjects. The two degrees, BA Hons and BA General, though not the same, were equivalent under the university regulations.

I accepted her proposal with great relief. Looking back at the anguished months I had lived through before this new arrangement came into force, I can only say that in the midst of all that misery the choice of history of art as one of my subjects was a blessing that fate bestowed on me. I was fortunate to be introduced to the study of the history of art by the eminent art historian and exceptionally gifted teacher, Professor Nikolaus Pevsner. Well known for his seminal work on English and European architecture, especially for his *Buildings of England*, he took the greatest care of his students: he imbued us not only with the appreciation of the human spirit as manifested itself in the works of art but also with the humility and respect with which we should approach them. We spent unforgettable hours with him: at the three hour evening classes he held in Birkbeck College which always seemed to be far too short and during the excursions when he took us with him to look at and examine every detail of the great English cathedrals. As for the German course, I survived it and somehow managed to pass the exams.

For the weekly Hungarian classes I became a student of Dr Cushing. There were two of us attending the classes. Under the guise of getting acquainted with the works of modern Hungarian authors, we spent the time translating literary passages into English. Searching for the most suitable words and most appropriate phrases, was a useful continuation of the intensive English language course. The other student, also a Hungarian refugee, took the opposite path to mine: she had been enrolled to study for a General degree as well, Hungarian being one of the subjects she had to read. She insisted, however, that she wanted to read English literature for an Honours degree. After the first year her wish was granted. Qualifying with a BA Hons, she continued her studies and obtained an MA in English.

And Anne, my room mate at Westfield, also decided to switch subjects. As soon as I was able to put two English words together, I kept talking to her about the crimes of Communism, the suffering we had to endure under the so-called Socialism and Soviet oppression. I told her what we were fighting against and what we were fighting for during the revolution and regaled her with the events of those exhilarating days. Listening to my outpourings she came to the conclusion that the road for her to understand the world led not through the study of English but the study of history. She gained a BA Hons in history and became a life-long history teacher.

By the end of January 1957 almost all "Quota" students knew to which university they had been allocated and the universities confirmed both the number of places and their future occupants, but the change of subjects and the transfer of students from one institution to another continued well into the academic year of 1957-58. A few students realized only after embarking on a particular course that it was unsuitable for them and requested permission to change it. The switch was often only possible by a transfer to another university. The CVCP and individual universities handled these requests with great flexibility and compassion. The University of Oxford, for example, not only allowed some of the students allocated to and being resident at Oxford Colleges to be registered for an external degree at London University, but continued to support them throughout their studies. Furthermore, it arranged for one of the students to transfer to another university while retaining all financial responsibilities for him. Parallel with the allocations, Lockwood urged the universities also to look at their entry requirements and how these could be modified, if necessary, for the admission of the Hungarian students. In his Second Memorandum to the CVCP he warned the universities that while some of the students might have documents to support their statements about their studies in Hungary, many of them might not. The university authorities had to rely entirely on the personal interviews conducted with the students by members of the central selection committee and by the tutors in their allocated institutions. In addition, some of the students had only recently started their university education, while others might be nearing the completion of their courses. All these details had to be borne in mind when matching the needs of the Hungarian students to the admission requirements.[13]

The Principal of the University of London asked the Academic Registrar as early as 22nd November – four days before the arrival of the first chartered aircraft with the students at Blackbushe – to scrutinize the

---

[13] Lockwood, J. F.: *Hungarian Refugee Students. Second Memoramdum of the Vice-Chancellor of the University of London.* 3 Dec. 1956. UoLA , CB3/2/1/2.

statutes for admission, including any changes made in the past twenty years and to explore how these might be applied to the current situation. The Academic Registrar in his reply divided the students into two groups: "advanced students" who had completed a minimum two years of study and "other students" who were in the early stages of their university courses. The definition "advanced students" had varied considerably in the statutes of the University over the years, the reduction of the number of required study years from three to two, for example, followed the influx of students from German-occupied countries during the Second World War – as already mentioned in connection with the registration of the medical students. He felt that the adoption of the 1947 rule would allow the registration of the Hungarian "advanced students" at London University. According to the statutes, however, students with less than two years' study in Hungary should, in addition to passing the English proficiency test, also pass GCE Advanced Level exams in at least two relevant subjects as the "Continental Maturity Certificates" were not recognized in Britain. Nevertheless, he suggested that the requirement to obtain two "A level" passes might be waived on the recommendation of the College tutors, and the students could be registered on an interim basis. This would enable them to follow the prescribed courses leading to the Intermediate Examinations. The problem was that the Intermediate Exams were to be phased out with effect from 1st May 1957.[14]

Faced with these complications, the Vice-Chancellor decided to call an emergency meeting for 7th December to draft recommendations for a scheme which, while adhering to the statutes, was simple and easy to apply. The draft would be considered by the Academic Council, the Council for External Students and the University Entrance and School Examination Council and, if passed, presented to the Senate for approval. The final version, duly endorsed by the Senate on 19th December, was brief and elegant. The preamble made it clear that it applied only to Hungarian students "who have been prevented from pursuing courses of study or have suffered interruption in their courses through political circumstances."[15] All students would be eligible for provisional registration as internal or external students on the recommendation of the Schools and Institutes at which they had been accepted for a first degree course. The Schools and Institutes could also recommend to the University a reduction in the course of the study or exemption from examinations on condition that the student would proceed to the final examination after completing

---

[14] Henderson, J.: *Memorandum to the Principal by the Academic Registrar.* 26 Nov. 1956. UoLA, CB3/4/1.
[15] University of London. Senate: *Minutes.* 19 Dec. 1956. UoLA, ST2/2/81.

no less than two years of study from the commencement of his studies. The scheme, together with guidance notes by the Academic Registrar, was sent to all Colleges and Institutes of the University in January 1957 in order to facilitate the formal registration of those students who might have already started their courses at the beginning of the second term in the current academic year. The guidance notes made it clear that the Senate's overriding consideration was to enable "each Hungarian student to embark on his chosen degree course with profit." For the assessment of the students' ability, the scheme relied on the judgement of academic staff and "the Senate was prepared to leave a wide measure of discretion to the Schools and Institutions."[16]

The other British universities treated the question of the registration requirements with similar generosity. They readily placed their confidence in the ability and diligence of the refugee students. The action taken by the Scottish Universities deserves special mention. On the recommendation of the Scottish Universities Entrance Board, and with the approval of the Senate of each university, it was agreed "that the students be granted provisional entry to the Universities, on passing an approved examination in English. Thereafter, on the completion of two terms' satisfactory work, the students will receive a retrospective attestation of fitness."[17] The Entrance Board duly delivered the certificates to the students at the end of the academic year 1957-58.[18] Other universities required even less. Oxford University, for example, simply left it to the Colleges to judge whether the students allocated to them would be able to follow their courses satisfactorily. Time would, in any case, sift out those who proved to be unsuitable.

Under the registration schemes accepted by most universities, a number of students were eligible for shortening their courses. For these students, after careful assessment by their tutors or departments, the relevant institutions submitted a request to the university authorities. Imperial College's Registrar, for example, was able to seek London University's approval for a rather bold plan concerning three undergraduates. They would be registered provisionally as soon as possible, begin to attend classes at once and take Parts I and II of the Final Examinations in June 1957. Part III could then be taken in June 1958, the

---

[16] Henderson, J.: *University of London. Scheme for the registration of Refugee Students from Hungary. Notes for guidance of Schools and Institutions.* 12 Jan. 1957. UoLA, CB3/4/1.

[17] Young, R. M.: Op. cit., p.23.

[18] Kálmán Száz, formerly a student at the University of Glasgow, kindly supplied me with the photocopy of the certificate he had received.

students technically completing their undergraduate studies for a BSc Engineering degree within 18 months. They would have to remain students of the College for another term in order to satisfy the University's requirement of completing two full years of study before being awarded their degrees at the end of December 1958. The work assigned to them in the last term could count towards a postgraduate degree if they wished to obtain one. The submission showed not only a remarkable confidence in the students' knowledge and academic potential, but also in their ability to adapt to a very different environment and cope with the inevitable "culture shock".

Two of the students completed their studies, as expected, by the end of the academic year 1957-58. They were encouraged to start researching for an MSc before receiving their degrees. The outstanding performance of one of the students, Gyula Székely, even led to unforeseen complications. In the mid-sixties he left for the United States to pursue his research and academic career. When he submitted an application for a full professorship at the State University of New York in Buffalo, he had to write to the Registrar at Imperial College requesting confirmation of his details as his CV had greatly puzzled the Americans. The CV contained a rather convoluted story of his obtaining an MSc before being awarded a first degree in chemical engineering. The Registrar set the record straight: the Department of Chemical Engineering, recognizing the exceptional ability of Székely, allowed him to start his research for an MSc as early as January 1957. However, he had to take the undergraduate exams first. He sat for Part II in June 1957 and Part III in 1958, and completed his thesis for the MSc by the end of the same year. It was then that the authorities discovered that he had not taken Part I of the first degree examination, so neither a BSc nor an MSc could be awarded to him. So, he had to take the first degree Part I exams in January 1959 and, on receiving the BSc, he could register for the MSc in June. He had to do a full year of research, at least on paper, to obtain it officially in June 1960. In the meanwhile he was transferred to study for a PhD and although he completed it in 1960, according to the regulations, it could be awarded to him only in 1961. Throughout this procedural ordeal the reports on his progress abounded in superlatives and the College was delighted to appoint him to the teaching staff in 1962.

The most generous application of the rules for the registration of the Hungarian students was almost universal in the British Isles. There were, however, a few dissenting voices, sounding a warning about the qualification of the students. It was suggested that their vetting and selection should be done with more background knowledge and care.

Some of them might not possess the right type of "Maturity Certificate" and their admission to higher education in Hungary might not have been based on merit but on an ill-disguised attempt at social engineering. And some of them might not have been students at all. These persons should be barred from the special treatment, so readily granted to all the presumed refugee students. These questions were raised, for example in Cambridge, notably by Dennis Sinor, a lecturer at the University, who was one of the first academics there to offer help with the reception of the Hungarian students. He immediately volunteered to teach them in the special English language course set up for them days after their arrival. Sinor, himself a Hungarian, was in a unique position to be able to form a close relationship with the students, learn about their background and assess their fitness – or lack of it – for entering higher education at British universities. He first commented on his observations at a reception on 19th December, given by the British Council, in a conversation with N. S. Wilson, the Adviser to Overseas Candidates for Admission at Cambridge University. In Sinor's view, the University should demand from each student the presentation of his or her official student card and, if possible, their exam booklet, called "index", in which each examination—all oral—were recorded and endorsed by the signature of the relevant examiners. Failing to produce any documents to prove their former student status, a letter should be sent to the rectors of the Hungarian universities, requesting that a certificate should be dispatched to England, in order to prove that they indeed, had been *bona fide* students at a particular institution. He added that he would be willing to approach the Rector of Budapest University, whom he knew well, on their behalf; as a letter in Hungarian from an old friend would surely elicit a prompt reply. (It is not clear what Sinor meant by Budapest University, since there were at least four universities in Budapest at that time; he might have been referring to the Eötvös Loránd University which had only Arts, Law and Science Faculties. This would have left all other students without the special help Sinor had offered.)

The following day Wilson sent a letter to the Registrary of Cambridge University, R. M. Rattenbury, who accepted responsibility for all the Hungarian students at Cambridge under the CVCP scheme. Wilson was not sure whether Sinor had doubts about the qualification of some of the students, or their ability to study at university level in England, or, he was simply expressing his willingness to help with obtaining the necessary documents from Hungary. However, Wilson was sure that Sinor referred to the CVCP students who had come to England with Flight IV, and who had been transferred to Cambridge on 14th December and for whom the

English classes had begun already on 17th December.[19] Yet, it is possible that Sinor was also influenced by meeting with the so-called "Roughton" students a couple of days earlier. These 25 students had been brought to Cambridge from the refugee camp at Wisbech, which normally provided seasonal accommodation for fruit pickers by Dr Alice Roughton—a doctor and wife of Professor Roughton—hence the name by which they were known.[20] Dr Roughton approached Rattenbury with the request to accept at least some of these students as Cambridge undergraduates, but he declined, being well aware of the CVCP scheme and Cambridge's commitment to provide places for 15 students under the scheme. (He gave, however, permission for four of them to attend the language course set up for the "Quota" students from the middle of January 1957.) The Roughton students were registered by WUS and their registration might give credence to the presumption that Sinor was acquainted with them. In his letter to Rattenbury, in which he expounded his reservations concerning the students and their qualifications at length, he specifically mentioned the registration form they had to fill in and its inadequacies. These—he observed—might have greatly contributed to the formulation of misconceptions on the students' background and abilities.[21]

Sinor was most probably referring to the WUS registration form, which he deplored in the strongest of terms: "I have seen the questionnaire which all these students had to fill in. I understand that the answers given to the questions contained therein from the basis on which they are being judged anyhow for the present. This questionnaire is, or pretends to be, the translation of an English original. Clearly, it is the work of someone who not only does not write Hungarian properly but has no idea whatsoever of the Hungarian educational system. Unfortunately it is not only teeming with grammatical and spelling mistakes, but what is worse, it does not convey any real meaning to the Hungarian students called to fill it in." He continued with the observation that it would be quite wrong to judge the students on the basis of the answers they provided to the questions, because not being able to interpret them properly, they put on paper

---

[19] Letter by N. S. Wilson to R. M. Rattenbury. 20 Dec. 1956. CUL/UA. Registry file R3445/56.

[20] Information kindly provided by István Selmeczi, one of the Roughton students. Several of the Roughton students were later admitted to universities; István Selmeczi attended the language course at Oxford University and studied at the University College, Cardiff.

[21] Letter by Dennis Sinor to R. M. Rattenbury. 7 Jan. 1957. CUL/UA Registry file R3445/56.

whatever came into their heads. The questionnaire should not be regarded as a source of reliable information.

Sinor gave a special warning about the two, substantially different "Maturity Certificates" currently issued to students in Hungary at the conclusion of their secondary education. One of them—which he called a "serious" certificate—was equivalent to the GCE examinations in Britain and students in possession of these should be admitted to British universities. The other certificate—for which he did not even give an English translation but referred to under its Hungarian name "szakérettségi"—was given to selected potential students of "popular origin", that is, to sons and daughters of working class or peasant parents. It was, indeed, a tool of social engineering, to be employed for changing forcibly the composition of the future middle classes. Sinor quite rightly explained that students with these "special certificates" might not even have completed their secondary education, or been pushed through their studies, or they might have failed the "Maturity Examination" but still received a certificate in order to engineer their admission to a university or to a higher education college. He called this examination and the certificate "phoney" and strongly recommended that students with such certificates should take some sort of entrance examination before being admitted to a British university. He concluded: "This examination could be conducted in Hungarian so as to give a fair chance to everybody and not to make the final result dependent on the linguistic capacity of the candidate." Were his recommendation to be accepted, he would be happy to help with the setting of the papers in Hungarian and with the evaluation of the answers. In conclusion, Sinor reiterated the desirability of obtaining the necessary documents from Hungary –either from the universities or from the parents of the students – which would testify to their previous studies and they should be required to submit these the following September in time for their matriculation. This could not be easier: the postal link between England and Hungary was excellent, the students only needed to write a letter requesting them.

Sinor was most probably right in assuming that some of the Hungarian refugee students selected by the CVCP or registered by WUS, had not been students at a higher education institution in Hungary. Their numbers, however, although cannot be verified, must have been small. Circumstantial evidence produced by the survey of Dare and Hollander, seemed to support this presumption.[22] The survey did not pose this question directly, but answers given to a number of other questions,

---

[22] Dare, Alan and Hollander, Paul: Op.cit., p.59.

provided enough information to settle the problem of the students' status in Hungary. To the question for example, "If you studied in a Hungarian university, for how many years did you study?" six replies said "None"; as these students had not been at university in Hungary.[23] This answer might be at first glance surprising, but in the light of another question quizzing the students about their age, it transpires that 14 persons of those replying, had not yet reached their 19th birthday in 1958.[24] These students definitely had been too young to attend any higher education institution in Hungary. To the previous question however, 54 students did not reply at all and this might have raised suspicions about their status. The authors, analyzing answers to two further groups of questions: "Are you continuing here the studies you commenced in Hungary?"[25] and "Have you in Hungary been interned, held under arrest, evicted, expelled from university, etc.?"[26] arrived at the conclusion that the number of those who did not follow university courses in Hungary must have been fewer than 42 persons, representing 15 per cent of the replies received. And this 15 per cent also included those who had not been admitted to universities because of their family background. Taking this fact and the age factor together, it seems obvious that the number of those who might have provided false information about their status in Hungary must have been insignificant compared to the total number of Hungarian refugee students in Britain.

Rattenbury asked Walters's opinion on the problems Sinor had raised in his letter. It was not surprising that Walters—who must have been deeply offended by the harsh criticism of the WUS form—replied rather tersely: "Clearly I am in no position to judge whether the WUS form for Hungarian students is written in the best idiom. I can only say that it appears to be effective since the basis of our interview has been this form and we have all found it useful." He then continued: "If men decline to fill in the form in which the intentions are clear, irrespective of its phraseology, then I would say such quibbling is a poor recommendation for candidates for admission to a British university."[27] The questionnaire had actually been seen and endorsed by Dr Cushing, who provided the guidance notes for its completion. And the students—reiterated Walters— had been interviewed in depth by leading academics in their field: the engineering students for example, by Professor Greig and the medical

---

[23] Ibid. Table 19A, p.XXV.
[24] Ibid. Table 47, p.XLIII.
[25] Ibid. Table 19C, pp.XXV-XXVI.
[26] Ibid. Table 36, p.XXXVIII.
[27] Letter by R. H. Walters to R. M. Rattenbury. 8 Jan. 1957. CUL/UA Registry file R3445/56.

students by the Deputy Vice-Chancellor of London University himself, who had previously been the Dean of the St Bartholomew's Medical School. Their judgement could be trusted and was, in fact trusted by the universities, since not a single one declined to accept a student on the recommendation of the CVCP interviewing team to date. He admitted that in the selection of the arts students, the team had been somewhat more vulnerable, but he had no doubt that the assessments had been reasonable.

As for the production of documents testifying to the former status of the applicants, Walters remarked that the students selected for the special flights either had some sort of identification papers in their possession, or, the other students had vouched for them and they had all passed scrutiny, although this might have been rather amateurish. Concerning the "U" students, he was convinced that the Home Office had acted with due care when admitting them to Britain. Overall, Walters echoed the general attitude adopted by the universities, who were willing to accept all the selected refugee students on the basis of commonsense and compassion without additional investigation into their past. They did not wish to force them to take special entrance examinations – notwithstanding the extra time and money spent on those students who, after the first year were forced to withdraw from their studies because they were unfit to follow higher education courses. While no one can doubt the genuine concern of Dennis Sinor, to act upon his recommendations would have caused serious delay in processing the students and might also have raised anxiety, even uproar among the students themselves.

However, there were no mitigating circumstances for the naivety of Sinor in suggesting that the students should write to the Hungarian universities or to their parents to send them the required documents. Surely, he must have heard from the students that reprisals had begun in Hungary; that all those who had participated in the revolution were in danger and that leaving the country was also regarded as a punishable action. He must have been aware that the students, whenever and wherever they were talking about their experiences chose anonymity because they feared that their parents and friends left behind would be punished instead of them. And the last thing the universities would be concerned about in the days of the growing persecution in the aftermath of the revolution was the dispatch of documents to hundreds of their former students who had "illegally" emigrated to the West. Nevertheless, it is always possible to find an example to prove the opposite. New College in Oxford for example, applied via the British Embassy in Budapest to the Eötvös Loránd University to supply them with the student index of Nicholas Krassó, the postgraduate refugee student allocated to them. The Embassy successfully obtained the document and sent it to New College. Krassó was delighted to have it and showed it to all and sundry as a proof that he had, indeed been a university student. The authorities of New College never learned that Krassó had no "Maturity Certificate"; he had never completed his secondary education, but had been issued with a special licence acknowledging his undoubted talent, and thus was admitted to university to study philosophy.

In conjunction with the admission requirements, Logan also raised at the mid-December meeting of the CVCP, the question of sending every student a letter of contract. This would be a common form of document, which would make it clear that a) admission to courses would be dependent upon the student having a sufficient mastery of the English language to undertake his course successfully and b) his continued maintenance would depend upon satisfactory progress being made by him in his course of study.[28] Logan was entrusted to draft the letter, which was discussed at the subsequent meetings. At each revision the tone of the letter became more and more stern in stressing the duties of the students: the need for hard work, ready co-operation and satisfactory progress. If a student were to fail the exams and could not supply an adequate explanation for the failure, it would be difficult, if not impossible to continue to provide financial support for him. The final version, together with a Hungarian translation was attached to Lockwood's Fifth Memorandum and sent to the universities. They were to hand it to their students asking them to read it carefully, sign the English version and return it to the authorities.[29] With the letter of agreement the CVCP wished to ascertain that the students were aware of their own obligations; that entry to higher education in Britain was not an automatic right and that were they to lose support they would have no recourse to legal redress. The CVCP however, was not in the position to force the universities to have the letter signed by their future charges. The Minutes of the 16th January 1957 meeting of the Oxford Hungarian Committee, for example, simply record the Committee's dissent regarding the letter: "It was decided that Oxford would ignore this letter, and that Colleges would make their own arrangements."[30]

Each university also had to gain the approval of their Senate for waiving all fees in respect of the Hungarian students. It was obvious that no tuition fees were to be paid; had they been charged, the maintenance

---

[28] CVCP: *Minutes. Refugee students from Hungary.* 14 Dec. 1956. CVCPA
[29] Lockwood, J. F.: *Hungarian refugee students. Fifth Memorandum by the Vice-Chancellor of the University of London. 21 Dec. 1956. UoLA, CB3/2/1/5.*
[30] Oxford Hungarian Committee: *Minutes.* 16 Jan. 1957. BLA UR6/OVS/H File 1.

allowance for the students should also have been raised by the appropriate sum. There were, however, several other fees the students normally had to pay: matriculation and examination fees, fees for the use of the laboratories and, at the end of their studies, degree fees. A very detailed table of the fees was drawn up the Oxford Hungarian Committee for the Financial Committee, which clearly indicated that the combined fees over three years of study amounted to quite a considerable sum: £43 for an arts student over three years, £132 for a science student during the same period rising to £174 for a four year university course. Medical students were required to pay the highest fees: if their course lasted six years, the accumulated fees could reach the sum of £336.[31] Waiving these fees would, of course, increase the financial burden on the universities. In spite of this, in the spring 1957 the Senate of each university approved the proposal, although at that time it was not yet clear that they might obtain additional funding for the tuition of the refugee students. The fees, however, were waived only for the "Quota" students. The CVCP expected WUS or any other funding body or charity to pay the fees, including tuition fees, in respect of the students they sponsored.

The students had little if any knowledge of these administrative arrangements. They read and duly signed the letter of agreement and sent it back to the university. Most of them diligently attended the daily language classes, while those who knew sufficient English started their proper university courses. In the meantime, they began to get acquainted with university life in Britain, acquired British friends and set out on the slow process of assimilation. The British university students and staff with commendable foresight decided not to make an exception of them. If they were not treated as a separate group, they would sooner and less painfully adapt to their new circumstances, becoming members of the "university family" with greater ease. As the Deputy Registrar of Edinburgh University said in his summary of the events: "…from being an isolated party of strangers, the Hungarians began to become part of the general body of students."[32]

The very same attitude prevailed at Imperial College. A note, jotted down by the Rector, Patrick Linstead, recorded that on 11th January 1957 he invited the five "Quota" students[33] to see him in his office. He welcomed them and explained to them which courses they were to follow

---

[31] University of Oxford. Committee on Financial Questions: *Agendum 2. Appendix A*. 19 Feb. 1957. BLA UR6/OVS/H file 1.

[32] Young, R. M.: Op.cit., p.22.

[33] It should be noted that in addition to the five "Quota" students, in the academic year of 1957-58 six other, non CVCP supported students started their courses.

in the next two to three years. He ended his talk with the words: "… that from now on they would be regarded as ordinary student members of the College."[34] With this he wished to express that the Hungarian students were henceforth fully accepted and incorporated into College life. They were no longer regarded as refugees, or outsiders, but as valuable members of the College with equal rights. Equally, the College had high expectations of them: hard work and excellent results. The same sentiment was expressed in the spring issue of the college magazine, *Phoenix*: "We have extended a welcome. There can be no doubt that we are sincere. May we never forget that this country is now *their* home too." Then it gave them the 'Student Toast': "Success in exams; excess to wine."[35]

---

[34] Note by R. P. Linstead. 1957 Jan. 11. ICA, Hungarian Relief, SS/1/4.
[35] Hungarian students welcomed. *Phoenix*, Spring, 1957, p.9.

CHAPTER VII

THE LANGUAGE COURSES

It would be both pedantic and somewhat futile to dwell on what had induced Lockwood to emphasize in the strongest terms the need to provide English language courses for the Hungarian students as of the absolute top priority. It may have been the reports on the language knowledge of the students that he had received from Vienna, or possibly his meetings with some of students soon after their arrival in Britain. "While one or two of the students have a reasonable command of spoken English and a number have more than a smattering"—he wrote in his Second Memoradum to the members of the CVCP—"I doubt whether any of them could profitably embark on work for a university degree without an intensive course in English lasting at least three, and probably six, months."[1] The Oxford Hungarian Committee reached the same conclusion. In his letter to the Heads of Colleges Norrington singled out the immediate commencement of English classes for the students as the most important task: "Almost all the students coming out of Hungary, whether suitable for our Universities, or for Technical Colleges and the like, know no English, and no doubt the two essential processes, of teaching them English and selection (and allocating) those of University calibre will have to go on side by side – with the learning of English as the first priority."[2]

Thanks to this overriding concern, the universities which volunteered to act as reception centres for the 150 students transferred from Vienna to Britain by the CVCP, not only set up English classes—practically within days—for the students they received for a short stay, but agreed to be designated as regional centres for the systematic English courses to be started as soon as possible in the New Year. The universities of Birmingham, Cambridge, Leeds, London and Oxford were soon joined by the University of Edinburgh, which did not act as a reception centre, but

---

[1] Lockwood, J.F.: *Hungarian refugee students. Second Memorandum of the Vice-Chancellor of the University of London.* 3 Dec. 1956. UoLA, CB3/2/1/2.
[2] [Oxford Hungarian Committee: *The recent revolution in Hungary...*] 28 Nov. 1956. BLA UR6/OVS/H File 1.

was entrusted to organize the language course for the 22 students allocated to the Scottish Universities and to the Queen's University of Belfast.[3]

As early as mid-December the CVCP debated the question of how the language courses should be organized, whether by every institution separately for its own students or for groups of students at designated regional centres who would then move on to their degree courses elsewhere in September or October. While most of the universities were very happy to divest themselves of the responsibility to set up language courses and readily agreed with the proposal on establishing regional centres, a few expressed the wish to cater for the language needs of their students themselves. Their wish, of course, was granted.[4]

The table drawn up by the Hungarian Sub-Committee to show the grouping of the courses reflected this division.[5] Every regional centre was responsible for its own students. Birmingham was also to take the students allocated to the Aberystwyth and Bangor Colleges of the University of Wales and the Hungarian students of Liverpool and Manchester. Cambridge offered language courses also for the students of Leicester, Reading and Southampton. Leeds catered for the students of the Durham Colleges, Hull, Newcastle and Sheffield. Oxford was responsible for the students who would be studying at Bristol and the Cardiff and Swansea Colleges of the University of Wales. Edinburgh—as already mentioned— was to teach English to the students of the Scottish universities and the Queen's University, Belfast, while London had to cope with the largest group of 34 students allocated to London University. The universities of Exeter, North Staffordshire and Nottingham would organize their own courses. Each regional centre would instruct between 20 to 25 students. The total number of students learning English was – according to the table - 154, that is, all the CVCP-supported "Quota" students were included at this stage. This distribution did not yet reflect the students' true knowledge of English as a few of them knew enough to start their university courses in January 1957; the numbers simply followed the number of students allocated to each university on the basis of the proportional distribution plan. The Sub-Committee soon had to make some modifications: among

---

[3] The Scottish Universities were allocated 20 and the Queen's University 4 students. However, the list of those who were to enrol in the language course named only 18 students designated to attend Scottish Universities. *List of students (as at 2 January 1957) to attend the English language course at Edinburgh.* UoLA, CB3/6/3/1/3.

[4] CVCP: *Minutes.* 14 Dec. 1956. CVCPA

[5] CVCP. Sub-Committee on the Selection of Hungarian Refugee Students: *Minutes.* 20 Dec. 1956. UoLA, CB3/1/1/2.

others, the inclusion of the universities of Newcastle and Sheffield in the "going alone" group as these universities, at the request of the Vice-Chancellor of Leeds University, also decided to organize the language teaching for their own students.[6]

In the documentation about the language courses for Hungarian students there are several lists which give varying information about their numbers. Those mentioned in the final report prepared for the Lord Mayor's Fund are probably the most reliable. The report was written by Walters and he quoted the following figures: Birmingham had 23 students, Cambridge 18, Edinburgh 24, Leeds 19, London 34 and Oxford 25.[7] The figures are very close to the ones quoted in the spring of 1957 and this is surprising, because a reasonable decrease could have been expected, due to the number of students who had no need to study English and were exempt from the courses (this figure, however, must have been fairly small) and to the number of students who dropped out before the exams. So, it was the "late-comers" who boosted their numbers. Walters only counted the "Quota" students which, of course, distorted the numbers even more. London University for example, was supposed to organize the course for its 34 allocated students – and this is the figure Walters gave in his report - yet, the records for the June 1957 examination listed 50 students who were to sit the exams. Most of these newcomers were Ford students. The same happened at the other regional centres: Cambridge accepted four Roughton students for the language course and Edinburgh also catered for a fairly large number of Ford students, some of whom carried on with the language classes until Christmas 1957, or even beyond.

Also among the students were those who were supported by the Free Europe, the Gulbenkian Foundation and by other grant-giving bodies—most of the latter attended the language course in London—and in almost every university there were students or even non-students whom the authorities decided to include in the English classes. In Oxford, for example, there was Sándor Éles, the student who in Hungary had studied to be an actor. He arrived on the first of the chartered aircraft and thus ended up at Oxford with all the others. He was determined to go on the

---

[6] CVCP. Sub-Committee on the Allocation of Hungarian Students: *Minutes.* 3 Jan. 1957. UoLA, CB3/1/2/1.
[7] The Lord Mayor of London's National Hungarian & Central European Relief Fund: *Report Nov. 1956 – Sept. 1958.* [1958.] p.63. Although the report on the Hungarian students is unsigned, it corresponds very closely to the article published in the *University of London Bulletin,* No.43, 1977 and to the several drafts extant in the University of London Archives' CB3 collection, providing proof of Walters's authorship.

stage and therefore, the University could not offer him a place so the Hungarian Committee referred to him as a "problem person". It decided, however, to include him in the English course, since as a future actor in England, he could do with some polishing of his pronunciation. Éles indeed became a well-known actor: because of his dark, slightly threatening good looks he mostly played, both on the stage and on television, foreign aristocratic villains with a distinguished Oxford accent. It would be fair to say that including the "Quota", Ford and other students, there must have been at least 200 people participating in the language courses organized by the universities.

Language courses for Hungarian refugees were also organized in most of the camps, normally under the aegis of BCAR Education Department, which commissioned the YMCA to make the necessary arrangements and to oversee the operation. The YMCA made use of a large number of volunteer teachers, who were keen to offer their help, but also appointed some professionals to the teaching posts, among them some Hungarian refugees. The story of Ferenc Lengyel might provide an example. Lengyel had been a political prisoner in Hungary, serving the fifth year of his sentence - the last three years in the coal mine at Csolnok - in the autumn of 1956. Soon after the outbreak of the revolution, Lengyel, together with the other political prisoners, was freed and at the end of October he travelled to Budapest, where he was involved in the fighting around one of the capital's telephone exchanges. From December onwards the secret police started to round up the ex-political prisoners and it had become clear to Lengyel that he had to leave the country. He crossed the border to Austria with four other ex-prisoners on 13th December. They were helped to escape by the Benedictine monks, who had previously taught Lengyel and his fellow prisoners. In Austria they too found refuge in a Benedictine monastery, staying there until mid-January, by which time their plans to go to England had been finalized.

All of them knew English reasonably well, which was evidently why they decided to apply for refugee status in Britain. They obtained the necessary travel documents from the British Embassy in Vienna. Through some friends they were also able to arrange that on their arrival in England they would be employed by the YMCA as interpreters in the Hungarian refugee camp at Hednesford. In addition, they were to run the cultural and entertainment activities in the camp. Travelling by train, with special coaches for the refugees attached to a scheduled train, they arrived in England on 25th January 1957 and were immediately transferred to the camp at Hednesford, where they were expected to start work at once. They were accommodated in staff quarters, together with the British members of the staff and used the staff dining room for meals. Thus, they were able also to start building their social life in Britain. Some of the people, whom they met at that time, have remained friends to this day.

The Hungarian university students in the camp formed a distinct group and presented a favourable image of themselves. They were regarded both with admiration and some curiosity by their British hosts. Lengyel and his ex-prisoner mates had been university students before their imprisonment and naturally they wanted to complete their studies in England. However, by the time they began to make enquiries about how to apply for a place at a British university, they were told that all places had been filled and there was little hope of continuing their studies. They received no official help and were left to their own devices. They took up the challenge. Having been informed that the American sponsored Free Europe University in Exile was offering scholarships, they applied for and were eventually awarded grants. Then they had to find and secure university places for themselves. Their employment in the camp contributed to their success in their search: Lengyel passed the entrance examination at the University of Birmingham with flying colours. He started his course in electrical engineering in October 1957 and obtained his BSc degree in 1961.[8]

It was the language courses organized in the refugee camps which helped many of the students waiting for a WUS grant to obtain a modicum of English, enough to gain admittance to a university. It also enabled those students to learn some English who, for whatever reason, were destined to continue their studies in the technical colleges. Today, it is only possible to gain information about these courses from the personal reminiscences of the students who attended them. The universities could not admit them to their courses; there was neither the necessary teaching capacity nor adequate financial means available to cater for them. However, the previously quoted correspondence between Lockwood, Logan and the Ministry of Education in December 1956 seems to imply that the universities would have been willing to accept some of these students for the language courses were their expenses fully met from other sources. Lockwood even summarized the conditions the universities had drawn up in some detail for the CVCP Hungarian Committee,[9] but the uncertainty and the ensuing delay on behalf of the Ministry on how to approach the problem meant that the project never got off the ground. Time was the key factor: the universities wanted to begin the systematic language courses as soon as possible, while the Ministry needed more time to reach a decision

---

[8] Written contribution by Ferenc.Lengyel. 25 Aug. 2004.
[9] CVCP. Sub-Committee on Hungarian Students: *Note by the Vice-Chancellor of the University of London.* 5 Dec. 1956. UoLA, CB3/1/1/1.

on the technical college students, and to make the necessary preparations for their admission, including their English language tuition.

Nevertheless, a few courses for the future technical college students were set up, some of which ran parallel with the university language courses. Where this happened, the university authorities were forced to draw a distinct line of demarcation between the two courses, indicating that they accepted no responsibility whatsoever for the technical college students. The two courses in Oxford also ran parallel. The course for the technical college students was under the direction of Dr G. J. Hervei, a Hungarian-English bilingual scholar, later a respected proof-reader at the Oxford University Press, and it was so highly regarded that the Oxford Hungarian Committee noted with some envy, that many of their own students would have rather joined Dr Hervei's classes than attended the course organized by the University: "The other course... with the bilingual Dr G. J. Hervei in charge, is very successful, and some of those in the B.C. [British Council] course are looking over their shoulders at Dr Hervei's popular course."[10]

Both of the two rather distinct types of language tuition recognized by the CVCP—for large classes at the regional centres and for individual students at a few universities—had their advantages and disadvantages. Those universities which did not wish to send their students to the regional centres but were organizing their English courses themselves received their future undergraduates in early January, under the "Operation Switch" transfers. These students then were given ample time to settle down in their new environment before starting their university courses, and the opportunity to discover and get used to the local customs, make friends and to get acquainted with the teaching staff. So, it seemed to be an ideal solution. Yet, in the early weeks of January most of these student felt lost; they were just emerging from the trauma of the crushed revolution, of fleeing from their homeland in fear of their lives and desperately trying to find a new home somewhere in the Western world. They arrived in England, a strange country with strange customs, where they could not even make themselves understood. Being sent to a university they probably had never even heard of, and finding themselves there alone, perhaps the only Hungarian student, deepened their feelings of misery. They were unable to feel or to respond to the welcome extended to them by the other students and this was not just because of their inadequate knowledge of English. For a Hungarian it took months, even years to discover that behind the mask of reservation feigning disinterest and

---

[10] Oxford Hungarian Committee: *Minutes.* 7 Feb. 1957.

detachment the English could be just as emotional as their openly demonstrative, wearing-the-hearts-on-their-sleeves, loud, tearful and wildly gesticulating Continental counterparts. The progress of these Hungarian students in mastering the English language might have been spectacular but they paid a heavy price for it by experiencing isolation and a sense of loneliness. It is not surprising that some of these students requested a transfer to another higher education institution – not necessarily to another university – during the summer or during the course of their studies. Those who could count themselves luckier were the ones who were joined by other Hungarian students, allocated to the same university or, in some cases, by a whole group of refugee students – such as the mining engineers supported by the National Coal Board.

The first months of adjustment to a new life were easier for the students in the regional centres, who, ensconced in the warmth and security of the "family" of their own little Hungarian community, did not feel cut off from the past and did not have to face the strange new world alone. They had shared in the exhilarating common experience of the revolution, and in the sorrow and anger of it being mercilessly crushed. They understood each other without words and they could rely on each other for help and advice. They discovered together what the new world around them offered, laughed about its oddities and sought the ways and means to understand it. They attended the language classes together and there was always one amongst them who could provide the necessary explanation concerning the English or even the Hungarian grammar – what was, for example, the difference between the usage of the definite or the indefinite article in the respective languages. Being together alleviated the pressure of the inevitable culture shock and, being well prepared, they were able to withstand it even if it hit them after they had left the regional language centre and moved to their final university places. And they had to rely on this inner strength, because for quite a large number of them this last transfer was the third or fourth move they would have to endure within the relatively short time of nine to ten months.

All the students who had travelled to England on the CVCP chartered flights remained in London for a few days during which they were interviewed. After this short stay they were transferred to the interim reception centres where they were looked after until early January, when most of them were moved to the regional language centres for the English courses. Finally, in September 1957, every student had to take his place at the university where he was admitted to study for a degree. The magnitude of all these transfers is well documented in the report submitted to the Senate of the University of Birmingham on the reception of the Hungarian refugee students. The University received 30 students arriving on Flight III on 8 December 1956. They were housed in the newly refurbished Park Grange hostel, but many of them enjoyed the hospitality of local families over the Christmas period. Of these 30 students only eight remained in Birmingham when, in the context of "Operation Switch" the others were moved to the relevant regional centres for the language courses. However, Birmingham itself being a designated regional centre, it received 12 other students, coming from diverse temporary accommodations. After finishing the course and taking the exams, the students were again dispersed, only six of them registered as undergraduates at Birmingham: four from the language course and two who had already started their university courses in January 1957. As R. T. Jones, Permanent Secretary to the Guild of Undergraduates and the compiler of the report wrote: "In all, some 44 students passed through Park Grange and five received private hospitality. By the end of July it is expected that the students will be dispersed to their universities of ultimate allocation and that Park Grange will have fulfilled its present function. Those of us who have been associated with the Hungarians will be sorry to see them go but will wish them the greatest possible success in their studies and for their future."[11]

The luckiest students were those who were able to remain at the regional centre as newly admitted undergraduates after completing the language course. Cambridge also experienced a constant turnover of Hungarian students on a scale similar to that of Birmingham. From Flights V and VI, the University received 19 students, 16 of whom left after the Christmas break, most of them going to Edinburgh to attend the language course there, after which they were to study at the Scottish universities. However, 16 other students were transferred from their respective temporary accommodations to Cambridge for the language course to be held there. The language tuition ended in September and six of the students from the course moved to their allocated universities, for which Cambridge had acted as the regional language centre. Of the various student groups, there remained 13 "Quota" students and two others at Cambridge. However, this was the university, which, right from the beginning, offered accommodation for all Hungarian students in colleges. Students in the first group, who arrived in December, were housed in King's and Trinity Colleges. When the language course started, the 19 participants were allocated rooms in almost as many colleges. (It was only

---

[11] Jones, R. T.: An account from the Secretary of the Committee of the help given to Hungarian refugee students in the University of Birmingham. In: University of Birmingham. Senate: *Annex to the Minutes.* 2 July 1957. Birmingham University Archives.

at St John's that two brothers were housed together.) Rattenbury assured the colleges repeatedly that they should regard this distribution of the students as a temporary measure, to be reviewed in the autumn and were they to express their wish for a change, it would definitely be taken into account. Nevertheless, when the new academic year started all of them remained in their respective colleges with the exception of a single student. The Cambridge solution seemed to be the ideal arrangement. Regarded as members of their colleges, the Hungarian students were accepted with more ease and speed as part of the local community. They made friends among the college's undergraduates and got used to the daily routine. All this familiarity paved the way for a painless transition to proper undergraduate life. At the same time, the language classes created another community, a virtual Hungarian "family", which served as a psychological underpinning by providing inner strength in an alien environment.

At Oxford, a few of the students—most of them from Flight I—were also given rooms in colleges. And just as in Cambridge, the Oxford Hungarian Committee strongly emphasized that after their matriculation their students might have to be moved to other colleges. The other students enjoyed the hospitality of local families and individuals who, wishing to participate in the common effort to help the Hungarians, offered accommodation for some of the students for several weeks or even months. Afterwards, the students moved into "digs" and with an increase in their weekly pocket money they had to learn to fend for themselves. They relished the measure of independence this arrangement provided, while—just as in Cambridge—the daily language classes satisfied their need for a familiar Hungarian background and for a network of Hungarian friends, on whom they could depend for support. Of the 24 students attending the English course, 15 remained at Oxford and, at the beginning of October, all of them moved into their allocated colleges. And even if for many of them this was the first taste of college life, they had already amassed a great deal of useful information from those who had been living in colleges since December 1956, enough to give them assurance to settle down with relative ease and confidence. They certainly fared better than those students who had to move to a completely new place for their undergraduate studies and to begin yet again the slow process of adaptation.

The first couple of weeks of language tuition—at the universities offering interim accommodation—were driven more by enthusiasm than by professional competence. Sometimes it seemed that everyone in Britain wished to teach the newcomers a few words of English. The English family who had so kindly invited us refugees from the camp at Aldershot to their home, felt the need not only to acquaint us with what might be called the English "tea ceremony", but to give us language lessons. They pointed at objects in the living room, or had some pictures in their hand depicting objects, which they named and we were encouraged to repeat the names after them. The situation was only slightly less improvised at the English classes held at the temporary student hostels; most of the people who volunteered their help were not trained language teachers. Norrington voiced his concern about this unsatisfactory state of affairs, but in those early days of the CVCP Hungarian student scheme, other organizational matters enjoyed priority while everyone was more than aware that systematic English courses must also be set up as soon as possible: "Our Hungarians now in Oxford have begun English classes on Monday this week"—wrote Norrington in early December—"which are at present on an improvised and amateur basis. We think that the problem of teaching English, up to university standard, even in the nine months between now and next October, is a difficult one and probably only possible with efficient professional help. You will realise that English for foreigners is the one subject that nobody in this University is qualified to teach."[12] There were, of course, exceptions: at the University of Birmingham Dr. Horne had begun, with the help of his Hungarian friends, to organize the language course in December, which was then carried on under his guidance until the summer. Similarly, Dr. Hervei started his much admired English language course for Hungarian technical college students in Oxford, which became a worthy rival of the university course. Not to mention the University of Cambridge, where the task was eagerly undertaken by the Bell School of English.

On behalf of the School, its director, Frank Bell, offered his services as early as 11th December to the University, both for the short-term and for the regular course. One of the teachers at the Bell course was none other than Denis Sinor, already mentioned in connection with the students' entrance requirements. The presence of Denis Sinor proved invaluable for the Hungarian students. Being a Hungarian himself, he could, perhaps more than anyone else, provide explanation on the questions of English and Hungarian grammar and elucidate the meaning of English idioms. Some of the former Cambridge students still remember him and his help with affection. Frank Bell himself made a special mention of Sinor's contribution in his letter to Rattenbury: "I should like to pay special tribute

---

[12] Norrington, A. L. P.: *Memorandum by the President of Trinity.* 13 Dec. 1956. BLA UR6/OVS/H File 1.

to the work of D. Sinor without whose help (mainly in the form of teaching English grammar in the Hungarian language) the task would have been very much more difficult."[13] In addition to his teaching duties at the Bell School—and presumably academic work—Sinor had immediately begun to compile an English-Hungarian dictionary comprising over 7,000 words, which was published in 1957 under the title: *A modern Hungarian-English dictionary.*[14]

Although in the preface Sinor claimed that the dictionary would have a much wider use, it was primarily conceived as a useful, indeed indispensable tool for the teaching of English to the Hungarian students: "Although the compilation of this dictionary was begun under the impulse of the events that took place in Hungary in October and November, 1956, it claims to be more than a convenient tool to help the Hungarian refugees arriving in this country. It claims to be the only Hungarian-English dictionary with some pretensions to scholarship published in Great Britain."[15] The Hungarian students in Cambridge were actually involved in the work and their help was acknowledged by Sinor in his the preface to the book: "The compilation of this dictionary has greatly benefited by the help of those Hungarian students who under the sponsorship of the University of Cambridge have been following an intensive course of English set up by the Bell School of languages. Some of these students very obligingly went through the galley-proofs and their remarks helped me to suit the dictionary to the requirements of Hungarians arriving in this country."[16]

Hervei, Horne and Sinor were of Hungarian origin and, like so many of the Hungarians who had been living in Britain, offered their help. Those at the universities with the teaching of the Hungarian students, others by looking after them and, *in loco parentis*, providing for them a home instead of the home they had lost. Special mention should be made in this context of the Reverend and Mrs King of Edinburgh. As a young man, King had maintained the traditional close links between the Scottish and the Hungarian Protestant Churches when he travelled to Hungary in the 1930s. The journeys undertaken in the 16th and 17th centuries had normally been the other way around: scores of young men of the Protestant persuasion, called "peregrines", came to the British Isles to learn and to gain experience before returning to Hungary laden with all the

---

[13] Letter by Frank Bell to R. M. Rattenbury. 22 Apr. 1957. CAL UA R3453/1957.
[14] Sinor, Denis: *A modern Hungarian-English dictionary. Modern magyar-angol szótár.* Cambridge, 1957.
[15] Ibid. p.vi.
[16] Ibid. p.vii.

books they could carry.[17] King spent some time in Hungary and on his return to Britain, he brought with him his Hungarian wife, Magda. In the turbulent months of early 1957 the elderly couple gave all that they could – sympathy, advice, encouragement - to the refugee students at the University of Edinburgh's language course in helping them to settle down. When talking to some of the former Hungarian students at Edinburgh, they remembered them in the warmest of terms.[18]

The systematic, properly prepared and professionally conducted language courses started in earnest in January 1957. Every regional centre however, followed its own method of tuition and administrative arrangements. From the references already made to the Bell School of English at Cambridge, it is obvious that it can be regarded as the most efficiently organized course. This is not surprising, since it was run by a well-established language school which also offered teaching English for foreigners. Its director, Frank Bell, was also very quick to approach the University with a well thought-out plan, which, if accepted, could be put into action without delay. Rattenbury himself gave an early warning about the need to set up English classes for the refugee students; in his letter to the Heads of Colleges, dated 27th November 1956, he specifically mentioned it.[19] Still, even before the first group of students arrived at Cambridge, Frank Bell wrote a letter to Rattenbury telling him that his School would be willing to commence courses for the students at once and would only ask for the reimbursement of costs. The experience gained by the professional teachers at the interim course run during the Christmas vacation, would enable him to provide tailor-made tuition during the main course which could start in early January and would probably last six months. Rattenbury accepted his offer. With this early action Bell also beat the competition: soon after his letter, the Davies's School of English and several individuals also sent notes to Rattenbury about their willingness to participate in the language teaching. Rattenbury referred them to Dr Roughton for the teaching of the "Roughton students"; with what success it is not known, although four "Roughton students"—

---

[17] See, for example: Trócsányi, Berta: Református teológusok Angliában a XVI. És XVII. században. [Protestant students of divinity in England in the 16th and 17th centuries.] In: *Yolland emlékkönyv. Angol Filológiai Tanulmányok,* V-VI, 1944, p.115-146.
[18] Interview with András and Kornélia Szabó. 19 Jan. 2006.
[19] Material on the Cambridge language course, including the correspondence between Frank Bell and Rattenbury is the file "English course" at CAL UA R3453/1957.

probably the most promising ones—were later admitted with Rattenbury's permission to the university course.

At the end of December Frank Bell sent another long letter to Rattenbury, in which he summarized his observations about the short term course and detailed his plans for the main course starting in the Lent term. He was convinced that the students must concentrate on learning English; as he put it "they have got to put their noses to the particular grindstone of mastering as much as possible of the English language." The costs were to be limited to the payment of the teachers: £3 per week per student and administrative expenditure of 15 shillings per week per class. The School would supply the books, but these would have to be returned at the end of the course. (It is interesting to note that the CVCP ordered sets of dictionaries for all the students from Collet's bookshop, which normally dealt with the sale of printed material from the Soviet Union and the East European satellite states and with the dissemination of socialist propaganda in Britain. The big profit suddenly reaped by Collet's and the Hungarian publishers was one of the unforeseen consequences of the crushing of the revolution and the exodus of thousands to the West. The students were expected to pay for the books out of their own pockets, but half of the cost was later reimbursed. Several British publishing houses either gave away books to the students free of charge, or sold them textbooks and dictionaries at a greatly reduced price. There were also many private donations made specifically for the purchase of books.)[20]

After asking the students to take a test in order to establish the level of their knowledge of English, Frank Bell divided them into two groups: beginners and advanced students. Their progress was frequently measured by written tests and an end-of-term examination in April 1957, with the participation of external examiners. Frank Bell expressed his satisfaction with what had been achieved during the term and reported that the teachers "attacked this new problem with enthusiasm". He hoped that after the completion of the course the School would prepare a report on teaching the Hungarian students which would be of special interest and value to all who teach English as a foreign language. As for the continuation of the course, he felt that more attention should be paid to pronunciation. The next set of exams were planned for 21st June and he was convinced that the students even in the advanced group should continue to have tuition during

---

[20] A remarkable example of providing money for books for the use of the Hungarian students was given by Miss Imogen Holst, the director of the choir of Imperial College. On her retirement she asked that the donations collected by members of the College for her present should be used for the purchase of books for the students living in the hostel set up for them. ICA, Hungarian Relief, SS/1/4.

the summer, preferably by participating in the vacation course for foreign students organized by the Board of Extra-Mural Studies, while for the beginners the Bell School would continue to provide English classes. The final report, issued at the end of August stated that while only a single advanced student attended classes during the summer, all of the students in the beginners group participated willingly in the Bell School's summer language course. Frank Bell concluded his letter with the words that the teaching of the students "has been an absorbing interest and I think that the progress made and the standards attained have been on the whole reasonable and in some cases remarkable."

The University of Leeds faced a particular problem regarding the establishment of the language course. Although the University was happy to act as an interim reception centre, the Vice-Chancellor, Sir Charles R. Morris felt unduly pressurized by the CVCP, and especially by Lockwood, to take on the additional role of a regional language centre. This was intended to provide a course for between 20 to 25 students for the universities of the North of England. The Vice-Chancellor objected to this plan for two reasons. First, he had already made an arrangement with the Leeds College of Commerce regarding the English course which, he thought, would be quite satisfactory. The College was to provide the tuition free of charge, but could only accept 16 students, most of whom would be expected to study at Leeds University. The University would, of course, make provision for their residence and pastoral care, including their early introduction to the departments which they would join in the autumn. Secondly, Sir Charles Morris wanted to have only the Leeds students attending the language course, as the correspondence between Professor F. S. Dainton, Head of the Department of Chemistry and Professor S. E. Toulmin, the Chairman of the Leeds University Hungarian Committee reveals. Dainton's letter was in response to a request for summarizing what preparations the Department had in mind for the integration of the Hungarian students. These would start immediately and run parallel with the language course. The plan included pre-arranged special tutorials, the study and interpretation of certain exam questions, attending selected lectures, conversation sessions with students in the Department to increase the students' technical vocabulary and supervised work in the laboratories.[21] These arrangements would, of course, make sense only for the Leeds "home" students.

---

[21] Letter by F. S. Dainton to S. E. Toulmin. 11 Feb. 1957. Leeds University Central Records Office

Sir Charles Morris, convinced that the above plan would be the best solution as it offered the greatest benefit for the students, and that all universities should act similarly, decided to take matters into his own hands. He sent a confidential letter to Dr. C. I. C. Bosanquet, Rector of King's College, Newcastle upon Tyne—today the University of Newcastle—in which he asked him to look after the five students allocated to King's College and also to arrange the language tuition for them locally, giving his reasons as follows: "I have always taken the view that on balance it would be very much better for the universities to keep their own students from now on and to make arrangements to teach them English at home. You will know why I have thought so from the Vice-Chancellors' Committee meetings and in any case the reasons are obvious. I have made it clear all along that whatever arrangements were made for other students we should want to have own Leeds students in Leeds."[22] A similar letter was sent to the University of Sheffield, for which Leeds was also supposed to act as the regional language centre. Both institutions accepted Sir Charles Morris's suggestion and the CVCP was simply notified of the change. Consequently, the short term language course for the 20 students arriving with Flight II was held at Leeds by the British Council, but after their dispersal, the course at the College of Commerce was organized for the 11 students of Leeds University (seven of them studying for a first degree, three of them postgraduates and one a student of the Leeds College of Arts) and three other students for whom their own university was not able to provide language tuition. Therefore, the Vice-Chancellor's wish to integrate his own students into the life at Leeds University as early as possible and to lay a rock-solid foundation for their future was granted.

The University of London allocated another house in Tavistock Square - to be used between 14th January and 26th September - for their English classes. Dr. Cushing accepted responsibility for the organization of the course and the teachers were drawn partly from the staff and students of the School of Slavonic and East European Studies—the institution where Cushing was a lecturer—and partly from the Institute of Education of the University of London. The latter received a large number of postgraduates from all over the world, who came to London to pursue their research and to gain some teaching practice. In the spring and summer of 1957, their practical exercises mostly consisted of teaching the refugee students English. The young teachers enthusiastically responded to the challenge; the relationship between them and the Hungarian students soon surpassed

---

[22] Letter by C. R. Morris to C. I. C. Bosanquet. 21 Dec. 1956. Leeds University Central Record Office.

the normal contact between teachers and their pupils: the teachers wanted to learn everything about life behind the Iron Curtain and the revolution and the students listened to the tales about the countries from where the teachers had come. Parties were thrown and friendships were forged, which lasted many years after the teachers had gone home. Initially, the London course was set up only for the "Quota" students, but they were later joined by the Ford students and by those who received grants from other sources. So, the numbers attending the course were boosted from the original 34 to 50 by the end of June examination. According to the records, a few students did not take the exam—they might have got cold feet at the last moment—19 passed satisfactorily and 19 were recommended to continue attending classes during the summer months. Some of the students failed, but even they were invited to a meeting to discuss their problems and to explore their chances for the future. The second and final examination was scheduled for the end of September. There are no records extant about the participants and the results they achieved, but according to the list of students studying at the colleges of London University, almost all the students successfully completed the language course. It was only a small group of the Ford students who were advised to continue with their language studies until the end of December.

The same success rate applied to Oxford, although the initial organization of the language course met with difficulties. This was surprising, since it was Norrington who insisted as early as November 1956 that setting up the language tuition was of paramount importance and that the arrangements for it should proceed without delay. The Committee already turned to the Education Department of the British Council for advice in December and received the recommendation from the Council to appoint Mr Edwards, previously an English teacher with excellent credentials at the British Council's office in Athens, to lead the language course, but with a warning that he would not be able to begin teaching before 18th January. Because of the unavoidable delay, the Committee regarded this proposal as untenable and after putting some pressure on the British Council, the supervisor of the teachers, Mr Cartledge agreed to start the course himself: "I am anxious to lose no time in starting the course and have therefore decided to take a hand."[23] Therefore, before the arrival of Edwards, the students were tested and divided into two groups: advanced, to be taught by Edwards and beginners, whose teaching would be undertaken by another language teacher. Both the British Council and

---

[23] Documents relating to the Oxford University's English language course for the Hungarian students is at BLA UR6/OVS/H File 1.

Edwards recommended Mr. Bayard for this post; he had also been teaching English in Athens—hence his acquaintance with Edwards—and had many years of experience as a TEFL (Teaching English as a Foreign Language) teacher.

The English course proper therefore began in the middle of January. The problems, however, continued, this time regarding the payment of the teachers. The salary of Edwards was actually paid by the British Council—which also provided the room for the classes at its offices at 1 Wellington Square—but it would not underwrite the payment of Bayard for his services as this should be the responsibility of the University. The Hungarian Committee applied to various committees of the University and to D. M. Hawke, the Vice-Chancellor himself, for the necessary sum, estimated at £500, but this was repeatedly refused on the grounds that the Committee had raised enough money for the Hungarian appeal to cover this additional expenditure. Furthermore, Hawke pointed out that the chairman of the British universities' main grant-giving body, the University Grants Committee, had made it clear that the government would not think it appropriate to spend the money allocated to universities for the education of British students on teaching the Hungarians English. Finally, a solution was found: the Hebdomadal Council approved the request that the Curators of the University Chest release the required sum from the Cecil Jackson bequest to cover Bayard's salary.

That Norrington's sustained campaign ended with success in obtaining extra funding is understandable, as both he and the other members of his committee were influential people in Oxford. They were relieved that at least at this stage, they need not touch the money the appeal had raised, since early in 1957 they were acutely aware that the fund, however substantial it seemed, would not cover the cost of the education the students allocated to Oxford unless additional financial help was forthcoming. A large part of the meetings of the Hungarian Committee was devoted to calculating and re-calculating the projected costs and it was noted with great satisfaction that the language course would not add to the expected expenditure. In the end the English tuition cost nothing: the BCAR transferred £20 000 to the CVCP in June and a further £28 230 was allocated from the Lord Mayor's Fund for this purpose, from which all costs met by the universities were reimbursed.

The personality of the two Oxford teachers could not have been more different. Edwards, with his spotless pinstriped three piece suit, elegant matching neckties and furled umbrella was the embodiment of the proverbial English gentleman. Never uttering a loud word, he kept order in the class by slightly raising his eyebrow. Bayard, on the other hand, was emphasising every phrase and every grammatical point he made with his whole body; wildly gesticulating, shouting and miming, he was, almost physically, trying to transfer the knowledge of English to his pupils. Both of them kept records on the progress of the students, sending their reports to the Hungarian Committee first weekly then fortnightly and a detailed description of the performance of each student at the end-of-term examinations with recommendations about their transfer from the beginners' to the advanced students' group, or their exemption of attending further classes. Bayard's comments were succinct, limited to brief notes on the achievement – or lack of it – of the students, while Edwards composed in a paragraph or two a complete picture, including a psychological insight, of each individual. "Has a fairly good knowledge of English"—he wrote about one of his charges as a first assessment soon after the commencement of the course—"which he imagines better than it is... Has a journalistic flair in his written work, though expression still lags behind content." And after correcting an essay written by the same student, some three weeks later: "Has been slightly shaken by the quantity of red-pencilling in his written work, but still wants to run before he can walk." Or, assessing the qualities of another student he wrote: "Actual knowledge more limited, but a quick learner with an amusing streak of fantasy... He is a curious and not unattractive blend of the gay and the pedantic." And finally, trying to discover the causes of the underperformance of an otherwise gifted student: "Suffers from morbid conscientiousness. Though a poor linguist, his real trouble is mental constipation, marked by the usual symptoms: polysyllabism, endlessly involved sentences full of abstract terms, inability to think simply and correctly. Is much too sensitive about his oral weakness. A bad examinee."

The first formal test was held at the end of March and as a result, the groups were readjusted. The next examination was planned for 14th June with the aim of exempting those who had passed the exam with flying colours from further language classes. However, only a single student was deemed to have reached the desired standard – László Jámbor, who then spent the summer months working in a laundry and earning some money for such luxuries as a radio and a tape recorder. All the other students were required to attend English classes throughout the summer. As Norrington noted in his report on the progress of the students at the end of May: "The continuation of the English course during the vacation... may interfere with vacation plans that are being made for some of the Hungarians, but the course should clearly have precedence over any such plans."[24]

Norrington was well aware of the causes which hindered some of the students in their language studies. Lists of students who missed several classes were regularly submitted by Bayard and Edwards to the Hungarian Committee with dire warnings about their ability to assimilate sufficient English for their university courses in the autumn. Then there were those students—most of them living in the colleges—who never turned up at the English classes. While some of the colleges were very concerned about their truancy and even recommending the Committee to send down the student in question, others cared little: if their Hungarian student proved himself to be a brilliant physicist, who would mind his faltering English? Exeter College on the other hand, decided to provide additional support by asking the College tutor to give extra language tuition to its Hungarian student. It was, because of these classes that the tutor, Mervyn Jones, a lecturer in classics, learned much about the revolution.[25] Not interested in politics, he only realized that something serious was happening in Eastern Europe when, one day, bumping into a newsvendor's placard he was struck by the headline: "Civil war in Hungary". Soon after that, he found himself teaching not one but four refugee students: the Exeter student and three others, among them Sándor Éles, the actor-student. Later however, he sadly admitted that the student at Exeter, for whom the language classes had been set up, was more interested in playing water polo than in immersing himself in the mysteries of English grammar. Mervyn Jones, however, intrigued about the mother tongue of his pupils, decided to learn Hungarian. He became an expert in 19th century Hungarian literature and in his books he explored the life and works of selected Hungarian authors, contributing a series of often strikingly original interpretation of their verse or prose and thus fostering their appreciation by English readers.[26]

The students who had missed their English tuition were collectively labelled "the bad boys" by the Committee and Norrington was entrusted with the task of severely reprimanding them, pointing out that their truancy, for whatever reason it had happened, would seriously jeopardize their future at Oxford. A few of the students in this group were also referred to as "the politicians", as they were still engaged in political activities spending days or even weeks away from Oxford, not only in London but also travelling abroad on a political mission. Norrington

---

[24] Norrington, A. L. P.: *Hungarian students. From the President of Trinity.* 29 May 1957. BLA UR6/OVS/H File.1.

[25] Interview with Mervyn Jones. 19 Jan. 2005.

[26] For example, Jones, D. Mervyn: *Five Hungarian writers.* 1966.

understood perfectly well how difficult—one might say impossible—it was for the students to erase from their minds the memory of the heady days of the revolution, to switch from trying to do something actively for their country—still seeking help from the West in the darkening days of the increasing reprisals—and to devote the whole of their time to nothing but to memorising the English irregular verbs. A few months earlier they had been, individually and collectively, demanding the end of the Communist regime and the demolition of the cold war structures through the recognition of Hungary's neutrality. They were ready to change the world. Instead, they were now being asked to bury all the responsibilities they had so gladly embraced under the heap of the fifty new English words they were required to learn each day.

Some of the students had left Hungary only to build personal contacts with student organizations in the West, asking them to intercede on behalf of Hungary with their governments, or with international organizations like the United Nations.[27] They felt that the *raison d'être* for their being in the free world was to spread the word about the true nature of Communism and the indomitable clamour for freedom by the people incarcerated behind the Iron Curtain. Almost all of the students who had escaped wanted eventually to return to Hungary, to help with the rebuilding of the country by using all the knowledge and experience they had gained abroad. They were convinced that they were simply on a study tour, not of their own free will but by the force of circumstance. To make the most of it, however, meant forgetting all that they thought the other half of their mission entailed; it was only possible to survive the brainwashing of the intensive language course by suspending all other activities as if the world did not exist outside the English classes.

It was the "politicians" who rebelled against this and Norrington sympathized with their predicament. Two of the Oxford students, György Gömöri and András Sándor had drafted an appeal to the students of the free world, asking for the expression of their solidarity with the students of Hungary, whilst still in Vienna where they had arrived as delegates of the Revolutionary Committee of the Budapest students. As the days passed they met with other students who were already contemplating the creation of a world-wide organization of refugee students, the Union of Free Hungarian Students (UFHS), which would carry the torch of the revolution onwards when, as expected, the MEFESZ (Union of Hungarian University and College Students), which had been set up by the defiant students themselves on the eve of the revolution, would be forcibly

---

[27] See the quoted works by Alpár Bujdosó, György Gömöri and Gyula Várallyay.

dissolved. Gömöri and Sándor arrived in England on the first chartered aircraft and after a few days in London, they were transferred to Oxford. They did not stay there long; in December they travelled back to the Continent, to persuade the officials of COSEC (Coordinating Secretariat of the National Unions of Students) at its headquarters in Leiden, Holland, to call an emergency meeting of all their members to discuss and advance the case of Hungary. COSEC being apolitical and slow moving, would not respond to their request as urgently as they had anticipated. The two students returned to Oxford somewhat disheartened, but were eager to seek fresh initiatives. Soon they formed a new organization, the External Committee of the University Students' Revolutionary Committee and attended several meetings on the Continent—for example the first meeting of the Hungarian Revolutionary Council at Strasbourg—as representatives of the refugee students. In tandem with their activity on the international stage, they and some other Oxford students such as László Jámbor or László Péter, were also busy setting up the local organization of UFHS in Britain.

I still vividly recall that wintry afternoon when we were asked to abandon the English classes in Tavistock Square and to hurry to the Student Union building, because some Hungarian students from Oxford wanted to talk to us. The first person to speak was an agitated young man, with blazing eyes and fiery words, György Gömöri. He said that we were now the last repository of the spirit of the revolution and it was our sacred duty not to allow its light to be extinguished. We must continue to remind the world of its missed opportunity to stand by the freedom-fighters; we should be the living conscience of the West. The MEFESZ should be rebuilt as the UFHS and he asked us to join its British branch there and then. Moved by what he said, we agreed with him and most of us signed up. Then we returned to the English classes and the commitments we had made soon became a hazy, ill-defined action which we were supposed to carry out, but which – we felt - could wait. It could be postponed until the completion of the language course, or of our university studies. In any case, little time was left for extra-curricular activities. The relentless daily routine slowly extinguished our enthusiasm and smothered our will to continue protesting. To submit ourselves totally to its iron-fisted rule gave us the only hope for completing at least our "study tour". (Yet, the UFHS in Britain lived on: its president, Gábor Schábert and secretary, Pál Hollander sent a letter of thanks to the CVCP on behalf of the association on the anniversary of the revolution in October 1957, for all that they had done for the refugee students.)[28]

The lack of interest in understanding the desperation of the refugee students by the international student organizations also hastened the students' disillusionment. By the time these committees went through the motion of considering and re-considering the requests of the Hungarians, it was too late for any effective action. The revolution was in the process of becoming history and the students' sole task was by then to prepare for their university studies. Norrington knew that it would have been futile to ask the "politicians" to abandon their convictions; time would solve the problem of the "bad boys". And truly, by late spring, they too were also busily turning the pages of the dictionaries and writing the essays, even if, almost surreptitiously, they still found a few spare minutes to attend political meetings, write an article or to compose poetry.

The transition from being involved in politics to becoming a sedate university student was also hindered by the admiration, or even reverence, with which the Hungarian émigré writers treated the refugee students. It was Zoltán Szabó[29] and László Cs. Szabó,[30]—to mention only the two most significant—who had the greatest impact on the newcomers. Neither of them, being abroad on the eve of the Communist take-over in the late 1940s—Cs. Szabó with a scholarship in Italy, Zoltán Szabó as cultural attaché at the Hungarian Embassy in Paris—decided to return home. To earn a living, Cs. Szabó found employment in the BBC Hungarian Section and Zoltán Szabó in Radio Free Europe, working in its London office. The position offered them the opportunity to continue writing and to keep in touch with what happened in Hungary. Cs. Szabó, a prominent essayist and the director of the literary program of Hungarian Radio before the Second World War, contacted the students arriving on the first chartered aircraft—the Oxford group—by turning up in the Lancaster Gate Hotel the next day and inviting four of them to participate in a lengthy, in-depth interview to be broadcast by the BBC Hungarian programme. For him, the students represented the authentic voice of the revolution, and for the students the interview offered the best chance to put their views and experience on record.[31] Zoltán Szabó, who as a young man had written the

---

[28] CVCP. Joint meeting of the Committee on Hungarian students and the Sub-Committee dealing with the allocation of the students: *Minutes*. 14 Dec. 1957. UoLA, CB3/1/3/6.
[29] See his obituary in *The Times*, 24 Aug. 1984.
[30] See his obituary in *The Times*, 1 Oct. 1984.
[31] A large part of the interviews are included in the book: BBC World Service: *A szabadság hullámhosszán: az 1956-os magyar forradalom története a BBC*

most incisive and influential sociological description of poverty in a Hungarian village[32] and who had bravely voiced his opposition to the road Hungary had taken when siding with Germany during the war, gathered the students interested in politics around him, to discuss and dissect world events and analyse how these might affect Hungary.

Some of the students were budding writers themselves who had had a handful of poems, short stories or newspaper articles published in Hungary and as newly-arrived refugee writers, they eagerly participated in the lively, often turbulent émigré literary life in London in the early months of 1957. They joined the P. E. N. in Exile, were founding members of the Association of Hungarian Writers Abroad - which came into being at a meeting in the Hotel Russell on 15th March - and wrote pieces for the burgeoning new periodicals and newspapers set up by the émigrés, including the *Irodalmi Ujság* (Literary Gazette) and *Magyar Szó* (Hungarian Word). In 1994, one of the former émigré writers recalled those stirring events and the student participants: "The young writers turned up at our meetings already as students at Cambridge or Oxford, bringing with them the spirit of freedom and sense of history of the ancient universities, of which they had not an inkling a year ago. Among them were András Sándor, the poet, who later became a university lecturer, a well-known expert of German literature and one of the founders of the Hungarian avant-garde periodical *Arkánum*, published in the United States; the always-alert György Gömöri, translator and propagator of Polish literature...; László Márton, author of entertaining and smoothly-flowing novellas and many others who truly began their career as writers in the newly re-founded *Irodalmi Ujság*."[33]

And it was just as difficult to give up, or even curtail the urge to participate fully in the unfolding exciting literary scene, to write freely about all that mattered to the young men, and to withdraw from émigré politics. Because this was the first time that they were able to say what they wanted, without fear of reprisal - and they were granted a responsive audience, both English and Hungarian. Yet, they acknowledged that Norrington's warnings had to be heeded, that common sense dictated the

---

elmondásában. Szerkesztette Pallai Péter és Sárközi Mátyás. [On freedom's wavelength: the history of the Hungarian revolution as told by the BBC; ed. By Péter Pallai and Mátyás Sárközi.] Budapest, 2006.

[32] Szabó, Zoltán: A tardi helyzet. [The situation at Tard.] 1936.

[33] Aczél, Tamás: Kezdők az Oxford Streeten: kísérletek egy korszak idézésére. [Beginners on Oxford Street: an attempt to recall an age.] In: *Az 1956-os Magyar Forradalom Történetének Dokumentációs és Kutatóintézete. Évkönyv III.* 1994. p.74.

suspension of literary activities, at least for the time being. They had to concentrate all their efforts on their studies if they wanted to obtain a degree and the first step for this was, of course, the need to pass the English examination. Political and literary ambitions had to be abandoned while sustaining the hope that the time would come when they could again write about the unforgettable days of the revolution.

Even those, who had willingly succumbed to the daily drudgery of the English classes, occasionally wanted to break the monotony by visiting a museum, viewing an exhibition, exploring the town, going to the cinema or reading a book. The students devoured any Hungarian book or journal they could lay their hands on. Émigré Hungarian publications were read from cover to cover. Books in English had to wait until late spring, when the students, elated by the progress they had made, tried, with the help of a dictionary, to follow a story in a work of fiction. The favourite book by consensus happened to be Hemingway's short novel—or long short story?—*The old man and the sea*. It is impossible to recall who had suggested it as suitable reading: one of the teachers perhaps? Or had one of the students had discovered it? It certainly helped to ease the linguistic torment of the past few months. Hemingway's style was terse, the vocabulary kept to the absolute minimum, the sentences were brief and to the point. The story was simple, yet monumental: the struggle and interdependence of man and nature. Others opted for the short stories of Somerset Maugham. They were entertaining yet sophisticated with an elegant but easy style. It was a first introduction to the way of life and attitudes of the English upper middle classes. Conan Doyle's *Sherlock Holmes* stories and the crime fiction of Agatha Christie were also much more than just a good read: the constant repetition, albeit always from a slightly different angle, of the scene of the crime, the appearance of the key characters, their motives and the words they uttered. All this greatly contributed to the retention of every linguistic twist and turn in the reader's mind.

There were, of course, plenty of blunders in picking suitable books. Dillon's bookshop in Bloomsbury, then still called the University bookshop, held a sale of paperbacks around Easter-time in 1957. I was living nearby in a student hostel, because my college was closed during the Easter break. Carefully eyeing the offer of Penguin fiction laid out on a tray, I decided after a few days to purchase a book, the title of which seemed promising. It was D. H. Lawrence's *Sons and lovers*. Its cover was dusty and slightly torn, but its price matched the tiny amount I could spare from the meagre pocket money I received. I settled down with the book in the built-in-cupboard in my room, near the hot water pipes. The central heating had been switched off and the pipes provided some protection against bitter cold of the merciless east winds. With a dictionary on my lap, I began to immerse myself in the story. This, however, proved exceedingly difficult as I could not find a whole host of words in the dictionary: mostly the ones peppering the dialogue. It took me a long time to discover that for the sake of authenticity, Lawrence preferred to use the dialect of the Nottinghamshire miners. No wonder that someone still in the early stages of acquiring English found this a rather disheartening experience.

To be able to read a book only with the help of a dictionary was, of course, inevitable for a long time. Albin Závody, an engineering student at the University of Sheffield remembered how boldly he had decided to buy the book which was of greatest interest: the newly published work by Arthur Bryant, *War diaries 1939-1943*, based on the war diaries of Lord Alanbrooke. He knew some English as his mother had been an English language teacher in Hungary and had also taught him, but it still took several months for him to read the book. Being a scientist, he could not help conducting an experiment: every day he noted how many new words he found on each page. On the very first page there were 33 words he had to look up in the dictionary, but on the last page he encountered only three unknown words. This he regarded as a genuinely measurable progress.[34] The progress made by the students in learning English might have been deemed to be slow, fast or just about satisfactory, but almost all of them passed the final exams at the end of September. They were ready to start their university studies.

---

[34] Interview with Albin Závody. 2 March 2006.

CHAPTER VIII

THE STUDENT YEARS

To arrive at an accurate figure of the Hungarian students enrolled in British universities is fraught with difficulties. The problem is not the lack of data, but its abundance. The numbers quoted in various reports and the numerous lists of names do not always correspond and while there is plenty of overlap, there are also obvious gaps, especially regarding the students studying in technical colleges. The survey carried out by Dare and Hollander might be mentioned as an example of how, even in a single document, the numbers constantly change and contradict each other. The authors first quote a figure of 350 students enrolled in British universities, then change it to 370. In one of the appendices, however, they refer to a more plausible figure of 391 students in total.

In their introduction Dare and Hollander outline their schedule and the progress they have made. The concept of the survey was formulated in early 1958 and by April they were ready to set up its basic structure. During the following two months a pilot questionnaire was tested on a selected group of 12 students and, after the authors had decided to gather the information by means of anonymous postal questionnaires, they sent them out in late June, with a covering letter explaining the aims of the survey and the methods they wished to use.[1] The Hungarian Office and WUS provided the addresses of the students to which the material was dispatched. In the letter Dare and Hollander strongly and repeatedly emphasized that the replies should be sent back anonymously, since they were aware of the students' reluctance to provide any information about themselves, let alone voicing their opinion freely about a range of topics, some of them rather personal. The experience of repeatedly being forced to supply details - mostly fabricated - about their background under Communist rule was still very much alive in their minds as well as the fear that anything they might reveal would, in some way or other, harm their

---

[1] Dare, Alan and Hollander, Paul: Op. cit., p.3.

parents, relatives and friends who had remained in Hungary. Anonymity—Dare and Hollander thought—would protect them.[2]

During the summer, the authors received 170 replies, well below the number they had expected. The reason for this meagre response might have been the students' feelings of insecurity or—as Dare and Hollander thought more likely—a problem with the postal delivery of the questionnaires, as the students had already left their term-time accommodation without providing forwarding addresses. They might have been travelling in Europe or working somewhere in Britain. On the advice of their supervisor, Dr. Himmelweit, they decided to send out the same questionnaire with a new letter in October. In this letter they specifically mentioned that they had sent out 350 questionnaires in June, "to all Hungarian students in Great Britain".[3] The response this time was more than satisfactory: 279 completed forms were returned, many of them with the name and address of the respondents. According to Dare and Hollander's calculation, the returned forms represented 78 per cent of the questionnaires they had sent out, high enough to validate their findings. (The 78 per cent response, however, also implies that they must have dispatched the forms to slightly more than 350 people—the correct figure should be 357—or, that they had sent a few forms to non-university students as well. The replies to the question "How old are you?" indicate that by October 1958 at least four of the respondents had not reached their 18th birthday; they must have been students in secondary education preparing for their GCEs.)[4]

Dare and Hollander completed the analysis of the replies and drew up their report during the spring of 1959 and submitted it on the 1st of May. In the introduction they described the parameters of the survey, and in order to place their sample in a world-wide context they provided the following figures: about 200,000 refugees had left Hungary in late 1956 and early 1957, among them approximately 6000 to 8000 university students, of whom 370 were currently studying in Great Britain.[5] The total of 370 students seems to be a revised figure—20 more students than previously mentioned—but it is unclear how the authors reached it, as it is not related at all to the student numbers given in the tables of Appendix III.[6] There the student numbers are tabulated by the grant giving bodies for the two consecutive academic years of 1957-58 and 1958-59. According to

---

[2] Ibid. Appendix I., pp.I-II.
[3] Ibid. Appendix I., p.III.
[4] Ibid. Appendix II., Table 47, p.XLIII.
[5] Ibid. p.1.
[6] Ibid. Appendix III. pp.XLV-XLVI.

the tables, the number of enrolled students in 1957-58 totalled 391 and in the following year 374. The latter figure included the 321 students who had remained from the first-year intake; the others had either completed their courses, had been suspended or had withdrawn. There were also 53 students newly enrolled in 1958-59. The information was supplied by the Hungarian Office and WUS and its validity cannot be questioned. It should, however, be noted that neither the Hungarian Office nor WUS kept records of certain categories of students, such as of those supported by various institutions or individuals. These students were, therefore, never included in the "official" figures. Furthermore, the tables list 85 students studying in technical colleges and polytechnics, which is a very low figure indeed, if the lists issued by LEAs or even the statement given by Walters to the Lord Mayor's Fund—in which he mentioned 140 technical college students—are taken into account.[7] Dare and Hollander did not add to the 391 students enrolled in 1957-58 the 53 students newly enrolled in 1958-59. Had they done so, the total number of 444 Hungarian refugee students in British higher education would have been much closer to reality. Still, in the absence of more detailed, reliable and currently accessible archive material, the figures quoted above provide enough proof that the number of students continuing their education in Britain was likely to be in the region of 500, especially if we add the missing technical college students, whose number, according to various estimates, probably reached about 60-70 persons. The validity of this calculation is supported by the fact that it closely matches the estimated number of places for which grants were available.

The most detailed information on the numbers and progress of the "Quota" students, directly under the control of the CVCP, is provided by the annual reports compiled by the Hungarian Office and presented to the CVCP's Hungarian Committee.[8] The students were listed by the universities where they studied or, in the case of a few individuals, by the institutions providing their grants. The tables include the subjects the students followed, the exams they sat and the results they achieved. A brief summary of the reports sent by the universities to the Hungarian Office highlights the perceived abilities and attitudes of the students and the progress they have made. These comments—often no more than a few of words—are revealing (good student, very conscientious, hard working, most satisfactory, acceptable college member, but also weak, failed all exams), especially if observed over the years. The progress reports note if

---

[7] The Lord Mayor of London's National Hungarian & Central European Relief Fund. *Report Nov. 1956-Sept. 1958.* [1958.] p.66.
[8] CVCP. *Progress reports.* UoLA, CB3/5/1/1-5.

a student has finished his studies and the class of degree he has obtained, or the estimated date of the completion of his studies. They also record whether or not students were allowed to repeat a year or were suspended for a period (some of the architecture students, for example, were advised to gain work experience before continuing their studies), or, if after repeatedly failing the exams they were dismissed.

It is surprising that the changes between the first lists of the allocations of the "Quota" students, drawn up in early 1957 and their matriculation lists were very few, although it is sometimes difficult to decipher and reconcile the various manuscript notes on the lists referring to the final destination of a particular student. Transfers were also kept to the minimum, but again, the university authorities were willing to agree with a recommendation to move a student somewhere else, if they found the argument for the change convincing. Other changes included the sources of funding. Some of the original "Quota" students were awarded special scholarships. At Cambridge, for example, Alfred Sperber received a bursary from Trinity College, or at Manchester University one of the Hungarian students was entirely supported by the undergraduates, while at Southampton University, a student received a grant from Winchester School. The vacant places were immediately filled from the pool of "U" students waiting for a university place. Conversely, three students who had been registered as privately funded were transferred to CVCP funding in October 1957.

Only a handful of students were barred from matriculation as they were deemed unsuitable to pursue university studies. Even in these cases however, the universities acted with great circumspection. The correspondence between institutions or departments clearly illustrates the care with which the potential of the student in question was repeatedly evaluated and some sort of solution for him or her was sought. Sometimes two universities agreed on the transfer of a student if they felt that the change might help him to continue his studies with a modicum of success. The records of Norrington's Hungarian Committee in Oxford are especially revealing of the repeated efforts made to help the so-called "problem students".

Among the Hungarian students at Oxford it was perhaps Antal Ormay who found it almost impossible to adapt to the merciless requirements of rapid assimilation to regular student life. A budding writer, he wished to remain a Hungarian writer in England too. There were many opportunities for the publications of his writings in the bourgeoning émigré newspapers and periodicals. He was a member of the circle of young intellectuals gathering around Zoltán Szabó who were keeping the spirit of the revolution alive, despairing about its suppression and outraged by the news of widespread persecution and reprisals. They were convinced that their primary duty was to serve the cause of Hungary and they cared little about starting a new life in Britain. The preparations for devoting themselves exclusively to university studies were abhorrent to them. And while slowly, one by one, they succumbed to the pressure of adhering to the demands set for them by the CVCP, Ormay was not willing to make any concessions. The language teachers complained vociferously about his non-attendance and his college voiced grave concern over whether he would be able to begin university studies at all. A solution for his problem was finally found – with Norrington's active participation – in the mutual agreement between the Oxford Hungarian Committee and Swansea College of the University of Wales. He was to transfer to Swansea where, under the guidance of his teachers, full of goodwill towards him, he would study for a degree in philosophy. However, Swansea was unable to contribute to financing his studies. Oxford therefore agreed to pay for his tuition and to provide for his maintenance. Ormay received no degree at Swansea. After years of vicissitudes, but strengthened by conquering his inner torment, he finally succeeded in obtaining a degree in philosophy and psychology entirely through his own efforts at University College London. Later he established a new branch of psychiatric practice in London, founded and edited a professional journal and is currently working as a psychiatrist in Budapest.[9]

The Oxford Hungarian Committee made it possible for several Hungarian refugee students to obtain their degrees at other universities, while continuing to accept responsibility for financing their studies. In addition to Ormay, three Oxford students studied for degrees at the School of Slavonic and East European Studies and all the Oxford based medical students who, while attending classes at Oxford, sat exams and gained their qualifications at the External Department of the University of London. No explanation can be found for this arrangement in the currently accessible files. Nor can the full documentation on the progress of the students be examined in the documents of the Hungarian Office deposited in the Archives of London University. Each university provided lengthy reports on the achievements of their Hungarian students annually, but the files containing the correspondence are closed until the middle of this century. So the success and failures of the students can only be glimpsed from the dry statistics and few scribbled remarks on the progress reports.

---

[9] Interview with Antal Ormay. 15 Nov. 2004.

According to the first progress report submitted at the end of the academic year of 1957-58, there were 154 "Quota" students admitted to university courses in October 1957 after they had successfully passed the language exams. By June 1957 six of the "Quota" students had completed their studies and obtained their degrees. This was a remarkable achievement even if these students had a reasonable knowledge of English when they arrived in England and had completed three or more years of study at a Hungarian university. The CVCP however, registered with regret that nearly a third of the "Quota" students—48 students—had failed the end-of-year exams. The Vice-Chancellors knew perfectly well that this dismal result should not be ascribed to a lack of effort by the students— their intelligence and hard work were much appreciated as revealed in the reports by their teachers—but to their inadequate knowledge of English. Already at the end of March, the Vice-Chancellors of Aberdeen, Glasgow and Manchester had voiced their concern about this at the meeting of the Committee recommending that further language courses should be organized and that those Hungarian students who might fail the exams should be allowed to repeat the year.[10] At the end of June 1958 meeting of the CVCP Lockwood offered some guidelines to the universities on how to treat the students who had failed: "Where it is clearly in the student's best interest not to encourage hopes of later success he should be told. His allowance should continue for up to two months and then cease. This should allow time for him to be helped to find a post by the Ministry of Labour. When the student appears to be more promising academically, it is felt that he should have the benefit of doubt."[11] That 29 students of the failed 48 were presumably encouraged to repeat the year and were keen to take up the offer, had considerably contributed to the overall success of the scheme.

Nevertheless, 19 "Quota"students withdrew from their studies at the end of the first year and a further 19 at the end of the second. In the following years, however, the number of dropouts began to decrease: in June 1960 a total of 12 students decided to withdraw from their studies and in the following year only three. At the same time however, the number of students obtaining their degrees revealed an opposing trend: 19 students received their qualifications in 1959 and in 1960 the number reached a record high with 39 students completing their studies. The following year showed a decline - 14 students receiving their degrees - but by that time the overall number of Hungarian students still pursuing their

---

[10] CVCP: *Minutes.*28 March 1958. CVCPA.
[11] CVCP: *Agendum 6. Memorandum by the Vice-Chancellor of the University of London.* 20 June, 1958. CVCPA.

studies was, relatively speaking, very small indeed. A final summary, produced for the CVCP in January 1962, lumped the "Quota" and Ford students together. This report analyses the results for both categories of students between 1957 and 1961 as follows: by the end of 1961 exactly 100 students had obtained their degrees, 30 were still studying, six had suspended their studies but were to return to university, 76 had withdrawn (but five had indicated that they would like to continue at a later date) and one had died.[12]

The Hungarian Office compiled separate annual progress reports for the Ford students, similar to those on the "Quota" students.[13] The decline of the Ford student numbers however, had already begun in Vienna. The Ford Foundation had offered to support 75 students studying in Britain, but during the interviews Walters and Professor Greig could only find 68 individuals whom they could recommend for acceptance by British universities. While in Austria, their number further dwindled to 55. Nine students decided to emigrate to other countries and by the time the travel arrangements had been made, four potential students could not be traced. Of the Ford students arriving in England, one returned to Austria almost immediately and seven others dropped out at the end of the first year. Drawing on the experience of preparing the "Quota" students for their university courses, the CVCP decided to lengthen the language tuition for the Ford students considerably; initially the course was to last until Christmas 1957, then it was extended to the summer of 1958. Many of the Ford students therefore started their university studies only in October 1958, a year later than most of the others but presumably much better prepared. The number of dropouts, however, showed a very similar tendency to the "Quota" students: by the end of 1961, 23 Ford students had withdrawn while 22 had received their degrees. A few students were still at university, and because the Ford grant was also available for postgraduates, some of them were still writing up their theses. Although there are no more progress reports after the end of 1961, it can be safely assumed that a fair number of those students still pursuing their studies beyond that date also obtained degrees. Furthermore, a few universities also reported that some of the Hungarian students, who, according to the progress reports, had dropped out earlier, had decided to return in the second half of the 1960s to complete their studies. It can, therefore, be stated that more than half of the "Quota" and Ford students finished their university courses and obtained their degrees successfully, and presumably

---

[12] CVCP: *Agendum 20. Analysis of results 1957-61: Quota and Ford students.* 26 Jan 1962. CVCPA.
[13] UoLA, CB3/5/2/1-5.

the same applies to the 89 WUS, 28 NCB, 9 Free Europe and 7 Gulbenkian students, as well as to the approximately 145-150 students studying in technical colleges – although there are scant records extant on the achievement of the latter group.

The reminiscences of the former students reveal that whatever subject they had chosen to study, it was the constant, never-ending and seemingly hopeless struggle with English that determined their progress, especially in the first year. Yet the survey by Dare and Hollander devoted little attention to this underlying problem. They questioned the students on their knowledge of English but only with the aim of establishing how effectively it had helped or hindered their integration into British society. The authors assumed that a student arriving with a good knowledge of English—which was further strengthened by the intensive language courses—found it much easier to settle down and begin, almost immediately, the process of assimilation. On the contrary, the lack of language ability slowed this process down considerably, compounding the students' problems. Nevertheless, Dare and Hollander tested the level of the students' language skills in six separate fields: the writing of essays, the ability to follow lectures, the reading of textbooks and of more general reading material, conversation and understanding plays, films and radio programmes. In each of these areas the students could choose from two possible answers to the question "Do you have any difficulties with the following?" - either a "fair amount or more" or "little or less".[14] Surprisingly, a large majority of the students replied that they encountered little trouble with English in almost all areas, the only exception being essay writing. But even faced with this onerous task 137 students declared that they had little difficulty in carrying it out and only 105 admitted that they found it rather troublesome. One can only assume that the students' bold expression of confidence in their language abilities must have been akin to whistling in the dark; it stemmed more from the need to bolster their courage by demonstrably shrugging their shoulders in the face of the problems they were encountering, rather than reflecting reality. It is true that some of them might have been over-confident. Edwards, the Oxford language teacher certainly expressed the opinion that they wanted to run before they could walk. In any case, the students filled in the questionnaire in their second year, by which time they had survived the worst. Fifty years later a rather different story has emerged from their recollections: all the students interviewed remember the superhuman effort and determination they needed to be able to roughly understand the lectures, to

---

[14] Dare, Alan and Paul, Hollander: Op.cit., Table 11A, p.XIX.

prepare the essays and submit them on time - in the hope that the tutors would be able to detect amidst the scores of grammatical mistakes what they wanted to say - and to pass the exams with luck.

We entered the university courses in October 1957 with great expectations. Yes, Edwards was right, we were full of confidence. After the exhausting language courses, lasting eight or nine months for most of us, we had passed the exam, obtained the Cambridge Certificate of English, read a handful of books cover to cover, were able to skim the daily papers and pick out what was of interest to us and to converse fairly fluently on any topic with our English friends. We were looking forward to serious study. So we took our place in the lecture hall, listened intently to what the lecturer said, tried to scribble down some notes and realized that we understood, if we were lucky, no more than a few words, at best a few sentences and perhaps the general drift of the lecture but little of the arguments. One of the students recalled that there was only one lecturer at LSE whom he could understand—most probably because he was a Pole— who spoke slowly and with a strong accent, emphatically rolling every single "r".[15] We knew that unlike in Hungary, in England there were no printed lecture notes we could purchase later or read at our leisure in the library; it was up to us to take notes to remind us what the lecturer had said and what we might be called upon to discuss at the tutorials or what might turn up as an exam question. Our note taking was a mixture of Hungarian and English—rarely including whole sentences—which we had great difficulty deciphering later on. We counted ourselves lucky if we found a relevant book by the same lecturer, providing some guidance for us. It was especially difficult for us to understand and write down names even if—as it later often transpired—we had already been well-acquainted with them, since their Continental and thus the Hungarian pronunciation differed so much from the English as to make them unrecognizable to us. A student, being quizzed about his knowledge of Latin, was asked what he had read by Virgil or Cicero. Sorry—he replied—he had never come across these authors during his years of study. It was only later, when he saw the names in print that he realized to whom the weird English pronunciation referred; by that time however it was too late to demonstrate his acquaintance with these Latin authors.

During the first year of the history of art course at Birkbeck College we were taught by Nikolaus Pevsner. He talked to us about medieval French architecture; how the solid, heavy Romanesque forms were slowly replaced by the lighter, almost transcendental pointed arches of the Gothic,

---

[15] Interview with Péter Pallai. 25 Nov. 2004.

representing the heavenward aspiration of the human spirit. He was standing behind us, at the back of the room, dropping the slides into the projector. When he wanted to point out a special feature, he grabbed his furled black umbrella, raced to the front, poked at the screen and repeated for us not only the name of the particular architectural element, but also the name of the town where the church whose picture we saw could be found. This was my salvation. Pevsner's method of hands-on teaching gave me time to write down the names, albeit I could only do it by following the rules of Hungarian phonetics. To give some idea of this rather individualistic note taking, I will give an example of what I had to do. The best example of the construction of ambulatory chapels is—said Pevsner—demonstrated by *Szan Szernín* in *Tulúz*, the magnificent church with the unusual dome—surely an Eastern influence brought back by the crusaders—can be found in *Perigő*. Then we confronted the massive façade of the Notre-Dame le Grande at *Poátyié,* the impressive regularity of the clerestory windows still discernible in the ruined church of *Zsümiezs* in Normandy and the bold architectural innovations in the cathedral of *Otőn,* well-hidden in the Morvan mountains. I spent hours with my scribbled notes in the Senate House Library, surrounded by English and French dictionaries, architectural textbooks and encyclopaedias, maps of France and guides to French phonetics until I was sure I had got the names right and understood the stages of slow transition from the earthbound Romanesque forms to the awe-inspiring airiness of the pierced walls of the Gothic cathedrals. And I knew very well that I should have devoted at least half of this time to my German studies. Still, it was with great pleasure when in the 1970s, touring provincial France during the summer holidays, I could greet my favourite churches in *Toulouse, Perigueux, Poitiers, Jumièges* and *Autun.* The other Hungarian students lived through similarly trying times. Recalling her student years in Edinburgh, where she studied German and philosophy, Kornélia (Markovich) Szabó lamented: "While the people were extremely kind, university itself was extremely hard for the first couple of years. I had to write down whatever the lecturer said in phonetics. When I got home I would look up the words in a dictionary."[16]

To burrow through the lists of set texts and suggested reading material presented its own problems. The lists were long and the books ran to many hundreds of pages. The students had to be selective, choosing only the absolutely necessary textbooks and the shortest articles. There were, however, times when even the most judicious selection could not help.

---

[16] Gilchrist, Jim: What Scotland did for us? *The Scotsman,* 5 Jan. 2007.

András Zsigmond, a medical student at Liverpool University, looked at the basic physiology textbook with desperation. He reckoned that to read it and to thoroughly digest all the information in it would take him a year instead of the allocated couple of weeks. And the physiology exam loomed in the not too distant future. He was, of course, familiar with the names of the parts of the human body from his student years at the University of Pécs in Hungary – but in Continental Latin. Thus, the only plan he could envisage for passing the exam was to take it in Latin. How he was able to cajole his teachers into accepting this plan is a mystery, but they agreed. So Zsigmond only had to take a crash course in the British pronunciation of Latin words to pass.[17]

The need to rapidly acquire the additional vocabulary needed to cover the various aspects of the subjects dealt also the science and engineering students a heavy blow. Tamás Csáthy, a civil engineering student at Glasgow University for example, not only had to learn English from scratch—his English knowledge barely covered basic communication—he also had to acquire and master the technical vocabulary required for his studies, namely the geological terms for a vast range of rocks and soil specimens. He had completed four years at the Technical University of Budapest and getting a degree should have been plain sailing for him anywhere, but because of the language difficulties it was two years of very hard work in Britain. He had relatively little time left for socializing, yet made many Scottish friends and enjoyed undergraduate life at Glasgow. Because of his steely determination however he not only obtained a first class honours degree in 1959 but was also awarded the Civil Engineering prize for graduating at the top of his class.[18]

Others had to re-learn the name of the elements or, if they studied biology, the names of the whole British flora and fauna. For the engineers, the measurements differed as well as the standards. Even in mathematics, while the results were expected to be the same, the methods of arriving at the right calculation, setting up an equation or presenting a rational line of thought were totally dissimilar to what the students had learned in Hungarian schools and universities. Even seemingly small things loomed as serious obstacles. One student confessed that whenever he met an acronym—and there were dozens of new ones cropping up daily with which everyone else seemed to be familiar—he was too shy to bother his fellow students by constantly asking them for an interpretation.[19] Those

---

[17] Interview with András Zsigmond. 17 Feb. 2006.
[18] Interview with Tamás Csáthy. 16 Feb. 2006.
[19] The problem is specially mentioned in a letter by Kálmán Száz, formerly a student of physics and mathematics at Glasgow University.

who studied a foreign language had an especially hard time. According to a former student "It was like waging war with blood and tears."[20] They scoured the libraries for English translations of the set texts and recommended literature and then, with the original and the translations side by side, they tried to get at least the gist of the story by reading both in parallel. Failing to understand even a single word could cause disaster. Csaba Juhász, a third year engineering student at Imperial College, was sitting an important exam when in a question on some aspects of fluid mechanics he found what he thought to be the key word: "sewer". He had no idea what "sewer" meant. The task was to measure the speed of the flow of water in the ominous "sewer" and while Juhász felt that he might be able to make the necessary calculations—the question otherwise seemed to be quite simple—not knowing what the liquid was supposed to flow through, he thought it was better to abandon it. Failing to answer one question did not, of course, result in failing the exam, but the mark he received was well below what he had hoped to get.[21]

According to the survey by Dare and Hollander it was essay writing that the students regarded as the most difficult task they had to grapple with. In addition, the pressure was relentless: a weekly or at best a fortnightly exercise for which they had to gather information, select and present it together with their arguments in writing and then discuss these lucidly at the tutorials. Although the topics offered were varied and challenging and their contemplation in normal circumstances would have given even pleasure, essay writing and the tutorials were for the Hungarian students an endurance test. Recalling her student days Kati Jámbor—and presumably this applies to most of the former Hungarian students—has confessed that had she known in advance what essay writing would entail, she would not have opted for the continuation of her university studies in England.[22]

The students felt ashamed when their papers were returned liberally peppered with corrections in red ink; these showed up basic grammatical mistakes by the dozen, the wrong choice of words as well as the clumsy formulation of sentences, inadequate for expressing their thoughts. Often it was well nigh impossible to give the right answer because it presumed the student's total assimilation to English mental processes and attitudes, acquired by the natives since childhood. "Marietta, you really should try to put yourself in the shoes of an eighteenth century English gentleman!" – cried a Cambridge tutor during a history tutorial. Yet, this was precisely

---

[20] Interview with András Sándor. 31 Oct. 2004.
[21] Interview with Mrs. Judith Juhász. 28 July 2004.
[22] Interview with Katalin Jámbor. 26 Jan. 2005.

the challenge to which Marietta Záhonyi could not respond, although she greatly enjoyed the history lectures, read widely in her subject field and was looking forward to the discussion at the tutorials.[23] It was even worse, when, analysing a literary work by putting it into a historical and social context, the students were accused of presenting a Marxist interpretation. They would have liked to rebut the charge—had they dared to contradict the teacher—by saying that is was he or she who had no idea what the tenets of Marxism were, and that the opinion expounded in the paper, instead of reflecting Marxist thought, would have earned the writer serious reprimand under a Communist regime. The torture of weekly essay writing however greatly helped the students to prepare for the final exams: the choice of questions was similar and also the way for presenting their arguments. If they had acquired the technique of marshalling their thoughts quickly and succinctly in writing, they stood a good chance of passing and obtaining the coveted university degree.

It was however, the nature of university education that presented the Hungarian students with the greatest culture shock: the totally different teaching methods and the high expectations from the students. Most of the students followed the same course in Britain as they had in Hungary. The replies to the question in Dare and Hollander's survey indicated that quite a small percentage—about 13 per cent—had initially toyed with the idea of changing their subjects. They were mainly those students who, for political reasons or because of their "class enemy" family status had been allocated to study certain subjects they might not have been interested in, and to retain their student status they had no choice but to comply with the allocation. In any case, not to deviate from their original subject areas increased the students' chances of obtaining a degree in Britain. The foundation they had received in Hungary, especially in science, engineering and medicine, was solid enough to successfully build on at a British university. If the same subject was taught in a different way, they could even turn the comparison to their advantage. It is not surprising therefore, that to the question: "Are you satisfied with your present course of study?" out of 279 replies 237 gave an affirmative answer.[24]

The survey intended to elicit the views of the students on how they perceived the different methodology in teaching, what aspects of university education they would regard as better in Britain and conversely, now with hindsight, better in Hungary. The authors felt the need to supply a lengthy introduction to Hungarian higher education. Only a thorough

---

[23] Interview with Marietta Záhonyi. 24 May 2005.
[24] Dare, Alan and Hollander, Paul: Op.cit., Tables 14A and 14.B., p.XXII.

understanding of the Hungarian educational system would provide the necessary context for the appreciation of the assessment given by the student respondents. Hungarian universities—most of them founded in the 19th century—were modelled on the German system, as regards both the curriculum and the teaching methods. Continuity was, however, disrupted by the major changes brought on by the Communist takeover after 1948, which affected all areas of life. Education, especially higher education, which was to shape the leaders of the next generation, was seen as a key instrument in changing society. Purposeful planning and, if necessary, brute force should be applied in this field to enable the Communist Party to strengthen its hold over the people. To achieve this, ideology had to permeate all aspects of education and the strictest control had to be observed. Apart from the careful selection processes (no "class enemy" should gain admittance to universities), higher education institutions were expected to fulfil their political role in several ways.

First—wrote Dare and Hollander—the university branch of the Communist youth organization (DISZ), was charged with the duty of ensuring the political integrity of the students; it spied on them and castigated them for any perceived aberration either in behaviour or in beliefs. Secondly, all higher education institutions were infiltrated by the secret police disguised as "ordinary" students. They also spied on their colleagues and reported any "unreliability" and signs of discontent to the Communist Party. Thirdly, all subjects, with the exception of the sciences, were imbued with Communist ideology, and overtly political subjects like Marxism-Leninism were introduced as a compulsory part of the curriculum. Fourthly, reading material was severely curtailed: only books selected and approved by the authorities could be read. Special textbooks were published in order to ensure that no other material than that with the prescribed views were available to the students, even in university libraries. Western publications could be read only with special permission, which was extremely difficult to obtain. Consequently, the formulation and utterance of independent opinions was regarded as dangerous and not tolerated for either in essays or in seminar discussions.[25]

Fear permeated university life; students did not dare voice dissenting opinions and if they did, or were denounced for doing so. They were privately admonished or—as more often happened—publicly pilloried or even expelled. No wonder that Tamás Csáthy found student life at Glasgow University blissful: "We were used to a totalitarian environment where you lived every moment of your life in fear of something very bad

---

[25] Ibid. pp.14-16.

happening to you. To wake up in the morning and not to have to review what I had run from… was such a tremendous feeling."[26] Control was all-pervasive. Attendance at classes—and there were far too many of them—were compulsory. Exams were held frequently; they were almost without exception oral exams, a mostly one-sided discussion with the lecturer during which students were expected to repeat, almost verbatim, what they had heard at the lectures or read in the approved textbooks and official printed lecture notes. In an examination booklet, called *Index*, the examiner made a record of the mark the student received. Documentation – date, place subject of the exam, marks given and the signatures of the lecturers – was regarded as more important than testing the knowledge of the students. This was what the students had to compare with the English higher education system, and their response to the survey truly reflected both their elation at ridding themselves of the all-pervading ideology and control and their bewilderment when they found themselves face to face with total academic freedom. They were expected to form their own, independent opinion without the ideological crutches supplied by their teachers.

In addition, for many of the Hungarian students the teaching methods were startlingly novel, even disturbingly alien. In the very first term of the academic year 1957-58 the set-text for my German literature class was a short story by a 19th century Swiss parson with the pen-name of Jeremias Gotthelf, entitled *Die schwarze Spinne*. From a distance of more than fifty years I cannot now recall how the black spider came into the story, but I still vividly remember my astonishment that we were expected to analyse this one novella for an hour each week over three months. We looked at the structure of the enfolding story, the naïve originality of the expressions the author used and the words and phrases he most frequently employed. We compared it to a sermon which Gotthelf, being a pastor, might have delivered and, assuming that his intentions were didactic, we tried to substantiate how successfully he incorporated his religious zeal into his writing. To read any other short story by the author was not required; we never discovered who or what might have influenced him, what books beside the Bible he might have read, or with whom he corresponded. There was no attempt to place him into the whole or at least in a segment of 19th century German literature or to discuss his innovations in the wider context of his contemporaries.

This approach seemed to me the exact opposite of what would have constituted a series of lectures or seminars on German literature in

---

[26] Gilchrist, Jim: What Scotland did for us? *The Scotsman*, 5 Jan. 2007.

Hungary. There we would have started with painting a wide tableau of historical events, dominant ideas and significant artistic movements and then placed the individual authors into their respective context. In England—I felt—we were building up a picture up from a single work, moving outwards into wider and wider circles, until it might cover the output of an individual, a group of people, a particular literary movement or even the aspirations of an age. In Hungary, there would have been first and foremost the authoritative canon, regardless whether it was Communist or non-Communist, to which everyone was expected to adhere. There would have been the commonly accepted milestones of events and the "giants" of literature, around whom, working inwards from the perimeter of the large picture through narrowing the perspective step-by-step, we would have finally woven the lesser individual authors into the big tapestry.

At Westfield College, even by the end of the third year, we had not formulated an overview of the history of German literature. It was a series of set-texts, similar to Gotthelf's short story, which provided us with useful demarcation lines in a rather hazy, ill-defined field. We were free to explore it, but it formed no part of the curriculum. The same applied to the study of English literature. When I asked one of my fellow students about her perception of the poetry of Byron she shrugged her shoulder. Byron was not among the set-texts and she was not interested in him enough to devote her time to explore extra-curricular topics. It was the methodology of literary appreciation and criticism that she aimed to acquire during her studies and then she could apply this to the analysis of any writer had she wished to do so. Byron and his fellow Romantics were not among them.

It is interesting that both approaches earned an almost equal number of good points in the answers given to the questions in Dare and Hollander's survey comparing the British and Hungarian educational systems: "If you think that any of the British/Hungarian system of university and technical college education is superior to the Hungarian/British system –what is it?" The British system was appreciated for its high academic standards (high theoretical requirements, deeper and more thorough knowledge, the absence of dogmas), for practical training (especially the excellent laboratory facilities) and for self-reliance, while exactly the same number of points were awarded to Hungarian education—43 points out of the total of 279—for its broader perspectives (wider knowledge, versatility of theoretical analysis, provision of a general picture and, in view of all this, a much longer course), followed by a higher level of systematic training.[27]

---

[27] Dare, Alan and Hollander, Paul: Op.cit., Tables 20A and 20B, p.XXVI.

In this comparative evaluation the highest score—51 points—was reached by the British educational system due to its greater academic freedom apparent in the free choice of courses and lectures, free formulation of views and ideas and their free expression and discussion. There was little compulsion and no imposed control; for each student however, the deliverance from constant and intrusive external control meant the voluntary and by no means easy acceptance of self-control and individual responsibility. In the fields of science and especially engineering, the students greatly appreciated the problem-solving approach of British education, providing practical training for their future careers. All the students benefited greatly from the tutorials; the strong personal links forged between tutors and students went far beyond the formalities and helped them to settle down. On the other hand, the students confessed to missing the constant feedback on their progress so strongly demonstrated by the marks and signatures in their Hungarian *Index* (documents were still regarded as more reassuring than verbal encouragement) and the oral examinations, where personality and eloquence played such a dominant role.

Rather oddly, according to 29 replies, some of the students thought that the standard of lectures, both content and delivery, was higher in Hungarian universities. Dare and Hollander, ascribed this view to the inadequate English knowledge of the students: "It is probable that many of those students who stated that the lectures in Hungary were of higher standard are those who find it difficult to comprehend lectures in English; that is, in saying that the lectures here are inferior they are making a judgement on the subjective basis of their own difficulties with the language."[28] In their analysis of the responses to the survey, the authors might have hit upon one of the causes of the dissatisfaction. Boring lectures and mumbling lecturers were not uncommon in either country, except that they were more easily avoidable in Britain, while they had to be suffered under duress in Hungary. To summarize: after a year of studying in Britain the Hungarian students admitted to a preference for the British system, albeit by only a very small margin. Perhaps it was too early to formulate a comprehensive judgement.

However, by the time they filled in the questionnaires, the first and most difficult year had passed. While their problems with English had not disappeared altogether, the students found them less of a hindrance in following of the lectures, coping with the reading material and writing essays. The students who were allowed to repeat the first year also

---

[28] Ibid. p.17.

benefited by able to lay a solid foundation in their respective subjects on which they could build in the subsequent years, and many of them easily passed the exams at the second attempt. The report produced for the CVCP in January 1961 noted that in the current academic year there were still 38 "Quota" and Free Europe students studying as well as 14 students with Ford grants. The remainder of the students had either completed their courses or had dropped out. The Hungarian Office also supplied an interesting annex to the report which listed the occupations of the "Quota" and Ford students, who had obtained their degrees and also those who had withdrawn but were still contactable.[29] The CVCP received this information with genuine interest and many of the Vice-Chancellors expressed their satisfaction at the excellent results; they felt that the outcome of the Hungarian refugee students scheme truly justified all the efforts the Committee had invested in it. Because of the fairly large number of students either finishing their courses in less than three years or withdrawing after the first or second year, the funding earmarked for their fees and maintenance grants over the full course of three years became available to be used for other purposes. As the CVCP was adamant that all the resources should be spent on the Hungarian students' cause, it was decided to finance also those students who were entering higher education in the late 1950s and early 1960s. They had arrived in Britain as teenagers who first had to complete their secondary education, gain their GCEs and then apply for places in universities and technical colleges. They were brought under the umbrella of the CVCP scheme.

In addition, the CVCP was keen to sponsor the Hungarian students who, after obtaining their first degrees, wished to study for postgraduate qualifications. An analysis of the results of the "Quota" and Ford students between 1957 and 1961, produced by the Hungarian Office for the CVCP a year later,[30] highlighted that during this period ten Hungarian students obtained first class degrees. This was a remarkable achievement not only because at the middle of the last century a first class degree was regarded as a rarely awarded grade and truly outstanding result, but also because some of these Hungarian students had no knowledge of English when they arrived in this country. Of the other students who had completed their undergraduate studies by the end of the academic year of 1961, 35 obtained second class degrees (11 upper second, 12 lower second and 12 second with no sub-division) and the CVCP, regarding also this result as a

---

[29] Present occupation of the original Quota students. UoLA, CB3/5/1/5; Present occupation of the original Ford students. UoLA, CB3/5/2/5.
[30] CVCP.: *Agendum 20. Refugee Hungarian students. Analysis of results 1957-1961.* 26 Jan. 1962. CVCPA.

strong academic achievement, encouraged the students to continue their studies and provided the funding for it.

The Hungarian Office had already compiled a list of potential Hungarian postgraduate students for the January 1961 meeting of the CVCP, together with an estimated cost of the sponsorship. The list contained the names of 52 students, the subjects they intended to research and the university places allocated for them. It is interesting to note that nearly half of the students, 25 individuals, were to continue their postgraduate studies at London University. During the following years the number of Hungarian postgraduates increased substantially; some of them obtained their degrees in the early 1960s and some who had completed their undergraduate studies earlier decided to apply for postgraduate courses after a short gap.

My recent research in the archives and student records of the universities has revealed that the number is closer to 79. This figure can be expected to increase, because some of the information on postgraduate students is still patchy. In addition, after gaining their first degree in Britain, a fairly large proportion of the students decided to relocate to other countries, mostly to the United States, where they pursued postgraduate studies and obtained further qualifications, generally PhDs. It would not be surprising if the final tally of students with higher degrees would reach about one hundred, an exceptionally high figure. Based on the currently available and verifiable data it is possible to provide the following summary of the results: approximately 500 Hungarian students enrolled in British higher education institutions in 1957-58 and the subsequent academic year. Of these students more than half, between 250 and 300 completed their studies successfully. Nearly a third of the qualified students continued their studies and obtained higher degrees. One can only agree with the final assessment of the CVCP that the Hungarian student scheme was, indeed, an extraordinary success. The leaders of the universities had devoted a huge amount of time and effort to help the students and the students had worked incredibly hard to overcome the difficulties in learning English, adapting to a new environment and a new system of university education and not losing heart in the process.

Furthermore, the above quoted figures could be expected to increase. The research carried out in the Archives of Imperial College might serve as an example for this. The main files initially listed five "Quota" students (actually six students as one of them left for Germany in early 1957), all of them undergraduates. With the addition of the students receiving Ford, Free Europe, WUS and LEA grants and the one privately funded student, their number grew to 12. As for the number of PhD students, the early records mention only two; both studying part-time, but two others soon joined their ranks. This was the most up-to-date data that I was able to present at a conference on British-Hungarian relations in April 2004.[31] The CVCP's 1961 endorsement of grants for Hungarian postgraduate students—found subsequently in the CVCP's archives at Warwick University—added no fewer than seven additional postgraduates to the Imperial list, three of them former Imperial undergraduates and four who had obtained their first degree at other British universities. Currently there are 11 verified students on the list who were awarded a PhD at Imperial College. If second degrees awarded in other countries could also be added to the list—such as that earned by Felix Allender, a Free Europe undergraduate at Imperial, who obtained an MBA at prestigious INSEAD in Fontainebleau, France[32]—the number of postgraduates associated with Imperial would rise to the relatively high number of 12. It would not be surprising if further research were to reveal new names which could be added to the total.

---

[31] Czigány, Magda: Treated as other students. 1956 Hungarian refugee students in the United Kingdom. A case study of Imperial College London. In: László Péter and Martyn Rady, eds.: *British-Hungarian relations since 1848*. London, 2004, pp.289-302.
[32] Interview with Felix Allender. 4 Jan. 2006.

CHAPTER IX

THE "SCALES OF ADAPTATION"

In the introduction to their report, Dare and Hollander give a detailed account of why they decided to make the Hungarian refugee students the subject of their sociological survey. They were intimately acquainted with the students' problems, Paul Hollander being a refugee student himself, and Alan Dare's research focusing on the study of refugee groups, of which the Hungarian students presented an especially interesting case. Both of them had first-hand knowledge of the difficulties the students were facing and of their attempts to adapt to their new circumstances. In their survey the authors intended to observe, analyse and summarize the degree of the students' adaptation, and to highlight the causes which could be perceived either to delay or accelerate it. For this they had to map out the students' background and learn about their motivation for choosing Britain as their new home. They wished to find a definitive answer to the question of what determined the scale of assimilation both of a particular immigrant group and of individual members of that group.

The structure of the so-called "adaptation scale" that Dare and Hollander set up is presented in some detail half-way through the report.[1] From the scores constructed on the basis of responses to three key questions—the feeling of loneliness and homesickness and whether the respondents were able to imagine themselves becoming members of one of the British classes—the authors devised a five point "scale of adaptation": adapting well, moderately, intermediately (neither well nor badly), poorly or badly. These scales were then used to examine the underlying causes of a relatively easy or a more problematic adjustment, which included among others a knowledge of English prior to coming to England, the students' Hungarian background, their expectations, and how far these had been fulfilled and their ease in establishing friendship with British people.

It should be stated that the responses were, in a large number of cases, no more than a reflection of the students' state of mind at a particular point in time, a snapshot of their transitory feelings. As one of the respondents

---

[1] Dare, Alan and Hollander, Paul: Op.cit., p.28.

observed: "The questionnaire was very useful because it raised several issues which I have previously had no opportunity to think about. The experience of my short stay here shows that views change a great deal even in one year. Success makes everything look bright, whereas failure can banish all hopes. If you were to ask these questions after another year, people would give different answers according to whether they had been successful or not. Such a questionnaire had only one disadvantage: some people may get the impression that a new cadre-classification has been started and that they are in the place from which they escaped."[2] The authors, however, noted with satisfaction that 56 per cent of the respondents stated that they had found the underlying idea of the survey "useful". It served as a tool for self-examination, helping to assess how far one had travelled on the path of assimilation and to what degree this had loosened one's ties to the mother-country.

The feeling of isolation and loneliness—as identified by Dare and Hollander—was one of the most significant elements measuring the degree of a newcomer's integration into an alien society. The Hungarian students were no exception. The ones who suffered most from isolation were those who, soon after their arrival, were sent to their respective universities where, at least for the time being, they were the sole Hungarian student. In addition, some of them spoke no English, so even the most basic communication was fraught with difficulties. They could not share information, discuss their experiences or raise each others' spirits when despair struck. Salvation came with the arrival of other Hungarian students. First impressions of Britain were rather bleak. It was winter-time, well before the general introduction of central heating in Britain. The rooms in the hostels and colleges were cold and damp. The eye-watering yellow smog which, at least in London, found its way through the smallest cracks in the window frames, left behind dirty patches on the wall. The small, inadequate gas fires, fixed to the wall, helped little: sitting close to them to get warm burned the front of one's legs and cheeks a livid red, while leaving one still shivering from the all-enveloping cold. In any case, most of them worked by feeding shillings into the slot and these shillings, being part of the meagre pocket money, were not to be spent without very careful consideration. Darkness descended by mid-afternoon and, as so many of the former students remember with a shudder, the yellowish light of the street lamps gave the whole town a ghoulish appearance: even the cheerful red of the buses faded into a nondescript murky grey and people walking in the streets looked like lost

---

[2] Ibid. p.7.

souls emerging from another world. Food, of course, was the greatest problem. Porridge, served up for breakfast, was almost impossible for a Hungarian to swallow, especially when instead of the addition of cold milk and jam to make it more palatable, it was liberally salted. Kippers proved to be a slowly acquired taste and lunch or dinner were not much better. The student dining halls had set menus and the Hungarian students found it a trial to eat greasy mutton chops, potatoes disintegrating on the outside but uncooked in the middle, or cabbage leaves boiled to death. To face all this alone, not able at least to share in the misery, was, indeed, a trial.[3]

It is not at all surprising that to the question "On the whole, do you feel lonelier in this country than you felt in Hungary?" almost half of the students replied with an emphatic "yes", even after spending nearly two years in Britain.[4] The authors, anticipating that one of the main reasons for the feeling of loneliness might be ascribed to the lack of close relatives and friends in this country next asked where their relatives were living. Some of the replies could, indeed, be safely predicted: a very large proportion of parents, brothers and sisters were living in Hungary. On the other hand, as far as the number of close friends is concerned, the survey reveals that the substantial majority was in Britain (113) as opposed to those in Hungary (61) or other countries (57). These figures refer only to male friends and, although this is not indicated in the survey, must have included new friendships, struck up in this Britain. Unfortunately, no further information can be gained about these new friends – whether they were English, Scottish, Irish or of other nationalities, or even newly acquired Hungarian friends - but it is certain that they helped to overcome the isolation and loneliness of the students. (There is a separate category of close female friends, but it is difficult to draw any conclusion from the figures, as the gender of the respondents is not indicated, and it is not obvious what relationship the 66 positive replies cover.)[5]

To describe the nature of homesickness they felt—to which 152 students admitted against 118—the students could chose from a whole range of combination of possible replies. Some of these indicated the frequency (permanently, almost permanently, often, not often, rarely) of being overcome by homesickness, while within the same set of replies another group noted its strength (intense, quite strong, strong, moderate, little). Selecting the appropriate combination from the set of responses might have been a complicated task and the tables reflecting the answers

---

[3] Interview with András Sándor, András Szabó, Kornélia (Markovich) Szabó, Béla Ulicsák, Péter Wonke, Albin Závody and many others.
[4] Dare, Alan and Hollander, Paul: Op.cit., Table 5, p.XVI.
[5] Ibid. Table 6, p.XVII.

do not, by any means, present a clear picture.[6] Nevertheless, it seems that the majority of the students had to cope with a moderate homesickness, which they felt occasionally. This assessment, in itself does not reveal much about the students' emotional life. However, Dare and Hollander, perhaps suspecting that more detailed revelations would be necessary for a valid analysis, also questioned the students about the causes of their homesickness. The largest group of the replies—as could be expected—named the absence of family and old friends, closely followed by the absence of the familiar, therefore friendly and secure environment (Hungarian landscape, Budapest, the Danube, etc.).[7] The deep-seated sorrow the students felt about not being able to see their families, perhaps never again in their lifetimes, and the feeling of guilt that they were unable to offer help to their parents when they needed it most, visited them unannounced and with great force. As one of them confessed: "So far I have been homesick only twice, but each time very intensely. For no apparent reason, I thought of my mother (that I might never see her again) then of the family, then everything, so much that I almost collapsed."[8]

A large number of students had sent in written responses to this question and the authors quoted abundantly from them to illustrate the many different causes which might trigger the feeling of homesickness. Some students for example, found the sudden challenge of taking full responsibility for their lives and actions, difficult to confront: "I would not call it homesickness. At home I went to school, did a lot of reading, writing, sport and chased after girls; money and housekeeping matters were my mother's responsibility. Here I have fewer of the former pleasures and more of the latter responsibilities." In this case homesickness was, at least partially, a test of adjusting to adult life, a process of emotional and intellectual maturing. Others, who found themselves without a circle of Hungarian friends, missed the comfort of speaking Hungarian and sharing the new experience with like-minded people: "I miss the company of people whose approach to problems is similar to mine. I have yet to find a group of people where I could talk on any topic as freely as I at home." Or, an excerpt from another letter: "I miss Hungarian books, especially the Hungarian classical works which are not available here. The problem is not alleviated even by the fact that I read and enjoy English literature." Being without familiar support might extend to feel dissatisfaction with the whole of one's surroundings: "And sometimes I find my environment somewhat cold and too quiet."

[6] Ibid. Table 7B, p.XVII.
[7] Ibid. Table 7C, p.XVIII.
[8] For the responses to the question of homesickness see: Ibid. , pp.25-27.

Homesickness could flare up then quieten down: "When the other students go home for the vacation I feel a little lonely. But I quickly acquire new friends and life again becomes pleasant." Homesickness could be a direct response to problems and to fear of the future: "I am not homesick as long as I am busy studying. But when I face difficulties with my studies or with anything, which at first seem insuperable then it crops up." The passage of time, the process of gradual adaptation to the new environment, the accumulation of small or larger successes in varied walks of life, the acceptance of exile and acquiescence to the unchangeable political situation slowly tempered – even if never quite extinguished – the feeling of homesickness. However, once the students gained British citizenship and were in the possession of a British passport, they could contemplate a visit to Hungary. From the mid-1960s onwards parents were allowed by the Hungarian authorities to travel to Britain to see with their own eyes how their children fared. The separation of families, the core cause of homesickness thus ended, and with it its nagging pain.

Many of the students suffered little from homesickness. The authors, however, did not query its absence, because they regarded it as self-evident. The feeling of homesickness in political émigré groups receded into the background, was even wiped out by the relief of having escaped from danger; they did not wish to return to the dreaded situation which they had successfully left behind: "...this applied to political refugees in general"—the authors argued—"in whose case the loss of familiar environment (including human) is counterbalanced by the realization of the benefits of human and political liberties and the removal of actual or possible persecution for political reasons." Amongst the many comments they quote is a brief but hard-hitting remark: "The Rákosi regime managed 'to purge' me of all homesickness."

Neither did Dare and Hollander refer to the terrifying dream common to all Hungarian refugees for a number of years after their escape to the West. Its basic pattern was described by Lóránt Czigány in an interview he gave in Budapest following the collapse of the Kádár regime: "The dream consists of three distinct segments. The person dreaming is back at home in Hungary, in what could be described as idyllic circumstances and is feeling rather happy. However, he suddenly he recalls a trivial task he has to undertake or an appointment he has to keep from his present-day life in exile – such as attending a tutorial, fetching a coat from the dry-cleaners, or an invitation to dinner next day. He is gripped by anxiety; as it is utterly impossible to get back to Oxford (or Heildelberg or the Sorbonne) by tomorrow. The problem is only resolved on waking when relief replaces anxiety. The interpretation of the dream does not, of course, require an in-depth knowledge of Freudian concepts in order to understand it, but I believe that it serves as an excellent example for the genesis of the Jungian 'collective unconscious'. Although on quite a different scale, there is little doubt that the 'spiritual reality' (*seelische Realität*), or the 'eternal myths,' that survive in the collective unconscious of an ethnic group or tribe also owe their origins to the memory of a shared calamity or catastrophe."[9] In addition, the repeated experience of escaping from Hungary which featured in most of the dreams, could be extremely bizarre and at the same time terrifying, as it is littered with numerous impossible tasks and obstacles similar to those found in fairytales, which had to be executed and/or overcome to ensure survival. The same topic surfaces in the poetry of the young poets who left Hungary after the revolution albeit in a fragmented form. It is a variation of the common myth of escape, survival and adaptation. A firestorm has devastated the earth and forced the people to flee underwater and thorough swamps as amphibians, by growing gills and scales. After reaching dry land, they have to divest themselves of their gills so they can breathe. Only the fittest and most determined are able to survive the repeated traumas, those, who at all times, are best able to adapt themselves to the new and ever-changing environments.[10]

Dare and Hollander presumed that the first steps to successful integration consisted of establishing new contacts and forging new friendships. They regarded this aspect of the process of assimilation so important that the first four questions of the survey were devoted to it. In answer to the question whether the students had found it difficult to establish friendships with British people, the majority replied with a "no".[11] To one of the following questions, however, which set out to investigate the closest ties the students had, two thirds of them stated that their best friend was Hungarian. The second best friend was British—no separate mention of English, Scottish, Welsh or Irish friends—followed by

---

[9] "Nyugatról nézve semmi sem tűnik annyira provinciálisnak, mint éppen európaiságunk örökös bizonygatása." Kérdez: Tóth Péter Pál. [When looking from the perspective of the West, nothing is more provincial than the constant reiteration of our 'Europeanness'. Interview by Pál Péter Tóth.] In: Czigány, Lóránt: *Gyökértelen, mint a zászló nyele: Írások a nyugati magyar irodalomról.* [Without roots like a flagpole.] 1994, pp.314-315.

[10] Czigány, Lóránt: Gyökértelen, mint a zászló nyele: a természetes világkép felbomlása az ötvenhatos nemzedék költészetében. [Without roots like a flagpole: the disintegration of the natural picture of the world in the poetry of the 1956 generation.] Ibid., pp.80-114.

[11] Dare, Alan and Hollander, Paul: Op.cit., Table 1A, p.XII.

other ethnic groups, but these with very low figures.[12] Establishing friendships with British people was mainly hindered, at least in the beginning, by a lack of language skills. However, a substantial number of students felt that a difference in outlook also played a role, not to mention the vastly different life experiences.

The majority of British students belonged to the middle classes and had enjoyed a sheltered life both within the family and at school. They had few challenges to face and were, therefore, little interested in the problems of the outside world. The Hungarian students on the other hand, had lived through the total upheaval imposed on them and on the population at large by the Communist regime, had learned to hide their family background and their true feelings and had had to adjust to the ever changing-demands of sheer survival. No wonder that they regarded the British students as juveniles, occupied with trivial problems, insensitive to and uninterested in wider issues. Only those students who had already served in the army were singled out for exception, as they were about the same age as the Hungarian students and, if they had been stationed abroad, displayed some knowledge of the world. It was possible to hold a political debate with them, to talk about the plight of people behind the Iron Curtain, to explore ideas for ending the cold war and first and foremost, to regale them with the stories of their experience of the 1956 revolution. Some of the students recalled during the interviews how they had sought out the friendship of these older British students for the above reasons, not to mention the fact that any sustained discussion had also helped them to improve their English.[13]

The refugee students represented to their British counterparts no more than a curiosity – at least this was what they often felt. They were invited to parties as a colourful addition to the usual crowd and were taken home during the vacations to be introduced to the family as "the heroes who fought with bare hands against the Russian tanks." Within a few months, however, their novelty had faded; there were new causes to champion and new acquaintances to show off. As one of the respondents wrote in his letter: "It is very easy to establish a superficial relationship with English people. Strangers, especially Hungarian students, arouse their interest at first, but this does not last."[14] Or, as another student observed: "The English word 'friend' means rather acquaintance in our terminology. In the English sense, it is not difficult to acquire a friend; but it is difficult in

---

[12] Ibid. Table 2A, p.XII.
[13] For example, interview with Péter Pallai. 25 Nov. 2004.
[14] Ibid. p.30.

the Hungarian sense. In the English sense of the word 'friendship' means superficial social contact."[15]

The expectations of what life in the British Isles, or what the British people might be like, were, if they were formulated at all, very hazy indeed. Under Communist rule Hungary, like other East European countries, was totally sealed off from the West. The meagre amount of information young people might have amassed about life in the Western countries was gained mainly from the Hungarian broadcasts by the BBC, Radio Free Europe and the Voice of America. (140 students identified the source of their information about the West as broadcasts by Western radio stations.)[16] The programmes, beamed at the Soviet satellite countries were, however, devoted mainly to the discussion of politics as far as it might have influenced events behind the Iron Curtain. More reliable, although rather dated information could be obtained from the stories of the parents of the students, who had visited England in the 1930s. Their number was surprisingly large, because a fairly large percentage of the refugee students came from the former Hungarian educated middle classes. The students in their replies also singled out the reading of books as the source of their information about Britain. These books, however, being mostly the works of the 19th century classics of English literature, must have reflected life in Victorian England. Most of the contemporary British authors were banned under Communist rule—their works were unavailable and forbidden—and the adventures of Mr Pickwick contributed little if anything at all, to the students' understanding of life and mores in England in the middle of the 20th century. Nevertheless, when they were asked to list three favourable and three unfavourable characteristics of the British people based on their own experience and observation, they automatically chose the well-known and widely accepted stereotypes.

First and foremost, the British were honest and reliable, calm, patient and well-balanced as well as helpful, kind, polite and well-mannered. Their outlook was conservative, governed by tradition while being tolerant and respecting individual liberty. On the other hand, their unfavourable characteristics included their stiff and formal behaviour, keeping their distance and withdrawing behind their own defences. They were cautious and hid their feelings behind a camouflage of indifference. It was, however, quite possible that they were truly indifferent, unimaginative, empty and boring.[17] In contrast, if the students were to list the good characteristics of the Hungarians for an English friend, these would have

---

[15] Ibid.
[16] Ibid. Tables 28A and B., p.XXXIV.
[17] Ibid. Table 4A, pp.XIV-XV.

included: friendliness,   a   communicative   and   generous   nature,
resourcefulness, talent and enterprising spirit and—not surprisingly—love
of freedom, courage, rebelliousness and independence. At the same time,
however, they were undisciplined: rash, inconsiderate, even egotistic,
leaning to extremes and far too emotional. They found it difficult to adapt
to new circumstances, which could be taken as a reflection of their current
condition. A fairly large proportion of the students—78 persons—were
unwilling to list the bad characteristics of the Hungarians at all.[18] The
replies certainly revealed an excessive measure of self-confidence and, one
might say, an innate national pride: against 401 favourable characteristics
possessed by the Hungarians, the British were able to register only 324.
Regarding the unfavourable characteristics, while the British reached the
relative high figure of 303, the Hungarians lagged well behind with 199.
As Dare and Hollander summarised: the respondents were much more
critical of British people than of the Hungarians.[19] (These ratios did not
change much over the following years. A survey on the 1956 refugees in
Britain, carried out more than two decades later,[20] arrived at the same
results. For example, one person simply refused to answer the question on
the faults of the Hungarians maintaining that they had none!)

The students' relationship with the country in which they chose to
settle was to a large extent determined by the official response of its
government to the revolution. Whether, in the students' view, the leaders
of the country had done whatever was possible in the circumstances either
to provide help to Imre Nagy's government or, through diplomatic means
to deter the Soviet Union from crashing the revolution. The response to the
question "What could the British government have done?" was uniform
and clear-cut: the Suez conflict had fully compromised Great Britain,
acting so demonstrably as a colonial power in its own perceived interest
that it could not object on any moral ground to the colonization of
Hungary by the Soviet Union in her sphere of influence as defined at
Yalta. As one of the respondents wrote: "The useless and senseless Suez
adventure should have been avoided...In that case the indignation of the
West concerning the Russian intervention would have been more
justified."[21]

---

[18] Ibid. Table 4B, pp.XV-XVI.
[19] Ibid. p.30.
[20] Sárközi, Mátyás: Ötvenhatosok Angliában. [1956 refugees in England.] In: *Új Látóhatár*, vol.32, no. 3-4, 1981. pp.459-465.
[21] On the students' views regarding Western reaction ot the revolution, see: Dare, Alan and Hollander, Paul: Op.cit., pp.55-57.

The refugees, including the students, arrived in the West full of anger and bitterness. They were unwilling to absolve the Western powers and the United Nations of the heinous sin of throwing Hungary to the Soviets without lifting a finger. They were, of course, unaware of the agreement between the USA and the Soviet Union—the relevant documents only coming into the public domain much later—not to disturb the strict demarcation lines mapped out between the great powers on their respective spheres of influence. They had to learn after the Russian invasion of Budapest that all the talk about the fight for freedom and the incitement to hold out as long as possible, broadcast by the Western radio stations, was no more that empty words. When the time for action arrived, the Western governments were willing to send only parcels of food and medication rather than observers and troops. "At any rate, the West could have done more than send medicine and second-hand clothes. In time they will also see this" – wrote a student. And from a more resigned response: "Since I left Hungary I realized that there is no idealism and courage in the West. Now I know that nothing could have been done!" Even the warmth of the reception given to the students, the efforts by the university authorities to help them with the continuation of their studies, the organization of their accommodation and the language courses seemed to them at times to be no more than an inadequate and tardy substitute for real action, the true aim of which was to appease their guilty conscience. It was, therefore, only natural to accept all the help and care without feeling or expressing undue gratitude. A year and a half after leaving Hungary was, however, long enough to still the students' anger. By then they had learned enough about the political and diplomatic mechanisms employed by Western governments to realize, albeit with a residue of bitterness, that the outcome could not have been different without risking the outbreak of a new world war: "From the perspective of two years it seems that the West could have done nothing; this is a very sad fact not only for Hungary but also for the West."

Regardless of the students' ambiguous feelings about the attitude of the West to the revolution, their slow adaptation to the new way of life in Britain and to the challenges of university existence had already begun. Although living in rented accommodation offered financial advantages—it was up to each student to decide how to spend his maintenance grant—most of them opted for living in colleges and halls of residence in the hope that it would be easier to forge friendships with the other students. (There was, however, at least one case, when the family offering accommodation to a Hungarian student requested the authorities to move him into a hostel, when they discovered that he had experimented on their pampered cat by swinging him around to see if he really landed on all four paws.)[22] Many of these friendships have lasted a lifetime, even if in their first stages it was by no means evident for the Hungarian students that the rather timid approach by English people signalled their readiness to engage in real friendship going beyond casual friendly contact.

This was how I became the "honorary member" of a small group of students, called the "plebs" at Westfield College. Most of the students at this so-called "ladies' college" were recruited from the English upper middle-classes, and those who felt that they did not automatically belong to this elite, might have felt excluded. From among these latter students a small group was formed; they had already become acquainted with each other by attending the admission interviews at the same time. They were the daughters of teachers, civil servants and white-collar workers, mostly from the Midlands, who felt somewhat "alien" among the other students in the college. The group was named the "plebs", its name signifying the committed defiance of elite attitudes and offering support to each other in face of the opposition. My room-mate, Anne Lois Evans, also belonged to the group and through her I was invited to attend the after-dinner meetings when, with a mug of cocoa in hand to fortify ourselves, we discussed the events of the day, expressed solidarity with each other and, to my surprise, exchanged views on current politics. Anne was a fervent supporter of the Gaitskellite Labour Party and the others, although I cannot recall the stance they took with certainty, also seemed to espouse some sort of socialist ideal which, considering their background, was not surprising. I represented the opposite view. They were interested in what really happened in Hungary under Communist rule, what the uprising was about and why the translation of socialist ideas into a functioning socialist society did not work. What were the obstacles and the problems? Because of my limited English, I kept silent initially, morosely drinking my cocoa with ill-concealed consternation. Soon, however, I tried to engage in the debate by expressing my own strong opinion that socialist ideology was not compatible with human nature and that its forced introduction would lead to the destruction of individual freedom and to the dysfunction of society. I am not at all sure that the members of the "plebs" listened to my arguments, or that I was able, even partially, to convince them. My friendship with Anne however—and to some extent also with other members of the group—has survived. Anne and I, although we seldom met, exchanged letters year in and year out and these revealed to me how much she appreciated our relationship. Yet, in the beginning I expected

---

[22] Interview with Albin Závody. 2 March 2006.

true friendship to be much more demonstrative and was little aware of the deeply-felt importance with which Anne regarded it, as she barely referred to it during our years together at Westfield College. The "plebs" also survived more than half a century. The yearly meetings of the members of the group over lunch at Oxford remind me of the natural openness with which they had welcomed and accepted me in the spring of 1957. They represented then, and still represent for me today, my full acceptance into a small community, providing me with the assurance of belonging somewhere.

Generally, the Hungarian students found the Scots and the Irish more open and easier to get on with; many of them recall with real pleasure the pub culture of their student days in Glasgow or Edinburgh. Some of them were given much more than the expected help and encouragement. Tamás Csáthy, for example, remembers with deep gratitude Professor Sutherland's efforts in securing him a grant to cover the cost of his ticket and initial expenses in Canada, where he had been offered a scholarship to study for a master's degree.[23] Péter Halmos, a former student at the Queen's University at Belfast, recalls the warm reception laid on for the refugee students by the whole university. He had spent four weeks at the language course at Edinburgh when, deciding not to wait any longer, the Dean of the Medical Faculty at Belfast travelled personally to Edinburgh to fetch Halmos and bring him to Ireland. Halmos's wife is Irish and their two daughters were born in Ireland. No wonder that, although he has lived in the USA since 1966, he still regards Ireland as his second "home-country" which he often visits: "I will always be grateful to Queen's for helping me with my education and try to reciprocate by supporting Alumni programs."[24]

As usual, British universities organized the annual fair of their clubs and societies in October 1957 in order to recruit as many new members as possible, especially from among the freshers. Many of the Hungarian students, just starting their university studies, also decided to join. They selected mainly the societies and clubs devoted to sport or cultural activities. As sport had been officially supported in Hungary and physical education compulsory even at university level, not only were they eagerly accepted by the clubs, but they soon excelled in their chosen fields such as football, water polo, fencing, rowing, swimming, athletics and chess, representing their universities' teams at national, or even at international level. After receiving his medical qualifications at Oxford, László Antal represented the University and Great Britain at pistol shooting between

---

[23] Interview with Tamás Csáthy. 16 Feb. 2006.
[24] E-mail letter by Péter Halmos. 12 Dec. 2005.

1969 and 1984, including the World, European and Commonwealth championships and at the 1976 Olympics. He was also a member of the British Olympic Committee between 1989 and 2003.[25]

Through participating in the activities of the cultural societies—film, drama, music and literature—the Hungarian students tried to regain what they had lost. Tickets for performances in Hungary were inexpensive and easy to obtain and outside Budapest all the major provincial towns also had theatres and concert halls which were patronized by the students. Dare and Hollander's survey revealed that most of the students felt deprived in this respect in Britain: even if the facilities existed in the towns where they studied, they were not able to afford the price of the tickets. Most of them admitted to attending cultural events much less frequently than they had done in Hungary. Although the university societies compensated them to some extent, it was films to which they turned for entertainment. According to the responses to the survey, they flocked to the cinemas and attended 25 per cent more film shows in Britain than in Hungary. At first they went to the cartoons; to understand the escapades of Tom and Jerry or Goofy and his mates required only the most rudimentary knowledge of English and the unrestrained laughter they provoked helped to ease, at least momentarily, the constant anxiety which tormented most of the students. As their knowledge of English improved, they graduated to enjoying films with sub-titles. It was much easier to decipher the brief summary of what was happening or what was being said on the screen than to take in the rapid-fire dialogues so common in the contemporary English and American films. The films with subtitles included mostly what are now regarded as the classics of cinema such as *The seven samurai* or *La strada* and similar foreign films which were barred from the audiences behind the Iron Curtain, so the students were kept busy by catching up with them. Finally, the golden age arrived: they were able to understand and enjoy the English language films. They saw most of these several times to make sure that everything was properly understood and correctly interpreted.

The most easily available cultural activity, the enjoyment of reading, was, of course, taken up by all the students. Dare and Hollander asked them in which languages they were reading. The vast majority replied that, apart from the compulsory set-texts required for their studies, they were reading books in English. The authors, however, did not enquire about the nature of the reading material: whether it was fiction, biography, politics,

---

[25] 50 years on – Hungarian uprising 1956. *the brick: newsletter for Keble alumni.* No. 38, Michaelmas term, 2006.

historical works or any other subject matter. This is surprising, because they listed a whole range of daily or weekly newspapers and other periodicals, and asked the students to state their preferred source of information.[26] Among the daily papers *The Manchester Guardian* was the most frequently chosen—it received double the number of votes than *The Times* or *The Daily Telegraph*—while among the weekly newspapers *The Observer* earned an outstandingly high vote. Among the weekly periodicals *The New Statesman* and *Punch* stood out as the students' preferred reading; a very large section of the respondents however gave no answer to this question at all. The survey obviously wished to elicit information on the students' political views by posing this question, and the replies regarding "general reading" produced at least a hint of it. "In asking this question"—summarized the authors—"we hoped to discover what were their political-intellectual interests, in so far as the reading of certain newspapers throw some light on these."[27] In the light of the answers, the political leaning of the students, as far as their reading of the newspapers was concerned, could only be described as tending to the left.

The survey also analysed in great detail the students' background (family and friends, belonging to a social class and its consequences, whether they suffered any discrimination or even persecution) as well as their views on and reaction to the major social changes brought about by successive governments after the war (land reform, nationalization of banks and big industries, school reform, improvements in welfare services). Dare and Hollander concluded that on the whole the students approved of the democratization process and the above-mentioned reforms, and that during the revolution or even after their escape, they were still convinced that its major achievements should be retained. Thus, it was no wonder that they also appreciated the major welfare reforms of the Attlee government, while, at the same time, expressing very strong anti-totalitarian sentiments and a firm belief in upholding individual rights. This political attitude, combining slightly leftist and some right-wing views stemmed directly from the students' experiences during their formative years. Their seemingly dedicated support of Labour policies was further strengthened by the fact that in the students' view Eden's Conservative government, totally preoccupied with Suez, had done nothing to help Hungary in her hour of need, while leading Labour politicians, first and foremost among them Denis Healey and Hugh

---

[26] Dare, Alan and Hollander, Paul: Op.cit., Tables 12 and 13A-D, pp.XX-XXIII.
[27] Ibid. p.23.

Gaitskell, forcefully demonstrated their solidarity with the Hungarian cause.

About the time when Dare and Hollander were compiling their report, a lengthy article appeared in *Népszava*, a Hungarian émigré paper published in London. It was entitled 'Long-standing problems: surmises and observations on the fate of the refugee students'.[28] The author gave his name as Pálos—most probably a pen-name—and, although he did not reveal his identity, he must have been a student, since he often used the first person plural when referring to a special problem or discussing a special issue. Summarizing his experiences over a year and a half, he made it clear that all he wanted was to reveal his own somewhat speculative view, a tentative exploration of how the Hungarian refugee students felt. They had been safely delivered from the frightening possibility of being left behind, largely forgotten, in the camps and they now occupied the rather rarefied space of the stateless by belonging nowhere. Pálos wanted to explore how they related now and might relate in the future to their new environment, while not erasing from their memory the home they had left behind. According to him, as the views of the generation of the 1956 students were formed during their youth in Hungary as well as by the revolution, they should not therefore forget their mother tongue, nor the experiences they had gained. Nor should they expunge from their memory the revolution when the nation, united as one, expressed its own identity and desire for freedom and political change. From among the problems the students might encounter, he selected only one, the dichotomy of love for one's home country and the compulsion to adapt to one's chosen new country, and he marshalled all his arguments around this single topic. He maintained that during the process of assimilation to their new home, memories of earlier years would inevitably fade and the ties still strongly linking the person to the past would gradually loosen. In contrast, unsuccessful attempts to adapt to the new circumstances would bring the past back into sharp focus, strengthening the ties instead of loosening them.

Pálos distinguished three different groups of Hungarian refugee students. In the first group were those who had been able or were even urged to study at a university in Hungary before the revolution and who could, therefore, have looked forward to a promising career and a secure future. They would, probably receive little extra in the West; indeed, it could be safely assumed that their future prospects in Britain were more

---

[28] Pálos: Korosodó problémák: találgatások és tapasztalatok a menekült diákok sorsával kapcsolatban. *Népszava*, 1 May, 1958, p.4.

moderate than they had been in Hungary. Under Communist rule the party had arranged one's whole life; so the students, after gaining their qualification, were placed into carefully pre-selected jobs, encouraged to settle down and helped to start a family. However, total control over their life was the price they had to pay for this pre-ordained security. In Britain, it was up to them to find a job and to work hard for their advancement. They needed a good measure of self-reliance and determination to succeed – qualities not easy to develop and maintain in a foreign country. The second group contained the students who had been committed Marxists in Hungary. Although their beliefs had been badly shaken by the excesses of the totalitarian Communist regime under Rákosi, and turning against him they had sealed their opposition by taking up arms during the revolution, they retained their Marxist conviction even after settling in the West. Currently they were engaged in separating Marxist ideology from its misapplication in Eastern Europe – a philosophical-political exercise few people in Britain were interested in. Finally, the third group consisted of those students who would have left Hungary before the revolution had they been offered a chance to emigrate. Pálos believed that this last group had the best chance of speedily assimilating to the new environment.

This superficially convincing classification of the 1956 students needs much adjustment and further expansion. For example, there were many students who did not belong to any of the above groups: they did not espouse Marxist ideology at any time, nor could they be labelled as belonging to the select few who had been handpicked by the Communist party to be trained as the future elite. Also, it had never occurred to most of the students to leave Hungary before the Soviet invasion on 4th November 1956; they only escaped when they thought everything had been lost. Nevertheless, these limitations do not detract from the strength of Pálos's arguments regarding the students successfully developing a "double identity" without suffering inner conflict. How far and how quickly—pondered the author—would human rights and individual freedom, the basic tenets of Western democracy, the high living standards, the feeling of security and the promising prospects for their future, distance the students from their past? Who amongst them would integrate into British society in a relatively short period of time and why? And who amongst them would resist it most? Behind this line of thought one can detect a barely disguised concern that the majority of students would lose their ties with their own past. The article nevertheless ends with a slightly upbeat optimism, that they might just be able to strike an acceptable balance between their present existence and their past life, their "old" and "new" homes and that for their future they need not sacrifice the memory of their past experiences.

Many examples may be brought up for the description of the varied manifestations of dual identity. The proposal submitted to the United Nations by two Hungarian students in the autumn of 1960 might serve as good illustration to cover some aspects of this seemingly, but not necessarily actual, split personality. The discussion of the so-called Hungarian question appeared yet again on the agenda of the UN four years after the revolution. The students, acting in the name of the Revolutionary Committee of the Hungarian Students Abroad, worked out a plan which, by easing the entrenched polarization of the world between East and West, offered a new solution to a range of political problems. They hastened to put their proposal on the table in time to influence, if at all possible, the tone and outcome of the debate. Their paper, with a covering letter was sent in four languages (English, French, German and Hungarian) to the foreign ministers of all the countries mentioned in the plan, on both sides of the East-West divide and also to the representatives of the major non-aligned nations. The proposal was published in the Hungarian émigré press[29] and in addition, in some English newspapers.[30] The plan, called 'A Hungarian proposal for depolarisation', was drawn up, after extensive consultations conducted mainly by correspondence, by Géza Ankerl and László Huszár. Both of them were fully engaged in studying and research; Ankerl as a postgraduate at the University of Fribourg, Switzerland and Huszár at the LSE, in London.

Working out the details of the plan, including the precise sequence of moves it entailed, required not only determination and dedication from them, but also an immense amount of time, which they could scarcely afford. Their action seems to prove the opposite of what has been several times referred to in the previous chapters. Namely, that the students, if they wanted to complete their studies in a foreign country the language of which they also had to learn from scratch, were forced to choose between devoting all their time to their studies or keeping their political aspiration alive. It was a situation of what could be described as "either/or"—that is making, albeit reluctantly, a choice—which Ankerl and Huszár boldly changed to "both"; that is, studying for their degrees while devoting time to write and promote their political pamphlet. Both of them had obtained their first degrees at the Faculty of Architecture in the Technical

[29] Ankerl, Géza and Huszár, László: Magyar javaslat a depolarizációra. In: *Népszava*, 1 Feb., 1961, p.4.
[30] For example: Hungarian rebels have three-stage scheme for Europe. In: *Evening Standard*, 2 Dec. 1960, p.32.

University of Budapest and had been members of the Students' Revolutionary Committee. After their escape Ankerl settled in Switzerland while Huszár chose England, where he was offered a job. However, he wished to pursue studies in politics and international relations and after several attempts he was able to secure for himself a grant and enrolled at the London School of Economics. He admitted that he had found the course difficult and had to work extremely hard to graduate in 1961.[31] At the same time Huszár was very active in the Hungarian émigré circle which had formed around the writer Zoltán Szabó, consisting mostly of like-minded young intellectuals. He also joined the Association of Hungarian Writers in Exile and published a series of articles on political topics. And throughout these years he had never lost contact with his friend, Géza Ankerl.

The idea of their UN proposal first emerged in the spring of 1960. During the following months they exchanged innumerable letters; most of these are still extant in the vast collection of Huszár's papers. Every statement, argument and proposal was debated in the minutest detail, all possible consequences mapped out, all potential reaction to the plan taken into account. They sought the views of the leading figures of the Hungarian émigré circles and, whenever possible, of English politician friends, but the final decision always rested with the two students. They accepted full responsibility for the proposal. It was the autumn of 1960 when the final touches were added to the paper, the first term of Huszár's last year at the LSE. He was well aware that he should have devoted all his time to studying in order to obtain his degree in the coming June. However, he felt that to finish the pamphlet and to dispatch it to all the recipients was equally important and deserved his most strenuous efforts.

The core of the proposal concerned the depolarization of the world through negotiation, which would ease the international tension and indicate a possible way out of the long standing impasse. Of course, the chief aim of the authors was the liberation of Hungary from Soviet occupation, but they realized that the question of Hungary could not be treated in isolation. It had to be a small but logical step in a major realignment of the world powers. This ambitious project envisaged a depolarization process in three stages. The first of these would be the diplomatic stage, which, through a series of negotiated agreements and mutual concessions, would establish new structures: it would, for example include the recognition of the two Germanys or the admission of China into the UN Security Council. The second stage would be military, the

---

[31] Interview with László Huszár. 7 Feb. 2005.

withdrawal of occupying forces from all countries and the setting up of a demilitarized and neutral zone in Central and Eastern Europe. The third stage would focus on political issues: the recognition of the right to self-determination and the building of new alliances. It would also be concerned with the development of countries after the military occupation had been removed. The authors stressed that the debate of the Hungarian question in the UN should, on no account, yet again descend into mutual recriminations, a verbal "tit for tat" between East and West, but it should signal the beginning of an honest search for feasible solutions, which, in the end, might also resolve the Hungarian problem.

Ankerl and Huszár received numerous responses to their proposal, among others from the Director of the Political Department of the UN, from Adlai Stevenson, the US delegate to the UN, from Professor George Kennan, former US Ambassador to the Soviet Union and Director of Advanced Study at Princeton University at the time, who assured the authors that he would draw John F. Kennedy's attention to the document. The French politician Mendès-France also sent a reply and responses were received from several British Labour politicians, including David Ennals and Denis Healey. Sending an acknowledgement of the receipt of the proposal and a few kind words of encouragement did not, of course, mean that it would be presented for serious consideration either at the UN or at government level. Nor could it be expected that it would influence any debate on existing international structures. This, however, should not detract from the valiant efforts of Ankerl and Huszár. They were imaginative, bold and willing to sacrifice precious time to such a project when the demands of their academic work should have been more than enough to occupy them fully.

CHAPTER X

INTO A WIDE NEW WORLD

Two further aspects of their conduct of life set the Hungarian refugee students apart from their British fellow students. First, the compulsion they felt to acquire certain goods which had gained an almost symbolic significance for them, and secondly, the irresistible desire to travel; to visit and explore the countries and the major towns of Western Europe, from which they had previously been barred. For both of these activities however, they needed substantial additional financial resources. They could only secure these by saving as much as possible from their grants, which did not amount to much, and by supplementing their savings with income earned by taking up any odd job on offer. Dare and Hollander quizzed the students at length about their finances, whether the grant and/or pocket money they received was sufficient to cover all their needs.[1] The answers to the questions were extremely varied and difficult to interpret. Some of the students lived in colleges or student hostels, mostly providing full board, and the bulk of their maintenance grant was transferred directly to the relevant bodies, so they only received an agreed amount of pocket money. On the other hand, some of them lived in rented accommodation for which they paid themselves from the full grant handed to them every month. Of the many statistical tables, drawn up by the authors therefore, the one summarizing the replies to the question whether the students were, on the whole, satisfied with the grant they received seems to be the most relevant: 241 students out of 279 felt that the amount they received, either the full grant or pocket money, was just about right and more or less sufficient for their needs. This referred only to the most basic needs. The survey, however, clearly indicated that the students did not expect to be given additional grants either for travel expenditure or for the purchase of what could be perceived as luxuries. They found it self-evident that for these "extras" they had to pay from the "extra income" they earned themselves.

---

[1] Dare, Alan and Hollander, Paul: Op cit., Tables 43A-F, 44A-B, pp.XL-XLI.

Most of the students arriving in Britain had only the clothes they stood up in – only a very small minority had had the time, thought and energy to put on two or three pullovers before their escape. It would have been, in any case, totally inadvisable to pack a suitcase as it would have been a sure sign, a perfect give-away for the police or the border guards that the people carrying them were planning to cross into Austria. Not to mention that the suitcases would most probably have been abandoned when they were crawling on their hands and knees across the frozen fields. The warehouses of the Red Cross and the BCAR were immediately opened to the refugees, offering a wide range of second-hand clothes and most of them helped themselves by selecting a few necessary items. (A former student, however, gleefully recalled that one of his colleagues found it rather difficult to close the doors of his over-full wardrobe.) The students at Leeds and Edinburgh were lucky enough to receive a full set of new suits, underwear, shoes and overcoats; the others had to wait until they had saved enough for a much coveted new dress or for a pair of shoes that really fitted. Not to mention that the charities would have raised their collective eyebrows had they found a refugee student in their warehouse searching for evening wear suitable for a black-tie occasion. Yet, the Hungarian students at Oxbridge resented being regarded as poor relations by the other students, and while having only a single respectable suit, some of them had a dinner jacket made by a local tailor to be paid for from their hard-earned pennies.

The first purchases by the refugee students, however, consisted mainly of electrical goods; the acquisition of a typewriter, a camera, a tape-recorder or a record player was very high on their list of desired equipment. These were followed closely by the purchase of a bicycle, and not just any old, rusty and rickety push-bike, which would have been perfectly adequate to get about town but, in at least in one instance, a brand new, superb racing bicycle, the appearance of which caused quite a stir among the British fellow students.[2] Some of the students, especially but not exclusively those who were exempt from attending the language course, had already sought employment during the summer of 1957: László Jámbor, for example—the only Hungarian student at Oxford who passed the language exams with excellent marks in June—worked in a local laundry and bought a wireless and a tape-recorder out of his earnings.[3] Dare and Hollander's survey did not include specific questions about the purchase of goods, but, based on their personal acquaintance

---

[2] Interview with Albin Závody. 2 March 2006.
[3] Interview with Katalin Jámbor. 26 Jan. 2005.

with a large number of students, the authors concluded that they were well equipped with these and apart from a very few exceptions, they enjoyed a "materially higher standard of living than they had in Hungary" and that "this relative material well-being was an important element in their present sense of security."[4] The psychological motivation behind the urge, normally exhibited by refugees to buy goods in order to surround themselves with them and thus create at least an illusion of a secure home, is self-evident. The Hungarian students, although they were well cared for and suffered no lack of basic necessities, still exhibited the same symptoms: the things which they selected and bought from the money they had earned stood for their own self-esteem, independence and security in their new environment.

The students' desire to travel as widely as possible was prompted, to some extent, by the same motivation. The survey produced some astonishing results: by the autumn of 1958 more than half of the refugee students had visited at least one, and many of them two or even three West European countries. The report noted that although the authors had no comparable statistics for the travelling custom of British students, it could be safely assumed that a much lower percentage of them travelled regularly abroad.[5] It also revealed that a relatively large number of Hungarian students—98 out of 279—had visited other countries before 1956.[6] However, as the authors themselves explained, these figures most probably also included those students, who as children had either been rounded up and forcibly transferred to concentration camps or, had temporary ended up in Austria or Germany after fleeing to the West with their parents near the end of the Second World War.[7] After the war, especially during the 1950s, Hungary, along with all other East European countries, was hermetically sealed off, and not only from the West, but also from one another. The only young people who were able to visit other countries were those who were—after being carefully selected by the Communist party—sent to study abroad, almost without exception to the Soviet Union, or represented Hungary at international Communist youth festivals or at various sporting events.

Their desire to discover the world might, therefore, have been much stronger than that felt by other students; travelling abroad freely was their chance to break the shackles imposed on them by the Communist regime. They were keen to see Paris, Rome, Berlin or any town in any county

---

[4] Dare, Alan and Hollander, Paul: Op.cit., pp.69-70.
[5] Ibid. p.73.
[6] Ibid. Tables 22A-C, p.XXXI.
[7] Ibid. p.22.

which they had the opportunity of visiting or were passing through. The student hostels and colleges in any case closed down for the summer, the students had no family to go home to in order to spend a few lazy months there, so, instead of renting temporary accommodation somewhere in Britain, they embarked on long, extended journeys on the Continent. They were reasonably well supported by the three months' additional grant they had collected as a lump sum, supplemented by the money they had earned during a part of the vacation. The information underpinning the organization of the tours was plentiful. Friendships, broken by the escape to the West and by settling in different countries, were quickly re-established: everyone seemed to know precisely in which country everyone else happened to live and at which university they were pursuing their studies. The new refugee student organizations helped to forge new friendships: large numbers of students attended the frequent international meetings and kept in constant touch by correspondence. Information was readily available through commonly shared knowledge: on student hostels open during the summer in Europe offering free or inexpensive accommodation, on the student refectories where the food was acceptable and where no one checked student ID cards too closely, or on the pubs and beer gardens frequented by the local refugee students with whom one could discuss life over a glass of wine. Travel costs were kept to the minimum. Hitch-hiking was the accepted mode of travel; it was wide-spread and relatively safe in those days, even for female students. Information on events and offers of places were exchanged quicker than now, in the age of the internet. The University of Heidelberg is offering free places on its summer course for five Hungarian students – if you wish to improve your German, apply at once! There is going to be a seminar for Hungarian youth, organized in Holland for refugee intellectuals – do come and participate in it!

One of the most generous examples of hospitality was set by the Hungarian students studying at the University of Leuven in Belgium: to help the other refugee students to share in the celebration of the World Exhibition of Brussels in the summer of 1958, they offered their own places in the student hostel as accommodation for those coming from abroad.[8] This exhibition was the greatest attraction for the students that summer. According to the statistics provided by the survey of Dare and Hollander, the country most visited by the Hungarian students studying in Britain was, rather predictably, France. It was, however followed closely by the Benelux countries—40 visitors in a year—and this popularity could

---

[8] Information kindly contributed by Kálmán Száz.

surely be attributed only to the overriding interest of the students in the World Exhibition. As András Szabó recalled, some of the Hungarian students studying in Edinburgh, for example, decided not to repeat their sea-side holiday of the previous year in spite of it being a huge success. Five of them had rented a cottage and spent the time swimming, larking about on the beach and roaming along the seashore. This time they began to plan early and carefully for saving up enough money to pay for their trip to Brussels. Szabó himself, the proud owner of a brand new bicycle used his increased mobility to set up a messenger and delivery service.[9] He was just one student of the many engaged in a great variety of temporary jobs during that summer.

Today, from the distance of half a century, the students remember those jobs with humour and a certain nostalgia.[10] One of the most favoured workplaces was the Wall's sausage factory on night shift. The salary paid was exceptionally good as the students did not mind working overtime through the night. The spirit of the workforce was high with an unrestrained display of good-humoured camaraderie. In addition, for the staff working in December—and this included the students working through the Christmas break—the management put together a Christmas hamper, filled with the goods the factory produced. It was not the management's fault that the students, being fully aware of what was the composition of the filling put into the sausage skins, could not face eating the factory's present.

László and Kati Jámbor—like many other students—were employed by their colleges to work in the kitchens and refectories. Their main task was laying the tables, serving the food, clearing away the dirty dishes and, as their biggest chore, the never-ending washing up in the sculleries. No wonder that they soon tired of it and changed their jobs. They began to work in a doughnut factory instead, where they had to stand at the conveyor belt for hours on end and inject jam with an oversized hypodermic needle into the endless rows of doughnuts. During the summer others opted to sell ice cream on the streets. At that time this was a one-man job usually sub-contracted from an Italian ice- cream manufacturer. They pushed their carts to what was supposed to be the best positions for selling the maximum number of cones. Many students brewed tea in the Lyon's Corner Houses, or the luckier ones made coffee

---

[9] Interview with András Szabó. 2006 Jan. 19.
[10] I am grateful for the information on their experiences freely given amongst others by Lóránt Czigány, Katalin Jámbor, Tamás Kabdebó, Péter Pallai, András Sándor, Száz Kálmán, András Szabó, Albin Závody, Iván Zmertych, András Zsigmond, Ferenc Zsuppán.

in the few "Continental" type coffee houses – the notion of what consisted a proper espresso was almost totally unknown at that time in England. One of the students felt he had won the lottery by being accepted for a job in a whisky distillery in Scotland, while another was loudly proclaimed as "the excellent shot who had fought the Russian tanks on the streets of Budapest" and who had recently been enticed to help out in the shooting gallery at the local fairground where his expertise was greatly appreciated by the customers.

The students living in the hostel in Tavistock Square applied for cleaners' jobs in the City. They had to start very early by walking across London to start their shift at 5 am—there was no public transport running at that hour—so that the offices for the white collar workers, arriving at about four hours' time, would be ready and spick and span. This unusual timetable suited the students well; by the time the language classes and later their lectures started they had finished their jobs and the rest of the day was theirs to be spent as they pleased. Many of the students found employment in hospitals. They wheeled the trolleys in and out of the wards, moving the patients in and out of the operating theatres. The saddest job was to move them at the end of their journeys into the morgue. The students in the hospital laundries had to catch the hot sheets as they came off the giant pressing-rollers; by the end of the summer they developed thick callouses on the tips of their fingers. Some were even offered entertainment as part of their jobs: András Zsigmond, a medical student at Liverpool University, worked as a speedway assistant at a dog racing track. His task was to sweep the dirt track between the races.

The construction industry also tempted some students. Many of them actually had appropriate experience as during the "building of socialism" in Hungary they had had to spend a part of their summer holidays—mostly without pay as "voluntary workers"—on building sites. Péter Pallai related that whenever he passed the newly erected building of the Islington public library he was filled with pride because as a labourer he had participated, together with his best friend, in its construction. In fact, they had worked with such enthusiasm that the foreman had to take them aside and warn them not to employ the "Stakhanovite" working methods in England, their over-eagerness dictated a tempo which the local workforce found impossible to keep up with. They were advised, if they wished to retain their job, to take it easy.

There were many other equally odd or amusing work experiences which could be added to the list. To the question posed by Dare and Hollander about vacation work, more than two thirds of the students replied that they found it necessary to supplement their grant by taking up jobs during the summer. However, even with the extra income, some of them could not make ends meet and faced financial difficulties every now and then. These included an early acquaintance with the institution of the pawn shop where they had to leave on temporary deposit their newly acquired and cherished equipment. The banks were quick to warn the students about overdrafts, although most of them opened their accounts much later. The Hungarian Committee of the CVCP had, indeed, advised the universities that they should, for the sake of uniformity, give the grant as well as the pocket money in cash to the students. They would find this much easier to handle than to struggle with the alien concept of a bank account, when they had so much else to learn. The exception, yet again was Oxford. The Oxford Hungarian Committee decided to open a bank account for every student explaining that their pocket money would be transferred there regularly. The weekly sum was set at half a guinea—so much more elegant than the 10 shillings the students at other universities received—and it only cost an extra six pennies per student, a trifling sum.

The pocket money was also what might be called a "trifling sum", enough to cover the basic necessities only. It was most probably set by the BCAR's guidance, as this was the weekly amount that the refugees in the camps received. One was able to purchase from it the essential toiletry items, maybe a new pair of stockings and a bar of chocolate supplementing the meals which the refugees found difficult to eat, but it was almost impossible make it stretch to cover the cost of anything extra, such as the daily packet of cigarettes. The CVCP accepted the 10 shillings pocket money as the norm and Logan informed the universities to this effect.[11] Yet, some of the students had truly legitimate extra expenditure. The London students living in colleges for example, had to pay the bus or underground fare when travelling daily to Bloomsbury for the language course. It might also have been misunderstood by some that the money put into the slot of the gas fires would be reimbursed at the end of the term. Not being aware of this, they would rather brace themselves against the cold than enjoy every now and then a shilling's worth of warmth. However, some of the universities and colleges offered work to the students. At Imperial College it was suggested that they help out for a few hours in the laboratories which they might enjoy and for which they would be paid. This could be taken as supplement to their pocket money. However, on hearing of such a proposal, Logan immediately sent a note to the relevant authorities, among them to the Domestic Bursar of Imperial

---

[11] Seaford, C. C.: *Hungarian students. Notes on instructions received by the Domestic Bursar of Imperial College from the Principal of London University, Dr. D. W. Logan, on Monday 3rd December, 1956.* UoLA, CB3/4/31.

College, instructing them that if the students' earnings would exceed 10 shillings per week, no pocket money should be paid to them. At that stage, Logan was of course worried that the universities would not be able to fully support the education of the students out of their own resources, so he wished to account for every penny spent on the students including the meagre pocket money. He thought that, for the sake of the long term benefits, the students might have to suffer some initial minor inconveniences. Nevertheless, he felt that he might have acted with undue harshness and ended his letter to the Bursar with the words: "I hope I do not appear to be too mean!"[12]

The very first estimates for the cost of maintenance of the students throughout their studies were, in fact, drawn up by Seaford, the Domestic Bursar of Imperial College, in a memo to the Rector, on 13th December 1956.[13] He calculated about £50 for lodging, based on the rental value of the rooms including overheads, £150 for meals, that is, £200 per annum for each student. This sum excluded the pocket money and any additional monies the students might receive. These were the figures submitted by Lockwood to the CVCP Hungarian Committee for consideration.[14] The Committee finally agreed that the yearly minimum maintenance grant per student should be £325, with the exception of Cambridge, Oxford and London where a higher figure should apply. This sum, however, already included the substantially increased pocket money—from £2 to £10 per month—relabelled as "other expenses". The increase was accepted at the insistence of Cambridge University on the grounds that the Hungarian students had no families to rely on and no homes where they could spend the breaks in the academic year. Eventually, a further £30 was added to the annual sum given to the students. This was meant to help them out during the vacations.[15] Although two universities still expressed their reservations

---

[12] Letter by D. W. Logan to C. C. Seaford. 8 Dec. 1956. ICA, Hungarian Relief, SS/1/4.
[13] Seaford, C. C.: *Hungarian students. Memo to the Rector.* 13 Dec. 1956. ICA, Hungarian Relief, SS/1/4.
[14] Lockwood, J. F.: *Hungarian refugee students. Fifth memorandum of the Vice-Chancellor of the University of London.* 21 Dec. 1956. UoLA, CB3/2/1/5.
[15] This additional "vacation supplement" of £30 is not mentioned in the minutes and other documentation of the CVCP and its sub-committees. It was, however, one of the main topics discussed at the extraordinary meeting of the Collegiate Council of the University of London on 4 January 1957. The Council even determined the method of paying the supplement: the students were to receive £10 before the Christmas and Easter breaks and the summer vacation. See: University of London. Sub-Committee of the Collegiate Council for Allowances: *Notes on a meeting.* 4 Jan. 1957. ICA, SS/1/4.

about the adequacy of the £325 to cover all the maintenance expenses of the students, the Hungarian Committee agreed to uphold it, at least initially, as a reasonable working proposal. The Committee also agreed to handle the expenses under three separate headings: university fees (waived by the universities but which appeared as debit in their budgets), maintenance (board and lodging which might vary locally) and other expenses (pocket money and vacation supplement issued directly to the students from which they were expected to purchase the books and minor equipment necessary for their studies). The CVCP endorsed the proposal at its meeting at the end of January 1957.

The endorsement however did not set the accepted figures in stone, and the Committee reviewed them several times before reaching a final agreement in October 1957. There were at least two counterproposals which merited serious consideration. One of them was the document issued by the Ministry of Education in 1955 summarizing the result of the triennial review of the maintenance grant for university students, payable by the relevant LEAs, which offered comparable figures to those set by the CVCP.[16] The grant and other sums were, as detailed in the report, much lower than the figures agreed by the CVCP (Oxford and Cambridge £283 plus £47 and10 shillings vacation supplement, London £252 plus £38 and 10 shillings, all other universities £225 plus also £38 and 10 shillings), but these were regarded as the basic contribution, to which a whole range of supplementary grants might be added (for example, reimbursement of travel expenditure, special grant for books and learning equipment). The students' access to other financial resources (e.g. private support), did not affect the level of official grant they received. Since these supplementary grants were not available for the refugee students, nor would they get any parental contribution to the costs, the CVCP felt that the sums they set were roughly in line with the Ministry's directive.

The other document submitted in early July to the CVCP for consideration was a letter and an enclosed explanatory note by the Director of WUS, A. H. Robson.[17] He was, of course, mainly concerned about the students who were to be awarded a grant from WUS—the Lord Mayor's Fund had just transferred a substantial sum of money to WUS for the provision of these grants—since the WUS students would also be

---

[16] Ministry of Education: *Administrative memorandum No. 502. Maintenance rates for students at universities: result of the triennial review.* 1955.
[17] Letter by A. H. Robson to J. F. Lockwood. 1 July 1957. In: CVCP. Joint meeting of the Committee on Hungarian students and the Committee dealing with the allocation of the students: *Minutes. Appendices B. and C.* 16 July, 1957. UoLA, CB3/1/3/3.

studying in the universities and their treatment should be the same as that of the CVCP supported students. Their tuition fees should be waived, accommodation in student hostels provided for them at a rate fixed by individual universities and the money they were to receive for "other expenses" should be calculated on the same basis. The CVCP's Hungarian Committee discussed Robson's proposals in mid-July but reached a decision on the matter only in October. It declined to waive tuition and other related fees for WUS students as this would incur further losses for the universities which they would not be able to afford, but it was ready to take Robson's arguments into account when finally setting the amount to be spent on maintenance and handed over to the students for "other expenses".

Robson's estimates on what would be the fair amount to cover all costs were distinctly more generous than those calculated by the CVCP or set by the Ministry of Education. In his note he argued that the Hungarian students should be treated differently to their British counterparts; they had no family or homes in Britain, they had to study much harder because of their insufficient knowledge of English, including studying throughout the summer vacation, and "because of their relative ignorance of British ways Hungarian students may find themselves less able than British students to conduct their affairs economically." In addition to board and lodging he earmarked appropriate sums to cover heating, laundry, clothing, transport, miscellaneous expenses – such as toiletries, haircuts, shoe repairs, writing materials and stamps – and, last but not least, as a most commendable separate item, money for cultural activities such as subscriptions, newspapers, non-study related reading material, entrance fees to cinemas, theatres and concerts and for the bus fares travelling to them and, quite surprisingly, for the weekly supply of cigarettes. He proposed replacing the CVCP's £325 average for these expenses by the much higher sum of £390 plus £40 for textbooks and for holiday purposes, producing the grand total of £430.

The Hungarian Committee was unable to accept this very high figure, but convinced by Robson's arguments, decided to raise substantially the overall amounts: up to £400 for Oxbridge students, £375 for the students at London University and £350 for students at all other universities. The figures were to serve as guidelines. Each university was to receive half of the relevant sum from the central CVCP fund and was expected to pay the other half from the appeal fund raised locally. Furthermore, the Committee agreed to reimburse the cost of expensive major pieces of equipment needed by the students studying science, engineering and medicine, but maintained that for books, stationery and related items, students would have to pay out of their "other expenses" grant.[18] As the result of a review after the first year, this grant was raised to £12 per month with effect from 1st January 1959. Robson's intervention and the consequent increase in the students' finances, however, did not mean that the students devoted the whole summer to studying. Instead, they opted to work in order to earn some extra money and then spend all that they had on material goods and travelling abroad. What they gained by it was real life experience.

Towards the end of November 1956 when the members of the CVCP enthusiastically endorsed the proposal of accepting about 150 Hungarian refugee students and ensuring that they would be able to complete their studies, they were confident that they could raise enough funds to underpin their efforts financially. Each university set up an appeal, involving not only their current staff and students but also the alumni associations. Within a few weeks however, it became apparent that the original targets had been set far too high—most of the people targeted had already contributed substantial sums to the Red Cross or to the Lord Mayor's Fund—and the universities would not be able raise enough money to fund the students' education without external help. The CVCP decided to turn to the Lord Mayor with a request for additional funds. Lockwood had already approached the Lord Mayor's Fund in early December; at this stage for a lump sum to provide for the transfer of the students from Austria and their reception in Britain. Almost immediately the Fund released £10,000 for this purpose which just about covered the initial expenditure. A few months later, at the suggestion of the Lord Mayor, the universities compiled a detailed submission on the expected expenditure of the education of the students over the entire period of their studies. The estimate was drawn up on the basis of 164 students participating in the scheme (the numbers actually varied from estimate to estimate between 150 and 164) and the total cost, excluding the tuition fees waived by the universities, just exceeding £180,000. At the same time, the donations contributed to the universities' own appeal funds, were expected to raise, at best, no more than £70,000, so the anticipated shortfall was a very large sum indeed. The universities calculated that they would need at least a £115,000 infusion of funds and, in addition to this sum, an instant £40,000 to reimburse them for the cost of the language courses and the maintenance of the students during the courses. The total amount of money therefore, for which Lockwood on behalf of the CVCP submitted a

---

[18] CVCP. Joint meeting of the Committee on Hungarian students and the Sub/Committee dealing with the allocation of the students: *Minutes.* 4 Oct. 1957. UoLA, CB3/1/3/4.

request to the Lord Mayor's Fund, amounted to £155,000.[19] In his letter Lockwood also drew the attention of the Lord Mayor to those 120 students already registered by WUS, whose future needed to be decided. He said that the continuation of their studies should be assured, and they should not be cast aside for lack of funding.

The CVCP had to wait rather anxiously for another two months before receiving the definitive response from the Lord Mayor's Fund. It was at its meeting scheduled for 24th May that Lockwood was able to inform the members that their request had been fully met: the Fund was to transfer £125,000 for the education of the students and £10,000 for the cost of the language courses. Furthermore, the BCAR was also to allocate £20,000 to supplement the latter sum, so, altogether, the CVCP would receive the required £155,000. The Fund also transferred a large amount of money to WUS for organizing the education of the not yet allocated "Unattached" students. This extremely favourable outcome resolved, at one stroke, all the problems the universities faced; the lack of financial resources no more hindered the full implementation of the CVCP Hungarian students scheme. The universities could concentrate all their efforts on the teaching of the students and to look after all their needs, both spiritual and material.

Towards the end of 1957 the Lord Mayor's Fund asked the CVCP to prepare a paper on their activities regarding the refugee students to be included in the Fund's report, scheduled to appear the following autumn after the closure of the Fund. The work was undertaken by Walters[20] and he included in his report not only the CVCP's Hungarian students scheme, but also the role played by WUS and the contribution given by various organizations which had provided larger or smaller funds for scholarships: the Ford and the Gulbenkian Foundations, the NCB, the Free Europe University in Exile, the United Nations Association and the Local Education Authorities. Thus he was able to paint the widest possible picture, pulling together and depicting all the strands of activities exerted for the reception of the students: the large and enthusiastic response from the people of Britain, whose donations had established the necessary financial resources for their education, the concentrated effort by the universities and other higher education institutions to receive them at short notice, teach them English and allocate them to the place where they were

---

[19] Letter by J. F. Lockwood to the Lord Mayor of London. 28 March 1957. In: CVCP. Joint meeting of the Committee on Hungarian students and the Sub-Committee dealing with the allocation of the students: *Minutes. Appendix B.* 2 April 1957. UoLA, CB3/1/3/2.

[20] Lord Mayor of London's Hungarian & Central European Relief Fund: *Report of the Fund November 1956 – September 1958.* [1958.] pp.62-67.

to continue their studies. He outlined the results achieved in the first year and gave a detailed account of the overall financial situation. His figures on the finances should be regarded as the most authoritative, and, in the light of this information, the figures quoted above should be slightly modified. The expenditure on the transfer of the students from Austria to Britain, their temporary accommodation, the language courses and maintenance provided during the courses amounted to £48,230 instead of the estimated £40,000. As the contribution requested from the Lord Mayor's Fund and the BCAR was based on the original estimate, the excess was paid by the universities from their own resources. These had fallen well below expectation: instead of the targeted £70,000, the final sum collected amounted to only £56,418. However, the sum projected for scholarships had also somewhat decreased, because the number of CVCP students enrolled in October 1957 was 154 instead of the 164 as envisaged earlier.

The Hungarian Committee therefore recorded at the October 1957 meeting its full satisfaction with the outcome of its dealings with the Lord Mayor's Fund. The Fund made further provisions, the largest being the already mentioned grant to WUS of £141,000, sufficient to cover scholarships for about one hundred students. Separate allowances were made for students studying music and fine arts – £17,000 and £1,000 respectively.[21] The accounts presented at the end of the first academic year in which the Hungarian students entered higher education provided clear proof that the CVCP's satisfaction regarding the financial situation was well founded. Substantial savings had been made, due to a large extent to the reduction of student numbers; a few students finished their studies by June 1958, while some of them had decided not to enrol at university. Others dropped out during the first year, although the savings made on the dropouts were, to some extent balanced by the support given to those students who had been allowed to repeat the year. Finally, the money invested had earned excellent interests.

Because of the good financial results the CVCP decided to increase both the pocket money and the maintenance grant as from January 1959 and to reimburse two thirds of the costs incurred by the universities instead of the initially agreed half. Yet, it was with some embarrassment that the CVCP recorded further savings the following year, although it was again mainly due to the prudent husbandry of the funds. Since the Hungarian Committee was determined to spend all the money in the CVCP's central Hungarian fund on the students, after reviewing the situation in December

---

[21] Ibid. p.82.

1959, new resolutions were reached on the best ways and means to achieve their aim. First—they agreed—they would be able to take over the maintenance of the Ford and Free Europe students as their funding would end after the second year. As some of the Ford students were pursuing research for a higher degree, no strict time-limit would be set for the completion of their studies. Secondly, the annual reports on many of the students studying for a first degree strongly indicated that they should be encouraged to continue to study for postgraduate qualification. There were ample resources available for their full support. Thirdly, for the students studying on a LEA grant, the CVCP was ready to set aside a sum for additional money to help them maintain themselves during the vacation and students with families were to receive an extra grant on application. Suitable part-time students might be given help with their travelling expenses. Finally, university fees would be paid from the central fund and the real cost of maintaining "Quota" students should be met in place of the notional figures in such cases where considerable difference existed between the two.[22]

The universities, especially those which had been able to raise substantial sums from their own Hungarian appeal, found themselves in an equally embarrassing situation. The more financial support they received from the CVCP's central fund, the more savings accumulated on their own Hungarian account and just as the CVCP's Hungarian Committee, they faced the problem of deciding on the best way to use the money in their ever-growing kitty. The main item discussed at the meetings of the Oxford Hungarian Committee during 1959 for example, was the examination of the current and future financial commitments the Committee had regarding every single Hungarian student at Oxford. The University had already been more than generous in its support for those refugee students who had not been eligible for CVCP or other grants. All postgraduate students at Oxford belonged to this group—without themselves actually being aware of it—and, if they were accepted by the colleges to study for higher degrees, the Norrington Committee provided their funding. These students simply appeared in the official lists as "off Quota" and in the 1959 review the Committee was willing to extend their scholarship for a further two or three years on the recommendation of their supervisor. It also paid the grant to the students who had left Oxford to study elsewhere, and, if they failed there too, the members of the Committee wondered whether they had been unduly harsh in their assessment and had not done enough for

---

[22] CVCP. Joint meeting of the Committee on Hungarian students and the Sub-Committee dealing with the allocation of the students: *Minutes.* 10 Dec. 1959. UoLA, CB3/1/3/10.

those who "through bad luck and excusable foolishness" forfeited their studies at Oxford. Should they now be "rehabilitated"? Finally, the Committee set aside some money for those too, who initially had come to Oxford on the very first charter flight but not being students had been turned away. Should they receive a small sum to help them into a good job?[23]

The other topic discussed by the Committee concerned the future of the students. A year earlier Norrington had already pondered on the jobs the students might apply for when they had completed their studies. In a letter to D. M. Hawke, the Vice-Chancellor of the University, he expressed his concern about it and said that it might be appropriate to begin considering jobs for the Hungarian students: "This may be comparatively simple for the scientists, but more difficult for the 'humanists' of whom I suspect that Oxford has a proportion above average."[24]

It would be fair to say that at that time the students themselves had no idea of and seemingly cared little about what they might do after they had received their degrees. To the question put to them by Dare and Hollander "What sort of occupation would you like to obtain when you have finished your studies?" 48 students did not even reply and to the following question on what else they might do, 53 respondents expressed pessimism about finding anything suitable, 53 said they did not know and 120 students did not send an answer at all.[25] Even the science, engineering and medical students, whose studies were geared towards specialist fields and who were not expected to have problems in finding suitable posts, had doubts about their future employment. They were convinced that being foreigners they would suffer disadvantages: "I know that because of my background"—wrote one of them expressing the views held by many of them—"and my language difficulties I could get a leading position only with a very great effort compared with English people; therefore I will be at a disadvantage."[26] Dare and Hollander interpreted this pessimism as an expression of insecurity which would disappear very slowly. A relatively high proportion of the students, however,—18 percent of all who replied—stated that they hoped to obtain an academic position in a higher education institution or a post in a leading research institute. The authors linked this choice also to the feeling of insecurity felt by immigrants: the notion of

---

[23] Hungarian Students Committee. Hungarian Students Scholarship Fund: *Report of the Treasurer to the Committee.* 2 June and 3 Nov. 1959. BLA UR6/OVS/H File2. Vol.2/3.
[24] Letter by A. L. P. Norrington to D. M. Hawke. 8 Dec. 1958. Ibid.
[25] Dare, Alan and Hollander, Paul: Op.cit., Tables 15A and B., p.XXIII.
[26] Ibid. p12.

security and prestige associated with such posts greatly appealed to them when considering their future. It might also be added that after coming to terms with studying in a foreign language, the love of, and interest in, their subjects might also have tempted the students to dream about continuing their research first as postgraduates then as members of the academic community and thus carving out a respectable career for themselves.

By the end of 1958 the students had also made the first tentative mental steps towards assimilation into British society: more than half of them had decided to apply for British citizenship.[27] The majority could also imagine themselves assimilating into the British middle classes,[28] and 215 students out of 279 were willing and ready to marry a non-Hungarian.[29] (This is not surprising as a relatively small proportion of the refugees were unattached females.) The students still hoped against all the odds that they might be able to return to Hungary one day, but only on condition that the Soviet Army had withdrawn from the country, free elections would be held and democracy established.[30] Of course, in their hearts they knew that this was no more than a dream, but did not dare to confess it even to themselves.

On the occasion of the 25th anniversary of the revolution Mátyás Sárközi carried out a survey among the 1956 Hungarian intellectuals living in Britain to assess the level of their assimilation and the measure of their success against their expectations after spending twenty five years in this country. He noted that compared to groups of other Hungarian immigrants who had arrived in Britain earlier, the career of the 1956 generation was much less spectacular and their achievements less outstanding, in spite of the magnificent help they had received for the continuation of their studies which most of them managed to complete successfully: "Compared to the Hungarian members of the House of Lords and to the notable industrialists of Hungarian origin, the exodus of 1956 produced only a handful of respected academics, one or two moderately successful film directors and musicians and a few entrepreneurs who had built up a reasonably prosperous business."[31]

Admittedly, it would be futile to search for millionaires, captains of industry, media celebrities or other well-known public figures among the 1956 refugees who have settled in Britain, especially among the former refugee students. Even in their wildest dreams the students fostered much

[27] Ibid. Table 40. p.XXXIX.
[28] Ibid. Tables 16A and B. p.XXIII.
[29] Ibid. Table 3A. p.XIV.
[30] Ibid. Table 34. p.XXXVII.
[31] Sárközi, Mátyás: Op.cit., p.459.

more modest expectations. They had been forced to escape from their homes and arrived in this country with the aim of completing their studies, of finding a job in which they could make the best use of what they had learned, of settling down, having a family and to becoming a respected member of the community which had so kindly received them. It was a secure and normal existence that they craved rather than riches; recognition if they excelled in their own field rather than adulation or notoriety. Furthermore, they still hoped, at least during the first couple of years, that one day they would be able to return to Hungary and to offer their services, the knowledge and experience they had gained in Britain for the benefit of their home country.

Looking back now from the distance of more than fifty years, after a whole working life spent in this country, it seems that the path they travelled more or less met their expectations. The degrees they earned here enabled them to become industrious members of the British middle class: engineers, architects, doctors, teachers and a proportionally large number of them university lecturers and scientific researchers. From the latter group many joined the brain drain: after obtaining their first degrees or higher qualifications, quite a few of the former refugee students left for the United States to settle there. As one of the students quipped in the early days at Oxford: "We are all preparing to go to the USA except we do not know it yet." Some of the students reached senior and responsible positions to crown their careers both in Britain and abroad and enjoyed the recognition with which their achievements were honoured. To give just one example: the former Hungarian refugee student at Oxford, György (now Sir George) Radda began his research career in the Department of Physiology, Anatomy and Genetics at Oxford University eventually becoming its Head. He filled the position of Chief Executive of the Medical Research Council between 1996 and 2003, and for his services to science he was knighted in 2004. He is still engaged in research at Oxford.

British society on the other hand had no specific expectations of the refugee students, apart from hoping that they would work hard and make the most of the exceptional opportunities that had been offered to them, and concentrate on finishing their studies. To quote the Rector of Imperial College again, the Hungarian students were to be treated as any other students; they were to enjoy equal rights, but expected to achieve equally outstanding results. And those at the universities who, not sparing time and effort, had organized the reception of the students and looked after them throughout their years of study felt that they themselves had lived through truly heroic times. The leaders of the universities, their staff and students, put aside any temporary misunderstandings and petty problems which might have divided them, and all worked together to bring the Hungarian students project to a successful completion. As Walters described it in the closing paragraph of the article which he published anonymously: "Those who knew and worked with the students throughout the country were pleased and encouraged to see how hard they worked initially with their learning of the language and latterly with their degree studies. A number were awarded such good first degrees that they were encouraged to proceed to higher degrees and the same resilience and enthusiasm was displayed. Many have kept in touch over the years and all have settled happily to work in this country and elsewhere."[32]

In the autumn of 1958 the students were asked by Dare and Hollander whether they regretted coming to this country. From the 279 respondents 271 firmly stated that they did not.[33] During the interviews I conducted for this book with former Hungarian students, the same sentiment was expressed. Yet, some of them arrived here only by chance. When recalling their reception, their student years and all the help they had been given, they said time and time again how grateful they felt then and feel even today to the British people for accepting them, providing for them and making it possible for them to enjoy a happy life.

Now, that they all can and may go back to Hungary—the Soviets after all left the country soon after 1989—most of them maintain the notion of belonging, without any inner conflict, to "two homes". It was therefore not surprising that the idea of publicly saying thanks to the British people on the fiftieth anniversary of the revolution first surfaced at an informal meeting of the former Oxford Hungarian students in Budapest. All those participating in the meeting felt that the publication of a letter in *The Times*, signed by as many students as could be contacted, would be the best way to do it. I was happy to accept the responsibility of organizing it.

The letter, with 49 signatories appeared in the leading British newspaper on 2nd October 2006 under the heading: 'The UK and the Hungarian Uprising aftermath'. It was brief and to the point: "This month we commemorate the 50th anniversary of the 1956 Hungarian Revolution. After its brutal suppression by the Soviet Army, a large number of Hungarians, among them several hundred students, were given refuge in Britain. On our arrival we were received with compassion by the staff and students of universities and other higher education institutions. They opened their doors and offered us the chance to complete our studies in this country. It was, however, the most generous contribution of the

---

[32] Hungarian refugee students 1956-1957. *University of London Bulletin,* No.43, Oct. 1977, p.6.
[33] Dare, Alan and Hollander, Paul: Op.cit., Table 35A, p.XXXVII.

general public to the Lord Mayor's Fund that enabled the universities to carry out this programme fully. We were taught English and allowed to enter courses, often without proof of our previous studies. More than 300 Hungarian students received their first degrees here and many of us were encouraged and supported in completing postgraduate studies. As former Hungarian refugee students, on the anniversary of the revolution, we would like to take the opportunity to express our gratitude to the British people in general and to the universities and other institutions of higher education in particular for so wholeheartedly helping us. It is our hope that we have been able to repay some of the magnanimous support we received, during our working lives."[34]

---

[34] *The Times*, 2 Oct. 2006, p.18.

LIST OF ABBREVIATIONS

BCAR	British Council for aid to Refugees
BLA	Bodleian Library Archives
CUL/UA	Cambridge University Library/University Archives
CVCP	Committee of Vice-Chancellors and Principals
CVCPA	Committee of Vice-Chancellors and Principals Archives
ICA	Imperial College Archives
LCC	London County Council
LEA	Local Education Authority
MOL	Magyar Országos Levéltár (Hungarian National Archives)
NCB	National Coal Board
NUS	National Union of Students
ULU	University of London Union
UoLA	University of London Archives
WUS	World University Service

SELECTED SOURCES

Archives

Archives of the Committee of Vice-Chancellors and Principals. Warwick University. Modern Records Centre
Birmingham University Library. Special Collections Department
Bodleian Library Archives. UR6/OVS/H Files 1 and 2
Cambridge University Archives. UA R3445/1956, UA R3453/1956, UA R3454/1957
Corporation of London Records Office. Ref. No. PD145.8
Imperial College Archives. Hungarian Relief SS/1/1-4
Leeds University Central Records Office. Hungarian students: films 127-128, 229, 259, 1569
London Metropolitan Archives. London County Council Education Committee. File EO/HFE/3/22
Magyar Országos Levéltár. MOL XIX-I-2-f-241. doboz
The National Archives. Coal Mining Records. COAL 21/9, 21/10
University of London Archives CB3: Records of the Hungarian Refugee Students Scheme

The following university libraries, archives and records offices provided detailed written information (their former names in brackets): Aberdeen, Bangor, Bristol, Durham, Edinburgh, Glasgow, Hull, Keele (North Staffordshire), Leicester, Liverpool, Manchester, Newcastle, Queen's University of Belfast, Reading, Sheffield, Southampton, Strathclyde (Royal College of Science and Technology), St Andrew's, Swansea

The colleges, schools and institutes of London University: King's College, London School of Economics, Queen Mary's College, University College, St Bartholomew's Hospital Medical School

The former London polytechnics and technical colleges: City University (Northampton College of Advanced Technology), London Metropolitan University (Northern Polytechnic), South Bank University (Borough Polytechnic), University of Greenwich (Woolwich Polytechnic), University of Surrey (Buttersea College of Technology), Westminster University (Regent St Polytechnic)

Periodicals

Heti Hírek (London)
Irodalmi Ujság (London)
Magyar Szó (London)
The Daily Telegraph
The Manchester Guardian
The Times

Books and articles

Bogyay, Katalin: *The voice of freedom. Remembering the 1956 revolution.* London, 2006.

Bujdosó, Alpár: *299 nap.* Budapest, 2003.

Dare, Alan and Hollander, Paul: *Past experiences – present attitudes.* London, 1959. [Typescript]

Gömöri, György: Oxfordi egyetemisták a magyar szabadságért. In: *Az 1956-os Magyar Forradalom Történetének Dokumentációs és Kutatóintézete. Évkönyv III.* Budapest, 1994, pp. 27-34.

The Lord Mayor of London's National and Central European Relief Fund: *Report of the Fund November 1956 – September 1958.* [London, 1958.]

Sárközi, Mátyás: Ötvenhatosok Angliában. *Új Látóhatár,* vol. 32, no. 3-4, pp. 459-465.

Várallyay, Gyula: *Tanulmányúton. Az emigráns magyar diákmozgalom 1956 után.* Budapest, 1992.

[Walters, H. W. R.]: Hungarian refugee students 1956/1957. *University of London Bulletin,* no. 43, 1977, pp. 4-6.

Young, R. M.: The Hungarian students. *University of Edinburgh Gazette,* no.16, Oct.1957, pp.21-22.

INDEX OF NAMES

216 Index of Names